# MANCHESTER
# PALS

# MANCHESTER
# PALS

16th, 17th, 18th, 19th, 20th, 21st, 22nd & 23rd
Battalions of the Manchester Regiment
A HISTORY OF THE TWO MANCHESTER BRIGADES

## MICHAEL STEDMAN

Pen & Sword
**MILITARY**

*To Vincent Sleigh*

*A real friend without whom this would not have been possible*

First published in Great Britain in 1994 by Leo Cooper
Reprinted in this format in 2004 by
**LEO COOPER**
an imprint of
Pen & Sword Books Ltd
47 Church Street, Barnsley,
South Yorkshire
S70 2AS

ISBN 1 84415 046 1

A CIP record of this book is available from
the British Library

Printed in England by
CPI UK

# Contents

# Introduction & Acknowledgements

War is a terrible and unforgettable experience. But for many people in my generation who have no experience of war it is all too easy to pass over the shared horrors, degradation and human cost of war. This book has been written in hope that the communal and personal experience of Manchester people in the Great War can continue to remind us that the lessons of the past are ones to learn from; not to be forgotten and buried with the passing of the generations who knew and lived within one of the most destructive and inhuman chapters in man's story.

Throughout the last four years I have attempted to record the life and activities of many thousands of Manchester and Salford men who joined the Pals, and many other units during the Great War, as well as the experiences of the women and other family members who stood alongside during these experiences. This has given me contact with literally hundreds of individuals and families who have, without hesitation, proffered help and support in a multitude of different ways. So many of these people have become friends that my own life has been changed irrevocably. I am indebted to all of these people and would like to record my personal gratitude to each and every one. But in particular I should like to record my debt to Vincent Sleigh. Vincent provided his sensible and calm guidance, support and great friendship throughout all our researches in Manchester, France and Belgium. It is a great sorrow to me that he has not lived to see the fruition of his efforts. His death in the prime of life leaves a gap in my family's existence which it will be impossible to fill.

Captain Bob Bonner of the Manchester Museum Committee of The King's Regiment untiringly arranged to provide a wealth of material, documents and photographs through access to the Manchester Regiment Museum's materials and archives. Alan Pawson once again allowed me access to his unrivalled collection of photographs of the Manchester Pals. My father, Frank Stedman, has been beavering away in the production of the details of valour awards and the charts identifying the fatalities suffered by each battalion during their active service abroad. This book would not have been possible to write without such selfless and unstinting help and the committed support of my wife, Yvonne, and two sons, Richard and Jonathan. At the publishers, Roni Wilkinson and Caroline Cox have unwaveringly proved helpful, expert and cheerful throughout this book's progress towards completion. To all of these people, I am very grateful.

In other ways the following people have provided their own treasures, willing help and professional guidance to assist my progress. They include:

Peter Hart and Nigel Steel of the Imperial War Museum's staff. The staff of the Astley Cheetham Library in Stalybridge. The staff of the Local History Unit within the Manchester Central Library. The staff of the Salford Local History Library. The staff of the National Archives in Kew. The staff of the Commonwealth War Graves Commission. The many members of the Western Front Association who have willingly helped. The *Congleton Chronicle*. The *Sandbach Chronicle*. The *Jewish Telegraph* and the *Jewish Gazette* in Manchester. The *Manchester Evening News*. The *South Manchester Express Advertiser*. The *Morecambe Visitor* (Lancaster and Morecambe Newspapers Ltd). Marjorie Andrews. Dave Atherton. Roland Atkinson. Peter Bamford. Richard Bland. Don Bradshaw. Tom Brophy. Eric Burke. Manuel Cansino. Joan Capper. Alex Chadwick. Tony Conduit. Mrs Etheliend Cunliffe. Neil Drum. Francis Fogarty. Reverend Dr C S Ford. Jean Flaherty. Harold Gilbert. Jocelyn Greenhill. Michael Guest. Philip Guest. Tom Haddock. Aileen Hargreaves. Eddie Harrison. Frank Horsfield. Mrs V Howarth. Albert and Hannah Hurst. Bob Jackson. Edith Jones. Simon Lamb. Maurice Leech. Margaret Mace. Graham Maddocks. Ian McInnes. Martin Middlebrook. Mrs Millett. Bill Moores. Phil Moss. Mrs Murphy.

The first of Manchester's Pals battalions to be raised was initially called the 1st City Battalion. This was then designated the 16th (Service) Battalion of the Manchester Regiment. Until the various battalion's departure for France I have, where possible, referred to them as 1st, 2nd City etc. After their arrival in the theatre of war and the terrible experience of the Battles of the Somme and the Ancre I have begun to change that designation to the 16th, 17th Manchester etc. where it seems appropriate, to represent the loss of these battalion's Pals character. In total there were nine Pals battalions raised under the auspices of the Manchester Regiment, eight in Manchester itself and a further Pals battalion from Oldham, the Oldham 'Comrades', the 24th Manchesters. Salford, a mere stone's throw to the west was responsible for four further Pals battalions. For those of you who may not be familiar with the organization of infantry battalions during the Great War, a battalion was a unit of roughly 1000 men, divided into four companies of riflemen and further section providing administrative, signalling, transport, cooking and supplies support. There were, when the Pals went to war, four battalions in a brigade and three brigades in a division. With all its support services, artillery and machine gun sections, a division amounted to roughly 17,000 men at full strength. All of the Manchester Pals, with the exception of the bantams, served in the 7th and 30th Divisions. The 23rd Battalion, the bantams, served within the 35th Division, the bantam division.

For those of you who would like to pursue the story and research particular events which are only lightly touched upon in the story, the National Archives are an invaluable starting point. I have identified below some of the documentary sources which I have found to be most informative. In all cases it is usually more profitable to look at the appendices, attached maps, operation orders and narratives which accompany the diary rather than concentrating on the diary's frequently terse and brief record. All documents are prefixed with a WO95 number. Thus:

WO95/2339 – War Diaries of the 16th, 17th and 18th Battalions.
WO95/2339 – War Diaries of the 90th Brigade HQ up to September 1917.
WO95/2337 – War Diary of the 90th Brigade HQ up to September 1917.
WO95/2338 – War Diary of the 90th Brigade HQ thence up to August 1919.
WO95/2310 – War Diary of 30th Division HQ up to June 1916.
WO95/2311 – War Diary of 30th Division HQ thence up to April 1917.
WO95/2313 – War Diary of 30th Division HQ from September 1917 to April 1918.
WO95/2316 – War Diary of the 30th Division's C.R.A. up to December 1916.
WO95/2327 – War Diary of the 21st Brigade HQ up to July 1917.
WO95/2328 – War Diary of the 21st Brigade HQ thence up to the end of the war.
WO95/2329 – War Diary of the 19th Battalion.
WO95/2469 – War Diary of the 35th Division, 1917.
WO95/2484 – War Diary of the 23rd Manchesters.
WO95/1630 – War Diary of the 7th Division HQ up to June 1917.
WO95/1631 – War Diary of the 7th Division HQ thence up to end 1918.
WO95/1661 – War Diary of the 22nd Brigade, 1917.
WO95/1663 – War Diary of the 20th Battalion.
WO95/1668 – War Diary of the 21st Battalion.
WO95/1669 – War Diary of the 22nd Manchesters.

After their transfer to Italy the 7th Division's unit records are re-numbered as follows:

WO95/4218 – War Diary of the 7th Division HQ.
WO95/4219 – War Diary of the 7th Division's C.R.A.
WO95/4225 – War Diary of the 22nd Brigade HQ.
WO95/4226 – War Diary of the 20th Manchesters.
WO95/4227 – War Diary of the 91st Brigade HQ.
WO95/4228 – War Diary of the 21st and 22nd Battalions.

For those of you who would like to find out the location of the memorial or cemetery where a relative, who served with any military until such as the Pals, is recorded or buried then that information can be obtained from the Commonwealth War Graves Commision, 2 Marlow Road, Maidenhead, Berkshire, SL6 7DX, telephone: 01628 634221. The CWGC will not, however, be able to tell you how that person died or was killed. Some biographical details of men are however available within the pages of 'Soldiers Died in the Great War, 1914-1919, part 59 – The Manchester Regiment' and 'Officers Died in the Great War, 1914-1919'. (Both published in 1919-1921 by the War Office.) Less reliable but occasionally more illuminating details can also be found in 'The National Roll of the Great War, 1914-1918, Manchester.' (Published by the National Publishing Company soon after the war.) Apart from being available in many Reference Libraries, 'Soldiers Died in the Great War' and 'Officers Died in the Great War' is available on CD as a complete record of 665,000 soldiers and 37,000 officers in a searchable digital data base from Naval & Military Press. www.naval-military-press.com telephone number 01825 749494.

*The construction and opening of the Manchester Ship Canal, and its vast freight handling facilities at the Salford and Pomona docks, during the last decade of the nineteenth century, gave the city of Manchester a huge advantage in its rivalry with Liverpool.*

# Chapter One

# A Premier and Vigorous City

*'...the second city of England,*
*the first manufacturing city of the world.'*[1]

S ince the earliest flames of industrialism were transformed into the massive smoking factories which dominated south Lancashire in the 1890s, the manufacturing prowess of Manchester had always posed a threat to the power and influence of Britain's capital. Indeed, by the middle of the nineteenth century Manchester had become the premier manufacturing district of the world. The city's vast industrial output, created astride the rivers, coal fields and human multitude which cradled the textile and engineering heartlands of Britain's prosperity, ensured that London had a substantial indebtedness to 'Cottonopolis'. The Manchester stock-markets and exchanges, banks and insurance empires which supervised and financed Lancashire's seemingly boundless hubble of enterprise, commercialism and manufacturing were second only to London's 'square mile'. The city's clerks and warehousemen arranged and oversaw Manchester's commerce and trade with care and precision. Shipping factors, freight forwarders, import and export merchants, commodity dealers and the offices of every major shipping line provided hundreds of opportunities for a steady stream of bright boys, fresh from the city's grammar schools. The raw materials required for the region's textile and engineering giants were manhandled through the Salford docks, just a mere mile away from the city centre. On the metropolitan boundary the Pomona docks at the very end of the great ship canal made Manchester an international marine port. Whilst the city centre was urbane, prosperous and obsessed with the challenges of success in trade, her outlying industrial satellites were often characterized by a dramatically different atmosphere. Those

*At the turn of the century the commercial centre of Manchester was second only to London in its aura of prosperity and the busy accumulation of profit.*

*The 1/2500 series 1905 Ordnance Survey Map showing the Albert Square and central commercial district of central Manchester.* Manchester Local Studies Unit

towns and their people were blackened with the smog of a thousand chimneys whose effluent soured and stained the great swathe of industrial workplaces which stretched eastwards across Oldham, Ashton, Hyde and beyond to the Pennines. For talented men from such communities any chance for upward mobility meant jobs in the commercial and financial districts of the city centre.

Those people left in the peripheral industrial communities had long become accustomed to accepting any business put their way by Manchester's cotton masters. In the eighteenth century this domestic system of work had often involved the squalid exploitation of workers behind a multitude of meagre front doors. However, the subsequent development of massive coal fired rotary steam engines had created Manchester's factory system. Close on the heels of this development came a simmering malcontent and the hesitant origins of organized and determined groups dedicated towards improvements in the quality of life and employment conditions of working men and women.

In August 1819 thousands of local people, cotton mill workers, artisans and their families had gathered on St. Peter's Field to hear the orator, Henry Hunt, speak against corruption and the Corn Laws and in favour of a radical reform of government. Panic among the local magistrates, who believed that an uprising was imminent, led to their call for intervention by the local Yeomanry. The resulting unprovoked attack by armed men on local workers, women and children came to be known as the Peterloo massacre and set the tone for almost a century of mistrust between disenfranchised workers and their political and economic masters. The Chartist movement, which followed on from the 1832 *Reform Act*'s failure to give employees the right to vote, revealed the depths of misunderstanding between London's allies in Manchester and the impoverished working classes who depended upon the city for their meagre circumstances. The living conditions of Manchester's poor in the mid-nineteenth century were unrelentingly abysmal. Within a stone's throw of the city centre one observer was able to record his impression,

> *...of the filth, ruin and uninhabitableness, the defiance of all considerations of cleanliness, ventilation, and health which characterize the construction of this single district [which] exists in the heart of the second city of England, the first manufacturing city of the world. If anyone wishes to see in how little space a human being can move, how little air – and such air! – he can breathe, how little of civilisation he may share and yet live, it is only necessary to travel hither.*[2]

*Men of the 3rd Battalion of the Manchester Regiment pose as a working party on the island of St Helena in the South Atlantic in 1903. St Helena was an important staging post and coaling station for vessels en route for South Africa. During the Boer War the island became an important encampment for Boer Prisoners of War.*

*Men of the 3rd Battalion of the Manchester Regiment, soon after the South African War, photographed on St Helena in 1903.* Howarth

Five miles to the east of this misery barracks in Ashton had been erected during the early 1840s, partly to ensure the proximity of reliable troops to an area where obvious discontent and frequent trade recession left many an unemployed man gazing enviously upon Manchester's central prosperity and those solid soaring buildings which marked her Victorian affluence. Since 1881, when the 63rd and 96th Regiments had been amalgamated to form the Manchester Regiment, the city's two professional regular battalions had served throughout numerous campaigns in India, the West Indies, Canada and, later, during the Boer War. These men had campaigned in defence of the colonies which provided the material resources for their Queen's Empire.

At the turn of the century the area around Manchester accommodated a tremendous diversity of status and class.

Confident of their superior position in life, Manchester's middle class army of clerks, managers and office staff thronged the commercial city's busy thoroughfares each morning and night, en route from the prosperous villa suburbs of Didsbury, Withington, Whalley Range and Prestwich, isolated both by geography and outlook from the sweating and fraught confines of the city's gross industrial heritage. For the most successful in industry and commerce the fruits of their enterprise gave rise to homes in idyllic Alderley Edge and Wilmslow, prosperous developments whose tranquillity and affluence epitomized the success of Manchester's elite. Trains at 8.05 am and 8.32 am, took a succession of these wealthy entrepreneurs into offices above the bustle of the city's commercial districts. For such men and their families Manchester was the source of an affluent and cultured way of life whose Edwardian style seemed secure. A number of these merchant families had made enormous fortunes from the industrialization and urbanization of the area. The wealth of the newly rich families rivalled and often exceeded the established local aristocracy. Typical of them was the Philips family whose home was in Sedgley, just north of Broughton. Their family fortune was based on the business of J & N Philips. Amongst the professional and managerial employees and shareholders of such industrial companies, living in Prestwich, Didsbury and a dozen other similarly tidy suburbs, a reassuringly familiar and self perpetuating lifestyle existed. Through dozens of local 'prep' schools their children aspired to attend a number of pre-eminent senior schools such as Manchester Grammar, Chetham's Hospital School, the Warehousemen and Clerks and William Hulme, all of which prepared young boys for the security of academic and commercial careers which abounded within the city and its prestigious Victoria University. Almost all these educational establishments provided military instruction and preparation through the ranks of an Officer Training Corps. The schools were elitist, and proud of the fact. On matriculating many of their pupils would be called upon to defend Manchester's first rate reputation for technical expertise, precision and innovation. For many successful students the huge local engineering combines such as Whitworth and Mather and Platt provided further opportunity in companies whose reputation for quality was simply second to none across the globe. Even the nearest competitor to this mighty city, Liverpool, had been dealt with effectively when the Manchester Ship Canal's opening in 1890 had successfully by-passed that port, guaranteeing Manchester's economic independence.

Surrounded by such circumstances during the first decade of the twentieth century Manchester boasted a city centre marked by the affluence of the Empire's wealth and abundance. Its commercial architecture was diverse, substantial and confident. Even the warehouses were artistic in their fusion of function and style. The great metropolis provided work, prosperity and opportunity for her assiduous middle class. It also provided a constant, if dim, consciousness of nearby industrial underclasses whose poverty and labour both sustained the city's wealth and surrounded it with a malevolent fringe of industrial chaos.

Into this world the children and youths of the city, whose destiny was to become Manchester's civic soldiers in the Great War, were being brought up. For some young men at the very base of this social pyramid circumstances were little better than the poverty witnessed by Engels, half a century earlier. The first decade of the twentieth century had already witnessed an erosion in the value of real wages paid to unskilled labourers in this area. Into just such a hard pressed family Tom Haddock was born in 1899. His birthplace was within yards of London Road Station, now Piccadilly. At eighteen months he moved to No. 2 court, No. 1 house, in Stand Street off Store Street, amongst the maze of stables and warehouses below the great Railway Station.

*In our family, including me mother and father, there was ten of us. There was not one of us children born in the same house. Every 18 months we moved house, sometimes to get rid of the landlord when we couldn't pay the rent. A moonlight you know! All born in Ancoats. They called Ancoats a dirty, lousy 'ole and very poor. Well, no doubt about it, it was...* Tom Haddock

*No expense was spared to make the Victorian Army's officer uniforms into a stunning array of brass and gilt decoration. The photographs show:*
1. *A 96th Regiment Officer's Shako Plate, worn between 1869-1878.*
2. *A 63rd Regiment Officer's Blue Cloth Helmet Plate, worn between the years 1881-1914. This plate is surmounted with the King's Crown, dating this to the early twentieth century.*
3. *A 63rd Officer's shoulder plate, worn from the mid-1830s.*

Outside in the court was a water pump. His dwelling had neither taps, gas nor electricity.

> *The toilets was at the back of the houses, back of the square court, and they was long wooden huts with partitions. Under seats there was running water and everything went away with it...* Tom Haddock

Among the families of unskilled railwaymen, porters, engine cleaners and yard labourers pay was a mere sixteen to seventeen shillings a week. Such men were underpaid. Their families were underfed. Their homes were often hovels. Clothing was utilitarian and simple. At the age of three Tom arrived at school, dressed in the smock which was standard wear for all infants under the age of four. Whilst the girls managed a pair of bloomers, the

> *...boys didn't wear anything. We just knocked about like that. And of course we was always in bare feet. We used to do all kinds of games as youngsters. For the boys it was either marbles or piggy and stick, for the girls it was shuttlecock and paddle or bobbers and kibs. That's how we used to amuse ourselves. And there's one thing about it, if ever we was playing any game, whether it was a lad or a girl, or a bunch of us all together, and they found someone cheatin', they used to get battered and they carted them out of the road and wouldn't play with 'em you see...* Tom Haddock

Cheats in such a close knit community could not be allowed to profit.

In other aspects of life the local employers made some attempt to alleviate the poverty and hardship of an Ancoats' winter.

> *...they used to go round all the district, every day in the week with box carts full of bits of firewood and dump it in the streets. And same with the Gas Works. Once a week they used to send four box carts out full of coke and dump it in the middle of the streets for you to help yourself. You didn't have to pay for it. Matter of fact, if you went to the Gas Works to get a load of coke you had to take what was known as a coal waggon, you paid thripence for the loan of it. You took it to the Gas Works and weighed it on the big weighing machine and went to the pile of coke and helped yoursel', piled it up, went back and if you came over the scale with more than a hundredweight of coke, they gave you a shillin' for it to take the coke away.* Tom Haddock

However, at the turn of the century, working class opinion was not yet influential in Manchester. By contrast, the whole of middle class Manchester's Liberal and Free Trade perspective was represented and reflected by the outstanding regional newspaper of the time, the Manchester Guardian. In its editor, C P Snow, the newspaper had a forthright and renowned champion of the city's heritage. But this was no mere local paper. The Manchester Guardian had a national and erudite readership whose influence on bourgeois attitudes was only surpassed by that of *The Times*.

One man whose influence and position in Lancashire life was often the subject of the *Manchester Guardian's* critical interest was Edward George Villiers Stanley, 17th Earl of Derby. Throughout south Lancashire his position at the centre of industrial, social and political life was unchallenged. Derby was often spoken of as 'The Uncrowned King of Lancashire'. His family history spanned close on nine centuries of activity at the centres of influence and power. Stanley's grandfather, Edward Geoffrey Stanley the 14th Earl of Derby, had been three times Prime Minister in the early nineteenth century. By the first decade of the twentieth century one hundred and fifty years of growth within Lancashire's industrial regions had generated fabulous wealth for the Derby family. Their enormous home, at Knowsley between Manchester and Liverpool, reflected this abundance and power. Apart from their ownership of agricultural lands, further enormous incomes derived from their property in the residential and industrial areas of Liverpool, Manchester, Bury, Colne, Salford, Bolton, Preston and elsewhere. His paternal influence was both admired and feared

*House Party at Knowsley attended by King Edward VII and Queen Alexandra shortly after Derby succeeded to the title.*

by the mass of people in this corner of the North West of England. Derby was one of the last great aristocrats whose standing and prestige was quite disproportionate to that of other men in the locality. Amongst his friends he counted the King and the Prince of Wales.

In 1892, at the age of twenty-seven, Derby had been elected as a Conservative Member of Parliament for the constituency of Westhoughton. He soon became a Tory whip in the Commons. During the Boer War in South Africa Derby served as Chief Press Censor to the British forces there. In his absence during the October 'Khaki' election of 1900 he was re-elected as MP for Westhoughton and was quickly offered the post of Financial Secretary to the War Office by the Prime Minister, Lord Salisbury. It was the start of many years of central influence upon, and involvement in, Government in Britain. However, in 1906 he lost the Westhoughton seat to a Labour opponent, the carpenter W T Wilson. This was a serious blow to a Cabinet member and the cries of 'bloodsucker' which greeted Derby's appearance at many meetings reminded him that times and deferential attitudes in south Lancashire were changing.

Nevertheless, two years later, in 1908, Stanley's world changed irrevocably when he inherited the estates, wealth and title of the Derby family. With the exception of a handful of other men, Derby was now the recipient of one of the country's most substantial incomes, at a time when income tax was levied at the standard rate of 1s in the pound (5%). Derby's succession to the House of Lords gave him access to public influence, although the reforming Liberal Government of the period ensured that he would have no post in Government until the forthcoming war years. In opposition Derby greatly elevated his esteem amongst the ranks of Lancashire Tories and working men by his constant opposition to the idea of food taxes and Empire Preference which were commonplace amongst his party leadership. During 1911 this policy of Derby's risked splitting the Tory Party but he was adamant that it would give great financial benefit to working class people in the area who wanted the benefits of cheap food and free trade. Derby's victory on the issue was therefore enormously popular in the Lancashire locality. During this period Derby also concentrated his energies upon service to the various communities of Lancashire and Liverpool, accepting posts as University Chancellor in 1908 and the presidency of the Chamber of

# THE GREAT WAR.

## GERMANY'S REPLY

### TO BRITISH ULTIMATUM

## ENGLAND NOW AT WAR.

### TITANIC STRUGGLE COMMENCES.

In the House of Commons yesterday (Tuesday) afternoon, Mr. Asquith said Britain had requested Germany to give a satisfactory reply by midnight that she will not violate Belgium's neutrality.

A Press Association message to the 'Visitor' Office last night, said:

"Sir Edward Grey has asked German Ambassador to see him at the Foreign Office this (Wednesday) morning.

## War Declared

Turkey is now mobilising, and their reserves in England have received notice to that effect.

Italy maintains her neutral position.

Three dirigibles have been seen flying towards Brussels.

The "Daily Express learns on high authority that heavy firing has been going on for some time in the North Sea.

The captain of a vessel which arrived at South Shields stated that he had had difficulty in keeping clear of warships, and that French and German vessels were engaged.

Several German warships are lying off Flushing.

*The photograph above shows soldiers of the Lancashire Fusiliers Territorial units, resting during a route march in Lancashire during the days before their departure for Egypt. Many of these Lancashire Fusiliers came from nearby Salford and other industrial communities to the north and west of Manchester.* Author's collection

*Territorial Soldiers of the Manchester Regiment assemble as soon as their unit is embodied, prior to their departure for preparatory training outside the city. Within weeks these men would volunteer for service overseas, and be dispatched to Egypt where they would relieve regular soldiers at the Suez Canal. [Manchester Guardian 6 August 1914]*

Commerce in 1910. On 10 November 1911 Derby was elected Lord Mayor of Liverpool. In so far as it was possible Derby was now the undisputed spokesman for, and conduit of, Lancashire's industrial opinion towards the Conservative party in opposition. As international tensions rose and militarism spread an influence to all corners of the country, Derby also became the Chairman of the West Lancashire Territorial Association. This post, his public esteem, and the fact that so many of his family had or were serving within the armed forces ensured that he would become a prominent figure in any future call to arms amongst the people of South Lancashire.[3]

    The year that Derby was elected Mayor of Liverpool had become memorable for the working class people of Manchester and nearby Salford for quite different reasons. In the sweated workshops which now abounded in the clothing and furniture trades centred around Cheetham, Strangeways and Lower Broughton discontent with low pay and lack of union recognition was widespread. Within the docks and great railway depots which serviced Manchester's trade the labourers were filled with anger at their cruel circumstances. Amongst the very lowest paid the start of the second decade of the twentieth century marked a period of 'Great Unrest' when waves of class conflict began to swell ominously beneath the seeming calm of middle class Manchester.

The mid-summer of 1911 saw the high water mark of unrest reached. A general strike pitched Salford into turmoil. The docks, Manchester's lifeblood, were closed. Transport and distribution were brought to a standstill. In an atmosphere of brooding violence the arrival of the Scots Greys, infantry and armed police during July eased matters, but the employers were forced to concede on many matters relating to pay, recognition and conditions. August proved to be an even more extraordinary month. In Liverpool strikes and violence had led to a general lock-out. The city was close to anarchy. 7000 troops and Special Police were sent to maintain order. Gunboats appeared on the Mersey estuary. Engineering labourers in Manchester, Gorton and Salford were on strike, demanding one pound a week as a realistic minimum wage. Strikes by miners and railway labourers meant that coal was neither produced nor stocks of it moved. As the source of their power dwindled factories began to close. By the end of the month many settlements to the array of disputes had been reached and it had become clear that organized labour was now capable of influencing the oppression which established order had so long maintained. When autumn drew in tempers began to cool. Liverpool elected a Mayor who could be relied upon to reassert authority.

The final summer months before the onset of autumn in 1914 were the last few paragraphs of Manchester's Victorian and Edwardian story. The scene was set for Manchester's youth to write its own covenant, proving that self seeking need not be the ultimate motive for men's actions. In these last weeks, as the Great War approached and Europe's politicians wrestled with the consequences and tensions of the Dreadnought arms race, Manchester was clearly an extraordinary place. In some respects its position as an unquestioned leader in the world's commerce and manufacturing had come under pressure, the rise of engineering excellence in Japan, Germany and the USA had seen to that. But, the city had survived. It had grown and prospered for more than a century at the hub of industrial revolution, Empire building and commercial expansion. The deference of its huge working class had now dwindled, replaced by a necessarily more aggressive self interest. But the middle classes were still driven by honourable traditions of work, effort and an almost Presbyterian zeal. In some ways Manchester's population was better equipped to provide an army of men to fight the forthcoming war than many a smaller European state in their own right. The city held a proud regimental history and was located at the centre of an area renowned for its steady supply of recruits into the Regular Army as well as the enthusiasm of its artisans for the Terriers.

Indeed, soon after the outbreak of war, more than 15,000 men and officers of the 42nd East Lancashire Division volunteered and were despatched, without hesitation, from the ranks of these Territorials into service in Egypt and later the maelstrom of the disastrous campaign at Gallipoli against Turkey[4]. Many of this Division's part time soldiers came from Manchester and close by, the Lancashire Fusiliers Brigade from Bury, Rochdale and Salford, the East Lancashire Brigade which included the 9th and 10th Manchesters from nearby Ashton-under-Lyne and Oldham, and the Manchester Infantry Brigade itself, consisting of the 5th, 6th, 7th and 8th Battalions. Alongside their two regular battalions, the Manchester Regiment had, therefore, already fielded six territorial units on the outbreak of war, and would go on to raise eighteen further active service battalions as well as numerous reserve, training and draft finding units.

It was to become, by the standards of any city, a remarkable contribution to the prosecution of the Great War.

### Notes

1 Frederick Engels. *The Condition of the Working Class in England*. Written in 1844/5 following his intimate observation of Manchester.
2 Frederick Engels.
3 *Lord Derby. King of Lancashire*. Randolph Churchill. 1959. Hienemann. London.
4 See *The 42nd (East Lancashire) Division. 1914-1918*. Frederick Gibbon. Country Life Library, 1920.

# Chapter Two

# The Rush to Enlist

*'...the type which one sees on Saturday mornings in the winter carrying lacrosse and football bags – clean limbed and strong...'*[1]

The preparation and departure of Manchester's Territorials, bound for their Pennine training grounds, was marked by scenes of great enthusiasm and anticipation in the city. These Territorial units were closest of any to the hearts and minds of their community at this stage of the war. Whilst nearby Salford's Terriers were sent to Turton, near Bolton, Manchester's part-timers soon found themselves at Hollingworth Lake outside Rochdale. The hectic bustle of these camps was close at hand and Manchester's community soon found that a day trip could reassure mothers and fathers of their son's thorough preparation. By 10 September the Manchester Regiment's six first line Territorial battalions were en-route for the Middle East, out of Southampton. They would fight in Egypt, Gallipoli, France and Belgium. All of these battalions subsequently raised second and third line units, all of which would also see active service on the Western Front.

However, during the August and September of 1914 the City of Manchester's Regiment also raised three service battalions, the 11th, 12th and 13th. The raising of these units, through the Regimental Depot at Ladysmith Barracks in Ashton-under-Lyne, was marked by none of the communal initiative and support which soon characterised the Manchester Pals. The reservations and concerns of middle class men meant that many held back, worried about the

*An officer's cap badge bearing the 11th Manchester's insignia. It is thought that identification badges of this quality, belonging to these early service battalions, had been privately struck by a group of officers wishing to emphasize the character and origins of their unit as well as the personal status of each officer.*

*Men belonging to the early, non Pals, service battalions entrenching on a beach near their camp at Eastbourne. These men were not marked by the stamp of middle classness which characterised so many of the Pals photographs.* Pawson

*Officers Mess staff belonging to the 13th Manchesters, photographed on 25 November 1914.* Jones

nature and background of their potential working class comrades. The enlistment and medical facilities were both inadequate and antiquated and the Victoria Street recruiting centre acquired an evil reputation amongst intending recruits who, on arrival,

*...must take his place in a crowd of men on the other side of the street and wait there for an undefined period, in something that looks like a strikers' meeting, until his turn comes. While he waits he must consent to witness a good many depressing incidents – tearful mothers giving hurried, incoherent messages to their sons, the coming and going of distressed, hysterical women, and a multitude of things that are calculated to damp his ardour. From time to time the policemen cross the road, and there is a purposeless, irritating general move-on to nowhere in particular. A recruiting sergeant arrives briskly at remote intervals, and lines up a score of men along the sidewalk by the entrance to the Exchange Station goods yard, marches them over the road, and sees them through the door of the office. They fill the stairs and the doors are shut. The doors are really iron gates, and the men on the lower stairs, looking out into the street, look already unpleasantly like prisoners of war. Manchester Guardian, Friday, 26 August 1914.*

*Unknown Territorial soldier of the 1/8th Manchesters, wearing the battalion identification flash on his right shoulder, below the brass Manchester scroll on his epaulette.* Jones

Such fine men's determination and depth of feeling should have ensured that the exploits of these early, non-Pals, service battalions were more closely followed by and associated with the city of Manchester. However, following their departure from the area and a scanty training at Grantham, the 11th were despatched from Liverpool, direct to the war with Turkey. Whilst the 12th were sent to France as part of Kitchener's 2nd Army, the 13th also found themselves initially in France and then onwards to the wasteful campaign in Salonika.

*Manchester Town Hall.*                                             *Lord Derby in 1912.*

Any improvement which could be made upon those stark and unwelcoming arrangements which created the early service battalions could only be to the advantage of the forthcoming Pals' movement. The route would soon open for the city of Manchester's proudest contribution to the war, born out of its uncompromising competition with nearby Liverpool. Although local and national recruitment figures during the first two weeks of the war had been encouraging, any initiative which could capitalise on local and community spirit was clearly destined to create the greatest success. Lord Derby was the man who captured that spirit's influence and in so doing carved himself a central place in the history of the Pals movement. On 19 August he had promoted the enlistment of an active service battalion in Liverpool. A week later, on 27 August, a further initiative of Derby's was published in that city's press, appealing for the enlistment of men,

> *such as clerks and others engaged in commercial business, who wish to serve their country and would be willing to enlist in the battalion of Lord Kitchener's new Army if they felt assured that they would be able to serve with their friends and not be put in a battalion with unknown men as their companions.*

Within hours the idea proved enormously successful. The appeal to friends who could ensure that they would not be placed 'in a battalion with unknown men as their companions' was a powerful and emotive one. The Pals movement was born in a welter of enlistment on Merseyside.

On the day after Derby's historic appeal in Liverpool's Press, a group of leading Manchester industrialists and local figures met in the city's great Town Hall. These men were already well aware of the inadequacy and unwelcoming nature of the general enlistment arrangements which the Army had so far made at Victoria Street. As the early Manchester Regiment service battalions became filled, hundreds of surplus men were being assigned to the Rifle Brigade, the Border Regiment and other distant units. Such a scattering of the locality's menfolk was thought of as belittling to the status and significance of the city's name. The group was already aware that a meeting of the Manchester Home Trade Association, held on Monday, 24 August, had thought that recruiting should be encouraged amongst the clerks and warehousemen of the city. The Manchester industrialists' resolution, at their

# Proposed Battalion
## OF MANCHESTER
# CLERKS & WAREHOUSEMEN

A BATTALION is being raised composed entirely of employees in Manchester offices and warehouses upon the ordinary conditions of enlistment in Lord Kitchener's army, namely, for three years, or the duration of the War. The Battalion will be clothed and equipped (excepting arms) by a fund being raised for the purpose.

We therefore desire to call the attention of all our employees between the ages of 19 and 35 years to the call of Lord Kitchener, which was emphasized by the Prime Minister in the House of Commons, for further recruits, and, in order to encourage enlistment, we are prepared to offer to all employees enlisting within the next two weeks the following conditions :—

(1) Four weeks' full wages from date of leaving.
(2) Re-engagement on discharge from service guaranteed.
(3) Half pay during absence on duty for married men from the date that full pay ceases, to be paid to the wife.
(4) Special arrangements made for single men who have relatives entirely dependent on them.
(5) The above payments only apply to those enlisting in the Ranks, and not to anyone who may obtain a commission otherwise than by promotion from the Ranks, but each case (if any) of those obtaining a commission, will be treated on its merits.
(6) The above offer is for voluntary service only, and should the Government decide on compulsory training later, the offer will not apply to those affected by such compulsion.

Names should be sent in to your employer. Recruiting for this Battalion will take place at the

# ARTILLERY HEADQUARTERS,
## Hyde Road, Ardwick,
# DAILY, from 9 a.m. to 6 p.m.

Signature ....................................

It is hoped that all employers will fall in with the above scheme and do all they can to encourage their employees to enlist.

Papers and recruiting tickets can be obtained from any of the following :

THE FINE SPINNERS' ASSOCIATION, Ltd., St. James's Square.
J. & N. PHILLIPS & CO., 35, Church Street.
TOOTAL, BROADHURST, LEE CO., Ltd., 56, Oxford Street.
A. E. PIGGOTT, Secretary, 56, Mosley Street.

*Advertisement for the Clerk & Warehousemen's Battalion.*

meeting held on the 28 August, was therefore to raise a battalion of men drawn from the city's many warehouses and commercial districts, to be known as the Manchester Clerk's and Warehousemen's Battalion. It was an appeal unashamedly designed to interest the city's middle class men. An organising committee was formed.[2] Before the meeting broke up a guarantee fund was set up to receive money to finance the provision of uniforms and equipment. Those present had already promised £15,000. This sum included the unprecedented guarantee of £7,000 from the Gas Company's reserve funds, an action which was immediately responsible for prompting the willingness of other benefactors to pledge further large sums. To the War Office a telegram was despatched offering to raise, clothe and equip a battalion of local men at the expense of the city. Lord Derby was invited to become the proposed battalion's Honorary Colonel, his position of pre-eminence in the commercial, political and social life of the area meant that there could have been no competition for the honour.

Within three days the die was cast.

Kitchener's reply was welcoming and to the point. War Office approval was granted without hesitation.

> *Your telegram just received. Hope you will be able to raise a battalion in Manchester and thus give your signal help to the armed forces of the Crown. Any men joining the battalion will be doing a patriotic deed, and I shall hope to welcome them in the army, where their comrades await them. Will give you every assistance. Let me know how you succeed. Kitchener.* Received 28 August. *Manchester Guardian*, 29 August 1914.

On Monday, 31 August the Lord Mayor's appeal was published.

> *The young men of to-day have an opportunity such as is given to very few generations. The response to the call for men is so far good, but there are still some hundreds of thousands of young men whose clear duty it is to help in the most momentous struggle in which the country has ever engaged. It would be an indelible disgrace to our manhood if we, who are spared so many of the worst horrors of war, hesitate to bear our full share with our gallant allies in this great fight for honour and liberty. Manchester Guardian*, Monday, 31 August 1914.

Potential recruits, the clerks and warehousemen who worked for companies supporting the Pals scheme, were confident of the assurances which would protect their position in society. Those Manchester merchants and employers had made abundantly clear to their employees that,

> *...in order to encourage enlistment, we are prepared to offer to all employees enlisting within the next two weeks the following conditions:*
>
> *1) Four weeks full wages from date of leaving*
> *2) Re-engagement on discharge from service guaranteed.*
> *3) Half pay during absence on duty for married men from the date that full pay ceases. To be paid to the wife...* Made public in the *Manchester Courier* and *Manchester Guardian.* Monday, 31 August 1914.

As soon as the first editions of the local papers were made available men clamoured at the gates of the Artillery HQ and formed a queue on Apsley Grove. Two thousand enlistment tickets were quickly printed for distribution to men who could prove that they were the bona-fide clerks or warehousemen of the relevant firms.[3] From noon on Monday, 31 August those tickets were available from The Fine Cotton Spinners Association, J & N Philips and Co., Tootal Broadhurst, Lee and Co., and other prominent local enterprises. Once this was realised the throng outside Apsley Grove rushed back to their workplaces to obtain possession of these vital documents before returning to queue. However, this first day's recruiting for the Manchester Pals proved to be little short of a disaster. Nothing much

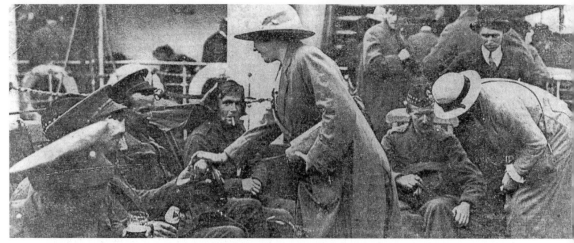

*The tone of many newspapers, by 29 August, was still an excited one, but the* Manchester Guardian *continued to be rather more considered than many of its rivals had been during the first few days of war. On 29 August the* Manchester Guardian *carried this photograph, 'Disabled but Cheerful', showing the arrival of wounded men at Folkestone. Images of this nature did no harm to the tide of enlistment into the Manchester Pals, which soon followed, during the first week of September.*

occured to suggest to these men that they were wanted. Hundreds were stood outside all day, unable to get inside the Drill Hall. Complaints and grumbles about military incompetence were rife. Inside the Artillery HQ Major Sington and Captain Bartram could not work fast enough to cope. Even groups who had joined the colours two days before on the Saturday were turned away in the crush. The authorities on this occasion were simply unprepared and the two doctors overwhelmed. Fewer than one hundred men were genuinely enlisted into the Manchester Pals that Monday afternoon.

Civic and commercial enterprises were nevertheless falling over themselves to donate funds and encourage enlistment. Aleady, by the last day of August, £7,000 had been donated from

*The throng of hopeful recruits, who waited outside the Artillery Headquarters on 31 August 1914.* MRA

the Gas Committee's surplus funds.[4] The raising committee was already sending letters, appealing for support in the form of funds, to every leading enterprise, merchant house and prosperous man. Advertisements were drafted, due for release to the local press, calling attention to the likely expenditure of £30,000 in clothing, feeding and housing the Pals and requesting donations from all responsible business houses towards these costs.

*Waiting to enlist.* MRA

By Tuesday, 1 September dissatisfied men were clamouring at the Town Hall, irritated by constant delays. The civic buildings were almost surrounded by impatient groups of men. Under threat of serious disorder the nearby Free Trade Hall, and the Albert Hall opposite, were taken over for enrollment and attestation purposes. A visit from the Chief Medical Officer of Western Command and the engagement of extra medical and clerical volunteers ensured a more speedy passage of men through the stages of inquiry and medical examination at Hyde Road. That day Alderman Sir Daniel McCabe visited the Artillery HQ and was able to swear in a further 800 men who were told that friends from the same firms and employers would be directed into the same companies and platoons. Outside in the streets many hundreds more men were milling about, wondering how to gain access. During the next few days further teams of doctors, clerks and magistrates were draughted in to speed and supervise the rush.

Over the next fortnight the esteem in which Manchester was held by its clerks, artisans and middle classes, would ensure the raising of three further complete battalions of infantry, creating the first of Manchester's two Brigades.

The first of these battalions, the 1st City Battalion, would later be designated as the 16th (Service) battalion of the Manchester Regiment. This distinctive unit was drawn exclusively from those men who proved themselves bona-fide clerks and warehousemen from the city's central commercial district. Shopkeepers, municipal workers and engineers were quickly encouraged by the press to purge their envy by finding '*a ready outlet for their feelings in emulation*'!

The 2nd City Battalion, the 17th Manchesters, were recruited on the 2 and 3 September. This period of September was characterised by an unrestrained and overwhelming enthusiasm for the idea of local and civic units which would soon form the bulk of Kitchener's Armies. The national recruiting figures for the period 30 August to 5 September were the highest returns for the whole of the war and this ardour was reflected in Manchester's record. On Thursday, 3 September 2,151 men enlisted in Manchester, second only to the 3,521 who joined the colours in London.[5] The processes of recruiting had, of necessity, been extended from the Artillery HQ on Hyde Road to the Town Hall and its nearby facilities. The men were assembled to enrol their names in the Free Trade Hall. They were then marched across Peter Street, in batches of fifty, to the Albert Hall opposite where they were attested. It had quickly become obvious, by Wednesday, 2 September, that recruiting for the second of Manchester's civic battalions would be speedily completed.

However, the Pals were not the only recruiting effort whose main thrust was directed

*The tents belonging to the Salford Lads Club which were the basis of the accommodation for Manchester's Pals under canvas.* SLHL

towards the area's middle classes. On Thursday morning, 3 September, a meeting was held at Manchester University addressed by J L Paton, High Master of the city's premier Grammar School, at which public school men and graduates were encouraged to join the University and Public Schools (U.P.S.) Battalions. This organisation's aims were to look after the ambitions of the,

> *...great number of old public school boys who are anxious to serve their country, but at the same time are somewhat chary of joining the regular army with the ordinary run of recruits...!*[6]

Paton was assisted at his meeting by Captain Lapage of the University O.T.C. and also by Captain Potts and Lieutenant Mumford of the Grammar School's O.T.C. Acting on his own initiative Paton opened a U.P.S. recruiting station at Manchester Grammar School. The

*Recruits, probably belonging to the 3rd City Battalion, being marched from the Free Trade Hall to be examined. Taken 3 September.* MRA

following day 117 men were attested there, quickly followed by many of Manchester's law students, architects and accountants. By Monday, 7 September more than 560 men had been 'accepted' and the U.P.S. in Manchester were able to say of themselves that 'The Grammar School Corps is about the surest way to a commission one can think of'! This initiative gave rise to the 20th Battalion of the Royal Fusiliers, almost all of whose men were professional men from the locality of

*The mayor's review outside the Town Hall, Saturday, 5 September 1914.* MRA

Manchester. The battalion quickly left the area to train at Leatherhead and Epsom although it is fair to say that many men did indeed return as commissioned officers in the locally raised Pals units, some being 'poached' even before leaving Manchester. Later that evening, 3 September, a similar meeting of members of the Caledonian Association and the St. Andrew's Society was undertaken to consider the establishment of a Manchester Scottish Battalion.

Although superior in tone, the sentiments upon which the University and Public Schools battalions appealed to their recruits very closely mirrored the appeal of the early Pals battalions to middle class men from the city of Manchester.

During these first few days of September many employees with families felt reluctant to renounce their work and spend time in unproductive queues until they were certain of a place in Kitchener's Army and their local Pals unit. A short cut was to visit the Town Hall and thence the Free Trade Hall where names could be left without the formality of medical examination and attestation. By the evening of the 3 September it was clear that a start had already been made on taking names in this manner for a second City brigade, the first battalion of which would, if War Office permission was given, be the 5th City Battalion.

On Friday, 4 September the Parks Committee of the Manchester Corporation gave its blessing to the idea of allowing the city's largest space of open parkland, Heaton Park, to be used for the men's encampment.[7] On that same day the processes of medical examination and attestation for the 3rd City Battalion was continued. As with Manchester's previous Pals battalions the quality of potential recruits surprised and gratified the hardened military recruiting staff. The men's physical strength and wellbeing contrasted markedly with peace-time recruiting, which was often blighted by the poor physical condition of intending soldiers. Pre war recruiting for the regular Army in South Lancashire had very often found extensive evidence of ricketts, coronary disease and malnutrition amongst their impoverished potential recruits, fifty per cent of whom were therefore frequently rejected on health grounds. By contrast, less than five per cent of the men who attempted to enter the 3rd City Battalion were rejected on health grounds. One influential local newspaper described the men as,

> *...the type which one sees on Saturday mornings in the winter carrying lacrosse and football bags – clean limbed and strong young fellows whom the recruiting officer eyes in vain in peace times. Manchester Evening News, Thursday, 3 September 1914.*

By the close of business on Friday, 4 September more than 750 men had completed their attestation into the 3rd City Battalion. That evening many of the Corporation's employees and members of the council's teaching staff met and handed in 210 names of men wishing to form the nucleus of another civic battalion, the hoped for Town Hall Battalion.

On Friday, 4 September and Saturday, 5 September the 1st City Battalion's men were placed in companies and the completed 16th Manchesters then paraded in front of the Mayor at the Town Hall. The Battalion marched from the Artillery HQ on Hyde Road in Ardwick under the command of Captain Walkley, the recruiting staff officer in Manchester who had taken temporary charge of this officer-less battalion of men. On the 9 September 'A' Company marched into Heaton Park under command of Major Sington to assist in the preparation of the tented accomodation. Throughout the day the Mayor and other officials encouraged the men and later dined with the few officers who were present. Three days later, on Saturday, 12 September, the rest of the battalion paraded at the Artillery HQ and marched off to Heaton Park's sodden fields. They were joined by 2nd City Battalion who arrived there a week later on 19 September.

The process of sorting the likely NCOs was left to the chance identification of men and boys with experience in the Boys Brigade, the Boy Scouts or the Territorials.

*...the Commissionaire asked me, 'Any of you fellows been in the Territorials?' I said, 'Yes I have'. He said, 'You take charge of this tent.' This is where all the fun begins because this tent was all J & N Philips where I worked, and of course there were young and older ones, and the older ones were my bosses. And of course I immediately became their boss... Scout Sgt. Bert Payne. 6310. No. 1 Platoon, 1st City Battalion.*

Between Saturday, 5 September and Monday, 7 September recruiting for the 3rd City Battalion was completed. Unlike their first two companion battalions the 18th Manchesters were initially trained at the White City, a sports and racing stadium in the Old Trafford area, and accomodated there in hastily erected and draughty constructions. Before those huts at the White City became available this battalion's parades were undertaken in the City Hall with route marches to and from Alexandra Park. The battalion only later moved to Heaton Park when huts became available there in February 1915. However, by the week beginning 7 September, it was clear that the Army was unable to cope with the continuing torrent of attestations which Kitchener's appeal had generated. Many men who had resigned their work were being placed on the Army Reserve at a nominal retainer of 3s 6d per week. This caused great hardship for many and its prospect certainly stunted recruitment in some less affluent locations where employment was hard to come by. By Tuesday, 8 September recruiting in Manchester was, by necessity, limited to just the Manchesters and the Lancashire Fusiliers, every regimental depot in other parts of the country being identified as full.

Apart from completing the 3rd City Battalion, Monday, 7 September also saw 565 men examined and attested for the fourth of Manchester's Pals Battalions. By now more than twenty doctors and eighty clerks were engaged in the processing of recruits and the men were being passed through very quickly. Charles Cain, who initially enlisted into the 4th City Battalion, was typical of the swell of enthusiasm which took many under age men into the Pals at this time.

*...I left the office where I worked, and went to Albert Square. At the corner of the Square stood a recruiting Sergeant, dressed in the Manchester Regiment walking out dress of navy blue, three gold stripes on his sleeve, a broad red sash draped across his body, and a red, white and blue rosette at the side of his peaked cap. I suppose in a way, all the men enlisting that day could well imagine themselves looking as smart as this man. I found him affable and informative.*

*'Can I join the Army, as a bugler?' I asked. 'A boy bugler, yes certainly' he replied,*

*Above: The arrival of the fatigue party at Heaton Park, under command of Major Sington.* MRA

'We have boy buglers in the Regulars, You will have to get your parents' permission.' This was a problem, for I had no father and my mother was working as a barmaid in the Isle of Man. I walked round for an hour, to think this out, and then came back to the Sergeant. 'Have you got your parents' permission?' he asked, 'Yes' I replied, and fortunately he did not ask for it in writing, 'Here's 2d, tramfare' he said, handing me a note and the money, 'Take this to Ardwick Drill Hall and see the doctor'.

On entering the Drill Hall, I was amazed to find nearly all the men walking about absolutely naked, I had never seen a naked adult man before, and to see several hundred suddenly like this was rather a shock to me, but I soon found myself without clothes waiting to be attested. The man who measured the height put me under a ruler, pulled down the top bit till it touched my head, 'four feet eleven' he muttered, and then out loud, asked a man who was writing down, 'What's the lowest height for the British Army?' 'Five foot three' came the reply. The sergeant picked up a small box, and asked me to stand upon it, took another measurement, and shouted, 'Five four and a half and when I stepped down he picked up the box, and said, 'I am very sorry, but you will have to carry this box about with you all the time you are in the Army, in case someone wants to know how tall you are.' The doctor gave me an examination, expanded my chest

**Members of the 1st City Battalion march into Heaton Park on the afternoon of Saturday, 12 September. During the afternoon and evening, the damp weather turned to a downpour which saturated the men overnight.** Jones

*Heaton Park Camp. This vivid panorama shows the enormous area of tented accommodation prepared for the first two of Manchester's Pals Battalions during September 1914.* Pawson

*Subsequent groups of men arrive to swell the camp.* MRA

*Men 'in training' pose for the camera! In reality, this period provided very few real opportunities for serious military training or the physical hardening of the men.*

from 27″ to 30″ slapped me on the back, and said, 'You're healthy enough but a bit small, but you'll grow.' I got dressed, much to my relief and restored dignity.

I was then taken with a party of men to the Free Trade Hall, where, before a Magistrate, twelve of us, after excluding a Jewish man, formed a semi-circle to touch a bible with about one finger and repeated the oath of allegiance to the King. The Magistrate then delivered a severe lecture on wine, women and song, after which he asked if there were any questions. I was the only one to ask 'What has wine, women and song got to do with going to war?' He called me to him. 'How old are you?' he asked '16 years' I said, putting a bit on. 'You'll soon learn' he said... Private Charles Cain, who enlisted into the 19th Manchesters, the 4th City Battalion. He was later forced to leave because of his youth, but quickly managed to re-enlist into the 2/5th Manchesters, a second line Territorial unit which contained many short stature Wigan miners. I.W.M. ref: PP/MCR/48.

In truth, the previous week's pressure was now slackening, especially in view of widespread rumours and reports of overcrowding and chaos at regimental depots. Nevertheless, by 16 September the 4th City Battalion was completed. Their drill and training was initially undertaken at the City Exhibition Hall, where they alternated with the 3rd City Battalion, and Hulme Cavalry barracks. By mid October a more satisfactory arrangement was made when Belle Vue Gardens were aquired. The men of this, the 4th City, battalion were however still billeted at home throughout this period, although arrangements were made for mid-day meals to be provided to ensure that a full day's training could be undertaken.

There is little doubt that the bulk of the Pals who had by now enlisted into Manchester's First Brigade, all ostensibly clerks and warehousemen but in fact drawn from a wider range of professional, banking, industrial and scientific circumstances, were filled with a belligerent optimism. They had been, quite clearly, drawn from the more prosperous ranks of the city's employees. Bowlers and boaters were noticeable in their abundance amongst the new recruits' headgear. These men felt themselves to be an élite force, certainly in terms of social status if

*Informal photgraphs abounded as groups of men from the same office and workplace rushed to send evidence of their wellbeing home to their families.*

*Left to right: RQMS Walker, Major Sington, Lieutenant Colonel Crawford and Arthur Taylor of the raising committee. Heaton Park, 11 September.* MRA

*Taken in the late autumn of 1914, this photograph shows officers' tented quarters, belonging to the 1st and 2nd City Battalions in the Heaton Park Camp.*
Pawson

OFFICERS QUARTERS.
HEATON PARK CAMP.

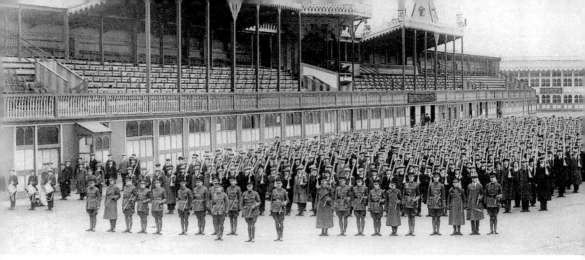

*The 4th City Battalion, the 19th Manchesters, at Belle View, complete with the officers and band. At this stage in the unit's history the men are not equipped with any uniforms and the rifles are, in many cases, a wooden 'dummy' for drill purposes.* Author

not in terms of military efficacy. And not only optimistic, but also firmly convinced of the true righteousness of their cause. The Manchester Pals' origins were in stark contrast to those of the nearby Salford Pals, whose battalions were drawn from the working class terraces, slums, docklands, mills and mines to the west of Manchester city centre.[8]

The close communal links were maintained by visits which many families made into the rather amateurish military routine and hectic activity unfolding at Heaton Park. Before the war it had always been a popular place for families in the summer months. Len Riley remembered the first deep impressions which the soldiers in the park made on his four year old memory. His father, Private William Riley, had enlisted into the 2nd City Pals. His mother had been mortified.

> *Eventually we were allowed to visit him in Heaton Park. When he met us he was still attired in his civilian clothes. I had expected him to be resplendent in a military uniform and was a little dissapointed, but very impressed with the 'Bell Tent' he lived in along with his mates, also dressed in 'civvies'. Heaton Park was alive with soldiers already in khaki, marching, parading, it all gave me quite a thrill.* Len Riley, son of Private William Riley, 8839, 10 Platoon, C Company, 2nd City Battalion.

By Wednesday, 9 September arrangements were well under way to establish the city's fifth Pals unit, the proposed Town Hall and Corporation Employees Battalion. This civic initiative

*Men of the 3rd City Battalion, the 18th Manchesters, pose in front of the bandstand at White City, where they were trained, before being moved to the encampment at Heaton Park.* Pawson

proceeded well in advance of any sanction from the War Office. Nevertheless, Houldsworth Hall, at the Manchester Church House, was taken over to accommodate the recruiting drive. Inadvisedly, the Lord Mayor took the opportunity to write to other local boroughs and corporations appealing to such authorities to send men of similar standing to enlist in Manchester's own Corporation Battalion.

> *If any officers and servants in the employ of your authority, about to enlist in Lord Kitchener's New Army, desire to enlist in a battalion which will be composed of men engaged in performing similar duties, and who, in this way, have a common interest, will they kindly send their names to Captain Walkley, of 67 Victoria Street, Manchester...* Manchester Guardian, Wednesday, 9 September, 1914.

The reality proved that the extraordinary surge of nationalism and enthusiasm seen the previous week was now slackening. Men from other localities would prefer the draw of their own local units. Enlistment at Houldsworth Hall was patchy, less than one hundred a day by Wednesday, 9 September. By contrast on 10 September, the U.P.S. battalion had enlisted its 858th man and were busy drilling at Chetham's Hospital School, under the shadow of Manchester Cathedral. The existence of this battalion and the Manchester Scottish did much to slow recruitment into Manchester's Pals during the second week of September. This was especially disappointing in view of the fact that men enlisting into the Pals were receiving a full allowance rather than the paltry 3s 6d which men recruited into the general service battalions received upon being posted to reserve. It was now clear that a Town Hall battalion could not generate sufficient numbers and the feeling was out in the city that the War Office had now received sufficient men for its likely requirements.

All, however, was not yet done. A further publicity drive and recruiting initiative in November did much to rescue the position. Permission to establish the battalion was only granted by the War Office on 7 November. The huge Victorian Town Hall was commandeered to replace the unsuccessful Houldsworth Hall location. Outside the municipal buildings in Albert Square a huge recruiting barometer and exhortations to enlist into local units called passers-by to the colours. The Corporation men found themselves as the nucleus for the 5th and 6th City Battalions. Recruiting started in earnest again on the 16 November and the 5th City was completed by the 18 November, with an excess of two hundred men. By Monday, 23 November only thirty six more men were wanted to complete enlistment into the 6th City Battalion and it was made public that the War Office had granted the city permission to embark on the raising of a seventh Pals unit. By the end of that day 200 men had indeed already enlisted into the 7th City Battalion. It was now becoming clear to recruiting officials that the Pals movement in Manchester was coming to the end of that supply of middle class men whose character had percolated throughout the first four battalions. In some respects these remaining battalions took on a different style with an increasing proportion of their recruits drawn from rather less prosperous circumstances.

The initiative which completed the Manchester City Battalions and therefore the Second City Brigade was made by Mr D E Anderson of West Didsbury, acting on behalf of the Manchester branch of the National Service League. Taking advantage of the enthusiasm of men previously rejected on the grounds of insufficient height, Anderson

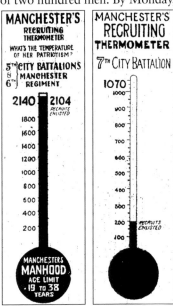

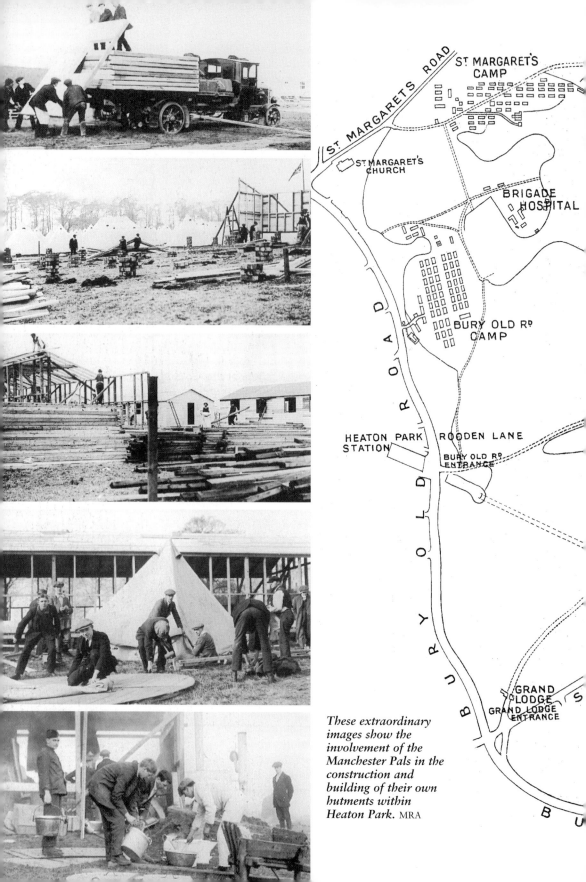

These extraordinary images show the involvement of the Manchester Pals in the construction and building of their own hutments within Heaton Park. MRA

HALL CAMP

HEATON HALL

# HEATON PARK

*Plan of the Heaton Park campsite showing the locations of each of the battalions which were housed within the parkland area.* Pawson

MIDDLETON RD. ENTRANCE

MIDDLETON RD. CAMP

MIDDLETON ROAD

OOT LANE

CHEETHAM HILL RD.

LEICESTER RD.

OLD ROAD

*Private Harry Westerman, 17795, 5th City Battalion. Unlike many of the distinctly middle class recruits to the 1st City Brigade, Harry Westerman came from the far less prosperous Ancoats area of central Manchester. He enlisted along with many other members of the Ancoats Lads Club football team who then, 'all swore never to accept promotion so that no-one would be giving or receiving orders from a friend'.* Westerman

began enrolling men's names for what became known as 'Bob's Own', the Manchester Bantams. By Wednesday, 25 November Anderson had the names of 1,208 men of short stature who would soon form the 8th City Battalion. Permission to raise the 23rd Manchesters had been given to the City's Lord Mayor by War Office telegram the previous evening. It was clear that attestation for the bantams would be completed well in advance of that for the 7th City Battalion, the 22nd Manchesters.

The completion of two Brigades was vivid testimony to Manchester's committment. However, it would prove impossible to accomodate and train all eight of these battalions within the confines of the city and the search was on to identify another location where the training and preparation of the 2nd Brigade could be undertaken. In the meantime the sight of so many men travelling by tram, en route for their drill sessions, ensured that the blue serge uniformed men of the 1st Brigade aquired the nickname 'the tramguards'.

As the 1st Brigade gradually filled Heaton Park, locations at Belle Vue, City Hall and elsewhere became available for drill purposes to the men of the 2nd Brigade, who would remain billeted at home during the November and December of 1914. Within weeks of their attestations the men of the City battalions were sufficiently smart to be reviewed and inspected by the Lord Mayor, on the 21 November, and their Colonel-in-Chief, Lord Derby, who travelled to Manchester to see the men on 24 November. By this time the first to enlist were beginning to find their feet. A tiny number of men already had the advantage of limited part time military experience. Before the outbreak of war Bert Payne had completed four years service with one of the Salford Territorial units of the Lancashire Fusiliers. It had been 'something to do', but the experience and expertise gained there stood him in good stead during the initial training of men whom he had previously regarded as his superiors at work. Now, in the world of military weaponry, training manuals and the potential difficulty of conversation with

unwilling French farmers, the twenty-one year old Sergeant was expected to take the lead.

*In my company, after I was appointed as scout I had three men from Brunner-Mond, scientists, intelligent men, who were given to me as scouts. We had to train as infantrymen and I was learning all the manuals. About twelve manuals I had to learn, Infantry Training, Cavalry Training, Musketry, Signalling, Field Engineering, Judging Distance, Map reading, sketching*

*Private James Adams, 22602, of the 8th City Battalion, the 23rd Manchesters. He is pictured in his Moss Side backyard with his wife, Alice, and son who has affixed one of his father's cap badges to his own waistcoat. He enlisted on 28 December 1914, having left his job as a painter and decorator, at the age of thirty-six. Before the outbreak of war he had completed a period of service with 1/9th Battalion, a Territorial unit of the Manchester Regiment.* Horsfield

*Officers of the 1st City Battalion at Heaton Park. To the right of the C.O. is the Adjutant, 6ft 6in tall Captain Southam. An ex-regular who had commanded a Camel Corps in Somaliland, Southam became a much loved Pals officer whilst managing to maintain a fearsome attitude towards military and regimental correctness. On the occasion of his initial review of his subalterns who were newly arrived and kitted in their hand tailored uniforms, Southam approached one 2nd Lieutenant who was wearing a gold tie pin. Southam's comment was withering 'Take that off young man. Officers in the Manchester Regiment do not wear jewelry.' The central figure in the back row is Wilfreth Elstob, a future commander of the 1st City Battalion and destined to become the most highly decorated of the officers who served within the Manchester Pals. Four to Elstob's right is his A Company commander and great friend, Hubert Worthington.* Worthington

*and trigonometry, estimating heights and gradients to get the culminating point in musketry, how to find the extreme range of a bullet, which is about 2,000 yards. I can't understand why they gave me the job, but they must have thought I knew something because I was good at musketry and I trained the men very well. I was the only one who had been a Territorial. I had a job of billeting. I had to find out how much hay a farmer had, and I would measure it by multiplying the length and breadth and dividing it by eleven to get the number of tons of hay in the stack. And how many horses he had because we may want to borrow the horses and we would want the fodder for our horses if we needed it. We had route marches at Heaton Park just to get us into fitness because we were very genteel sort of people, we weren't rough tough guys.* Scout Sgt. Bert Payne. Ist City Battalion, 16th Manchesters.

Negotiations were in fact well advanced for the 2nd Brigade's relocation to the seaside. Since 10 December Morecambe's Council had established a sub committee consisting of John Birkett, JP, who was the Mayor of Morecambe, Alderman Brown and Councillor Escolme, to make arrangements for the billeting of troops. On Monday, 14 December these three men travelled to Manchester to receive final confirmation of the decision. It was to prove very agreeable for the seaside town and one which generated great excitement there. Much trade was at stake.

By 16 December Lieutenant Colonel Arnold of the 20th Manchesters confirmed the impending arrival of his men.

> Husbands and sons and brothers too — they want to go. Will Manchester's womenfolk hold them back at this critical hour? — the hour when the fighting man is the vital need.
>
> Let Manchester's 7th and 8th City Battalions supply the answer.
>
> Bid the menfolk enlist NOW. Send them along to the Manchester Town Hall **to-day.**
>
> The War Office have sanctioned recruiting for a 7th and 8th City Battalion. Manchester can quickly raise them if her young men come forward now. In memory of the late Lord Roberts the 8th will be known as the "Bôbs" City Battalion, and the height standard is from 5 ft. up to 5 ft. 3 in. Other conditions as usual. Minimum chest measurement, 34½ in. Age 19 to 38.
>
> For the 7th City Battalion the previous height standard still holds good, 5 ft. 3 in.
>
> R. TOOTAL BROADHURST. A. HERBERT DIXON. } *Special*
> R. M. PHELPS. ARTHUR TAYLOR. } *Sub.*
> KENNETH LEE. VERNON ELLOURNE. } *Committee*

*An advertisement for the 7th and 8th Manchester.*
Manchester Guardian *Thursday, 26 November 1914.*

*Above: Photograph 315 by the local Manchester photographer, Tuson, clearly reveals the relative wellbeing and affluence of many Manchester recruits through the appearance of their casual civvies.* Pawson

*The Lord Mayor of Manchester reviewing his troops on 21 November 1914.*

*Wilfred Walton in civilian dress with men of the 1st Brigade in their 'tramguards' uniforms at Heaton Park. Walton was later commissioned into the Salford Pals.* Walton

CITY BATTALIONS MANCHESTER REGIMENT. HEATON PARK.

These two photographs were taken during the occasion of Lord Derby's inspection of the 1st and 2nd Manchester Pals on 24 November 1914. In the photograph below Lord Derby is accompanied by Lieutenant Colonel Crawford. The men nearest to him, A Company of the 1st Pals, have been issued with rifles. Whilst the rest of that battalion are equipped with their blue uniforms, the 2nd Pals are still dressed in their civilian clothing. In the background of the top photograph is the haystack under which aspiring NCOs were asked to make their calculations about forage for horses and practice suitable negotiations with French farmers. Walton

Another group of Pals, probably men of the 2nd City Battalion, wait patiently for the arrival of their Honorary Colonel, Lord Derby. Capper

*A Public Notice announcing the prospective Billeting of troops in Morecambe.* MV & HC 9 December 1914

Provision merchants anticipated a considerable windfall of income. Breakfast for billeted men would consist of 6ozs of bread, butter and jam, 1 pt of tea with milk and sugar together with 4 ozs of bacon or fish. Dinner would include 1 lb of meat ('previous to being dressed, or equivalent in soup, fish or pudding'), ½ lb of bread and half a pound of potatoes or other vegetables, together with an 'optional pint' of beer or mineral water to the same value. Tea was a light meal of 6ozs of bread and butter, another pint of tea and potted meat or cheese.

On 23 December the town's good fortune at Christmas was made public.

*All Schools and Entertainment Halls to be Utilised.*
*Free Tram Rides to and From Drill Grounds.*
*2s 6d per head per day for Billeting.*
*2,040 Coming on Dec. 30 and nearly 3,000 on Jan. 2.*

*They are composed of better class men, many of whom are well to do, and have private means apart from their army pay...* M.V. & H.C. 23 December 1914.

Never before had the seaside resort of Morecambe been busier during a pre-Christmas week. The atmosphere was expectant and enthusiastic. The first Manchester battalion to arrive in Morecambe was the 5th City, the 20th Manchesters. On the penultimate day of December, in mid morning, their train left its parent city, the carriage sides daubed with messages of cheer. 'To Berlin, via Morecambe' was popular with many of the graffito artists, as was 'To Berlin via Ypres'! Well before mid-day large crowds had gathered at the London and North-Western Railway station buildings in Morecambe to witness the seaside arrival of the Pals. A short while after the 5th City left home the 6th City Battalion commanded by Brevet Colonel W W Norman were following in their footsteps.

On the second day of the new year the 7th City Battalion, commanded by Lieutenant Colonel Etheredge D.S.O., and the 8th City Battalion, commanded by Lieutenant Colonel Cook, arrived in Morecambe.

Within hours all of these men's impact upon the life of the town was being felt. Billeting parties formed queues at every street corner. Landladies, housewives and families welcomed two, three, four and often more strangers into their homes.

*Local suppliers lost no time in incorporating the troops' arrival into their advertising!* MV & HC 30 December 1914

*A typical billet. These two photographs show a group of men from D Company of the 7th City Battalion (note the indication on the door) with their landlady, husband and twin daughters. The second photograph shows the same group of men in a rather more martial pose a few seconds later.* Pawson

*In some of the front houses, particularly Eidsforth-terrace, six, eight, twelve and fourteen men are billeted in one house. The men will have no need to fear that they will not be properly looked after, for as one landlady put it, 'They will be all right, sir, here. Send me some good lads and I'll treat them right.'* M.V.& H.C. 30 December 1914.

Bugles, drums and the sound of marching feet became a commonplace experience for excited schoolchildren. Reveille was sounded at each battalion's HQ at 7.00 am, after which each company's bugler marched through their men's streets, playing a series of jaunty tunes to ensure that no late sleepers dwelt too long within the comfort of their billets. Breakfast at 7.45 am, dinner at 1.00 pm, and tea at 5.00 pm. The adopting mothers found their new charges much to their liking. Not quite as free spending as the normal summer trade, but militarily guaranteed and, for the most part, more dependable in manners.

Morecambe itself proved to be ideal.

It was fresh. Open spaces abounded. The beaches and surrounding countryside provided every conceivable opportunity for exercise, training and recreation.

Fields turned into sports grounds. Country tracks were thronged with route marching companies. Football and sports equipment sales broke all records and the town's piers provided many excellent vantage points to witness the endless stream of soccer and improvised sports on the sands. The Y.M.C.A. and the churches took the interests of the men to heart, providing reading rooms, free letter writing paper, newspapers, draughts, chess and dominoes. Enterprising locals quickly grasped the opportunity to erect refreshment stalls where 'coffee and eatables can be had at nominal cost.' The culturally more adventurous men were able to embark upon Monsieur Menetriere's French evening classes, courtesy of the Belgian refugee community hosted by the town of Morecambe. One penny a session ensured sufficient fluency to cope with most continental requirements and one hundred and thirty enthusiasts set out on the rocky road towards multilingualism.

The Royalty Theatre was contacted by men of the 6th and 8th City Battalions, the 21st and 23rd Manchesters, with a view to giving vent to their commercial and entrepreneurial talents. From these battalions committees of men organised themselves to promote tournaments and competitions. £3 for the winners. £2 for each second place. Substantial prizes like these ensured a large entry for a series of boxing and wrestling events.

Throughout the town's entertainment halls the soldier's tastes and purse were well catered for as Morecambe came to realise the advantage of its commercial good fortune. The Whitehall Picture House offered *Fighting Death*, *The Naval Secret (3000 feet)* and additional features including *The Mysterious Shot*. The Alhambra's custom was called to witness *Little Soldiers of Rome... A Military Drama of Absorbing Interest*. Just down the road, at the Palladium, Lancaster's

*...finest Photo Play House, offered Mother of Men... A Fine War Drama, and Guarding Britain's Secrets... A Great Military Drama.* M.V. & H.C. 13 January 1915

During the first few short days of January every available moment of daylight was used in interminable drill and marching. Files of men were seen everywhere, marching, inclining, turning, at the double, forming fours and squads, constantly under the intent gaze of an inquisitive schoolchild's eyes, ready to draw shrill attention to every unfortunate who failed to fulfill his N.C.O's wishes! Companies in 'civvies', some in blue, a minority mostly consisting of experienced NCOs in khaki. They did not look much like an army yet.

Infantrymen who were able to glimpse a copy of the local *Visitor*, a week after their arrival, marvelled at their officer's fare, a contrast with their own rather more straight-forward victualling.

*The officers are billeted at the Grand, Midland, Clarenden and Park Hotels at the rate*

*Above and below: These photographs show Alfred Bland being trained at Berkhampstead in the December of 1914, before being commissioned into the Manchesters. Alfred Bland was a graduate of Queen's College, Oxford and had begun to work as a historian for the Public Record Office with colleagues from the University of London. In 1914 his first book had been published.[9] Although not a lawyer he had, along with many other educated and middle class London intellectuals, joined the Inns of Court OTC who were later responsible for sending hundreds of these young men on to regiments such as the Manchesters. By February of 1915 Alfred Bland was with the 7th City, the 22nd Manchesters. By virtue of its later establishment and recruiting the Second City Brigade was far more dependant upon the supply of OTC men than had been the case with the First Brigade, who had been able to recruit a higher proportion of experienced and regular Officers and NCOs from Reserve. However, in action, the courage, leadership and commitment of these relatively inexperienced officers was beyond praise.* Mace

*of 4s.6d. per day. Their schedule of meals is:- Breakfast: Porridge and two dishes, tea and coffee. Lunch: Hot and cold meats; sweet, cheese. Afternoon tea: Bread and butter and cake. Dinner: Soup and fish, joint, sweet, cheese.* M.V.& H.C. 6 January 1915

Presiding over the whole was Brigadier General Kempster, D.S.O., who arrived to take command. He had retired from military service in 1902 with the rank of Colonel but had been gazetted Brigadier General to supervise the progress of Manchester's 2nd Brigade. He had joined the army in 1876 and served in the Afghan war during 1880. Further service included Bechuanaland in 1884/5 and the Soudan Frontier Force in 1887, where he was

mentioned in despatches and awarded the D.S.O. He was promoted to the rank of Lieutenant Colonel in 1896 and served on the North West Frontier in 1897, where he was again mentioned in despatches. Kempster's senior battalion commander, Lieutenant Colonel A J Arnold, had an equally traditional and military background. Out of a public school into Cambridge, Arnold had enlisted into the Dragoon Guards in 1886. By 1893 he had become a 2nd Lieutenant in the 3rd Hussars, from whom he joined the Royal Niger Constabulary in 1894. He served during the Niger Sudan campaign in 1897 during which he was promoted to the rank of Captain and awarded the D.S.O. His career with the British army had ended in the Transvaal in 1901 after which he had followed a career as 'Inspecteur-General d'Exploitation Mozambique Company' until 1913, during which time he had developed an enthusiasm for 'Big Game Shooting'!

Of course not every one of Manchester's Pals managed to steer the straightest of courses throughout their training.

On Friday, 12 February John Drummond, a ship's cook from Cheetham with the 7th City Battalion, appeared at Morecambe Magistrates Court charged with stealing a purse and £4 17s 6d, being the weeks billeting monies for himself and five other Pals who were living with Mrs Marshall of 63 Westminster Road. Private Drummond claimed at the hearing to have used the money to travel to London, Newcastle, Barrow and Manchester in search of work on a merchant ship.

At Manchester Assize Court, one week later, Private Drummond was sentenced to three years 'penal servitude'. Sentences for crimes committed by these volunteer soldiers were usually of a punitive and firmly deterrent nature although they were usually commuted in order to allow each man to continue service with his battalion in return for an undertaking of future good behaviour.

Another of the Pals, Private Edward Hanson, 'alias Marcus Bowyer', a printer by trade but now with Bob's Own, had been committed at Manchester's Quarter Sessions on 6th April charged with stealing a bicycle. Having hired the machine from a Morecambe dealer Private Hanson failed to return and was later picked up by Manchester Police, the bicycle turning up at Victoria station. Having admitted stealing the machine the twenty five year old bantam said in his defence that he had no intention of keeping the machine 'permanently'. After borrowing it he had pedalled to Manchester because he was 'in trouble' with a woman.

Sentenced to three months hard labour!

For athletes and competitors among the Morecambe men, opportunities to compete in cross country races were a welcome relief. Saturday, 6 March saw one such race started at 3.00 pm. It was sponsored by a number of local people and the Morecambe hotel who between themselves had donated prizes including gold and silver medals, a silver cigarette case and a case of safety razors. Market Street's tobacconist, Mrs Baird, donated a fine silver mounted walking stick and the first bantam past the post would receive a framed photograph of the competitors. Truly an eccentric collection of sports prizes.

Problematically, the outcome of the race was something of a foregone conclusion since numbered among the Manchester Pals was one C E Bergemeir, an Australian and World half mile running champion! Nevertheless, 175 enthusiastic athletes braved the late afternoon winter chill to tackle the five mile course, laid out by Sergeant Daniels and Corporal Gannon of the 5th City Battalion. All hoped for the celebrity which would follow a victory over the speedy antipodean.

By 4.40 pm, the gold medal was safely numbered amongst Private Bergemeir's collection, the course having been covered in 32 mins 45 secs. However, for those forced to be content with the places there was always the Brigade's Sports Day to fix their hopes on.

The Second Brigade had, by the beginning of March 1915, experienced two months of

*The bantams take their ease, whilst in the middle of digging trenches within the confines of a farm behind the seafront at Morecambe.* Pawson

*The 23rd Manchesters engaged in Swedish Drill, on the seafront at Morecambe. Behind the men, straining to look comfortable whilst resting casually on one arm, another company of Manchesters are marching, perhaps smiling to themselves at the photographers exhortations to the men to stay still for just one more picture!* Pawson

*The typical photograph of a Manchester Pals platoon, before their training and uniforms transformed their bearing and stature. This photograph shows platoon XI, C Company of the 4th City Battalion, the 19th Manchesters. Like literally hundreds of other photographs this was the work of the photographers Tuson, taken at Heaton Park in October of 1914.* Chapman

training together. Like many other units raised locally the Second Brigade had been 'billeted on themselves' whilst in Manchester, and then continued a similarly informal arrangement within homes and boarding houses amongst the welcoming people of Morecambe. Whilst avoiding the capital outlays associated with permanent camp hutments, such arrangements had distinct disadvantages. Time was wasted whilst the men assembled for each days drill and training. Time was lost in making feeding arrangements. It proved more difficult to develop the sort of *esprit de corps* which units hutted together could develop at their leisure. Material shortages and delays in the fabrication of khaki uniforms meant that the men were still attired in their much disliked 'tramguards' kit in early March. And finally, being distant from their parent locality, and its raising committee, the Second Brigade was lost to its community early and came to be looked upon as the less favoured of Manchester's two Pals Brigades.

However, the spring of 1915 saw continued urgency in the training and preparation of Manchester's battalions. The news from the Western Front remained dour. Casualties among the regular battalions raised in the Manchester area had already been heavy. The ill conceived disaster along the Dardanelles would soon leave hundreds of local families benefit. Regular and the many Territorial battalions whose origins were in Manchester, Salford, Rochdale, Bury and other nearby localities suffered terrible casualties at Gallipoli. The Helles memorial at Gallipoli records the names of 1,329 Lancashire Fusiliers and 1,177 men from the Manchester Regiment killed during the campaign and whose bodies were either never recovered or are buried in unmarked graves. These numbers far exceeded in their disastrous local impact the casualties suffered by any other area as a consequence of the Gallipoli fighting. Just seven months into the war it was becoming starkly clear that the hundreds of battalions in Kitchener's Armies would soon be needed to hold their own grim places on the battlefields of France and Belgium. For many Manchester families there was already a deep and personal feeling of retribution to be attended to in these matters.

## Notes

1 *Manchester Evening News*. Thursday, 3 September, 1914.
2 Vernon Bellhouse. E Tootal Broadhurst. A Herbert Dixon. Kenneth Lee. Sir Daniel McCabe. Edward M Philips. Arthur E Piggott. Arthur Taylor.
3 Or employed by other responsible 'houses' whose owners were prepared to vouch for their men's status with a written statement of support.
4 In all there were seven donations to the guarantee fund in excess of 1,000. Throughout this early period of the war there was an extraordinary enthusiasm for the idea of encouraging civilian enlistment into the armed forces, from all of the area's major employers. Mather and Platt, for example, held numerous recruitment meetings on their own premises, addressed by Sir William Mather, designed to foster enlistment. Throughout the entirety of the war 1,230 from this engineering company alone joined the armed services, 175 being killed.
5 Simkins. *Kitchener's Army*. Manchester University Press. 1988. pp 66.
6 Anon. *The History of the Royal Fusiliers*. UPS University and Public Schools Brigade. (Formation and Training) Times Publishing Co. London. 1917.
7 Although the influence of the old aristocracy was on the wane in Manchester one of these families indirectly exerted a great influence over the armed forces raised by the city in 1914. The Egertons (later the Earls of Wilton), whose ancestral home had been at Heaton Park, sold the land of the park and the hall buildings to the City of Manchester in 1902 for a fee of £230,000. In the years before the outbreak of war Heaton Park had become a favourite recreational haunt for the people of Higher Broughton, Prestwich and Cheetham Hill.
8 Stedman. *Salford Pals*. 1993, Leo Cooper.
9 *English Economic History,* Select Documents. A E Bland, P A Brown & R H Tawney. Published by G Bell & Son, 1914.

## Chapter Three

# 'Its a case of just going over to put the lid on it'[1]

*'...every man was so keen and so intelligent. For the man in the ordinary army I suppose it was just a job for them but our men were really civilians turned into soldiers and every man was really each other's friend.'[2]*

Whilst life in Morecambe provided a healthy, recreational and domestic familiarity for the Second Brigade's men, their partners in the first four battalions were being forged in a quite different atmosphere at Heaton Park. The park's proximity to the city and the men's families meant that the First Brigade became the darlings of the community. Within that Brigade the first to enlist, the 1st City Battalion, was everybody's favourite. The railing outside the camp, and the numerous pathways which ran through, provided ample opportunity for children and well-wishers to glimpse the constant physical preparation of their civic soldiers, throughout each day. Many friends and children visited within the camp and in the evening the sounds of merriment and music enlivened the

*The First City Brigade were the objects of frequent review and inspection during late November and early December 1914. As the showpiece of what the city's recruiting effort had achieved the men's visitors included the Lord Mayor, who reviewed his troops on 21 November, and Sir Henry Mackinnon, G.O.C., Western Command on 1 December.* MRA/Pawson

*Lieutenant Colonels Crawford and Johnson at Heaton Park, together with the 1st City Battalion's adjutant.*
Pawson

camp scene. For more clandestine meetings it was always possible for men to meet their many 'admirers' and girlfriends within the local pubs during free evening hours. However, during the winter months of late 1914 the damp fogs, for which Manchester and Salford were renowned, hung heavily in the great bowl of Heaton Park. Underground, the impermeable subsoil and rock meant that the hutments soon acquired a reputation for tedious mud and slushy conditions.

The 2nd City Battalion had arrived in Heaton Park on 19 September. They and their sister battalion, the 1st City, were reviewed by Lord Derby on 24 November, and on 1 December by General Sir Henry Mackinnon, G.O.C. Western Command. The 4th City Battalion, who spent their early weeks within the New Armies billeted at home, identified details of forthcoming parades and marches from the pages of the *Manchester Evening News*. On 15 October the Zoological Gardens at Belle Vue were taken over for the purposes of training. In front of disinterested ranks of sea lions, monkeys, penguins and parakeets the men received their initial arms drill and exercises. Whilst the casual human visitor to the gardens was enthralled by the spectacle of hesitant drilling, the men were less enthusiastic about the close proximity

*Groups of men belonging to the first brigade at Heaton Park, on a frame from which suspended ropes provide a challenge to strengthen limbs during inter-platoon competitions.* MRA

*Officers at revolver practice in one of the purpose built ranges at Heaton Park.* MRA

*Route marches through the rain sodden streets of Manchester tested the men's durability and temper. Complete care, with the few rifles which were available, was still not fully understood. 'Watch that rifle son!' The photograph on the left shows the field kitchens which provided refreshment during another wet day's training.* MRA

of critical and vociferous children throughout the daylight hours. On 30 November the 4th City Battalion joined their Pals of the 1st and 2nd City at Heaton Park. Whilst gaining the pleasure and security of comradeship, the 4th City Battalion now lost those evening dances and relaxation to the melodies of the Belle Vue band which had marked so many autumnal evenings for this group of men. In the January of 1915 the First Brigade received its own staff, the Brigadier being Lieutenant Colonel H C E Westropp.[3] That same month also saw the delivery of the final blue uniforms and great coats to the 4th City men. It was not until 7 February that the 3rd City Battalion, the 18th Manchesters, emerged from their unpopular and draughty accommodation at the White City in Old Trafford to concentrate with the rest of the Brigade at Heaton Park.

Though still without khaki dress, the men were now able to embark upon specialist section training: scout groups, signallers, administration, stores, platoons of riflemen and machine gun sections. It was no matter that service weapons were not available. Throughout February the correct service dress and equipment items were delivered and the transformation into something that at least looked like a military unit was effected. As preparations began for the anticipated review by Lord Kitchener, the pioneer sections continued to work overtime in the creation of as many wooden rifles as were required to kit each man who would be without their drill pattern or Lee Metford rifles.

The unrelenting pressure of preparation was accelerating, albeit slowly.

## The review by Lord Kitchener

A fine spring morning, Sunday, 21 March dawned bright and clear over north west England. It was a day filled with frenetic preparation, both in Manchester and Morecambe. Upon arrival within the city Lord Kitchener, Secretary of State at the War Office, and more than anybody associated in the public's mind with the raising of the New Armies, was to be met by the Lord Mayor. Alongside were the Town Clerk, the Chief Constable and civic representatives from Salford and other nearby towns whose own battalions were to parade. Already that day Kitchener had witnessed a massive review in nearby Liverpool. It was imperative that Manchester's efforts at least matched those of Merseyside.

On the platform constructed on the Town Hall steps, apart from Kitchener and the civic parties, would be Lord Derby, General Sir A. Murray, General Sir Henry Mackinnon and a number of battalion commanding officers. Already, by early morning, many families were gathering in the shadow of the great Victorian edifice, hoping for a grandstand view and the chance to greet and cheer their own brothers, fathers and sons. Above the swelling numbers a massive board charted recruiting for the County Palatine Engineers. Friday had been a poor day for recruiting, the worst since the previous August, and it was hoped that Kitchener's presence would boost the figures.

In the small hours of morning the Morecambe men entrained for Manchester. Like the Heaton Park contingent, they arrived outside the city centre far too early. The battalions had been joined, en-route for the square, by a number of Lancashire Fusilier service battalions, including parties of the Salford Pals as well as bantam units from south east Lancashire. Over eleven thousand men were forced to wait beyond the confines of Albert Square while K's party assembled on the Town Hall's steps. For well over a mile the men sweltered in the heat of an unusually hot spring morning. Their arrival,

> ...surprised many people at their mid-day meal, but the halt enabled them to catch up with events, and a few, whose houses were on the line of the route, had the happy thought of bringing out their dessert to share it with the Pals in the street. They showered oranges and apples on a thirsty company, for marching in the sun, though there was a wind, was warm work, especially for those of the men who, coming from Morecambe and not counting on such a glorious beginning to spring, had brought their greatcoats with them. It was a day of unqualified beauty. Manchester Guardian. 22 March 1915.

At the appointed hour Kitchener's arrival in the square was marked by an enormous roar of approval. For a few moments he had surveyed the sea of inquisitive faces who, in their turn, studied his features, comparing them with the legendary lines and eyes which had made a million recruiting posters unforgettable to the nation. A persistent sweep of greying hair was noted, his face a little fuller and his eyes more tired than the myriad posters suggested.

Kitchener was to watch an unprecedented proof of Manchester and Salford's commitment

*Men waiting, outside suburban houses, for the chance to move on towards their review by Kitchener.* Pawson

to the war effort, an unbroken hour of marching soldiers. Starting at half past two the two City Brigades had been followed by detachments from the 15th and 16th Lancashire Fusiliers, the Salford Pals, who had returned from their camps at the Morfa outside Conway, two bantam battalions from Chadderton and Bury which formed the Lancashire Fusiliers' 17th and 18th service battalions, together with the, as yet, incomplete 19th Lancashire Fusiliers, the third of Salford's Pals battalions.

For the first time the First City Brigade wore their khaki service dress and leather field equipment in public. Six months training had seen an enormous development of their physique and precision. But it was the 2nd Brigade, still dressed in their 'Kitchener blue', who startled all with their healthy complexion and vitality. The sea air had worked wonders.

The lines of men which Kitchener reviewed represented many strands of fraternity from the areas which surrounded the city centre. Without doubt the greatest pride was felt for the eight battalions which represented the best men which Manchester could field, their two Brigades. Within the great square the marching and attention to detail was marked by precision as men, eyes briefly turned left, waited the almost imperceptible nod of recognition from K. Elsewhere, on the routes away from the square, the greetings were more personal and pertinent to the civilian army which, a few weeks before, had been the warehousemen, artisans, clerks, salesmen and engineers of Manchester's commerce and industry. Sisters and parents shouted greetings, a 'Jack' or an 'Ernest', guiding it to the man in question and, away from the formality of the Town Hall review, recipients turned briefly to smile. This was family business.

Within fifteen minutes of the parade's end Kitchener was on his way. For him it had been a long day. In the morning he had seen a similar March Past in Liverpool, providing him with a first opportunity to see a number of bantam units. Kitchener had also taken the chance

*Designed to capitalize on Kitchener's visit, this recruiting appeal was published in the* Manchester Guardian *on the 22 March, the day after the review.*

afforded by his visit to hand a pointed letter from the Government to James Sexton, General Secretary of Liverpool's Dock-Workers Union, warning him of Governmental displeasure at continued industrial unrest there. This was grave business.

The following day the *Manchester Guardian* identified the many heartfelt emotions of the city. Their leading article was an extraordinary testimony to the position of the Pals within local society.

*Only now and then in these months of war has it been forced fully home to us that we are living history, but the dullest could not see the march of the twelve thousand yesterday without knowing that of this his children's children will be told. Nor could he see it without a deep and quickening sense of his personal relation to the facts behind it. For Manchester's army is Manchester, and the New Army is Britain, in a way no soldiers ever have been before or, it is hoped, will ever need be again. The people who cheered and the people who marched were not spectators and a spectacle. They were kin in the truest sense, and every eligible man who watched the City Battalions swing by must have felt it an incongruous thing that he was not on the other side of the barrier.* Manchester Guardian. 22 March 1915

Morecambe's newspaper took a somewhat more parochial view of the event, taking the opportunity to emphasize the bracing attributes of the west coast clime. Their article recalled the,

*...cold January afternoon when the Manchester men arrived. How pale and delicate many of them looked...*

But now noted that, at the review,

*...the Heaton Park men were ruddy compared with the average city dweller, but the countenances of the Morecambe men constituted convincing evidence of the superiority of seaside air. They were tanned and reddened as though they had been on foreign service.* M.V.& H.C. 24 March 1915

The men of both City Brigades were now just one month away from their departure from initial training. They would be concentrated into the more rigorous and demanding regime which awaited at Belton Park, near Grantham, Lincolnshire. Before their departures the men celebrated their physical prowess at two sports days.

That for the Second Brigade was held on 7 April. Open ground behind *Bare's Elms* hotel was the scene. Again the *Morecambe Hotel's* Mr Daniels had been active in providing facilities whilst the arrangements were made. The organizing committee settled upon admission charges of 6d and 1s. Substantial prizes were on offer and, thankfully for the home grown talents, rumours were in circulation that Private Bergemeir was injured. Again the weather was cold but this could not prevent a crowd of over 5,000 spectators from gathering.

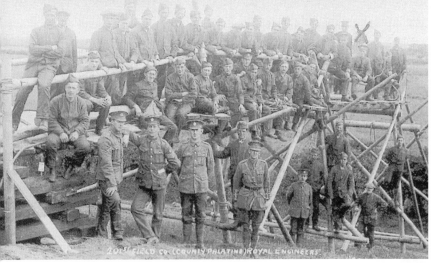

*The County Palatine Engineers. The massive hoardings outside the Town Hall in Manchester had charted the enlistment of these men, alongside the County Palatine RFA. Although these men served within the Royal Engineers, they were in effect a Manchester unit, very similar in composition to the city's Pals units.* Pawson

*Before and After. Two remarkable photographs of Sergeant Fletcher of the 18th Battalion, show the dramatic effect that a few months of serious training had on the appearance of a man. The first picture shows him as a Lance Corporal at the White City, the second a fully fledged Sergeant in his full uniform soon after the Kitchener review.* Pawson

Collections and badge sales made this into a profitable day for the local Red Cross Society to whom the proceeds went in order to support their work amongst the many injured and crippled soldiers, a steady stream of whom were arriving at the town's hospitals. In competition the Whitehead brothers had a particularly profitable day, cleaning up the prizes in both the 220 yards handicap and the half mile race, gathering a number of silver cups and yet another silver mounted walking stick!

Four days later, on 11 April, the First Brigade held their final church parade, every inch of space within Manchester's Cathedral being filled to overflowing with the ranks of men, their civic sponsors and other well wishers.

Back at Heaton Park, on 21 April, the First Brigade's sports were held in front of 20,000 family members and spectators. For many relatives and friends this was a final opportunity to witness the public spectacle of the Pals Battalions. Departure arrangements were already in hand. The following day, confirmation of the Second Brigade's imminent leave-taking was made when the Inspector of Infantry, Major General Dickson, reviewed the progress made by

*One of the many thousands of family portraits which were taken in Manchester, after the issue of the khaki field dress and before the men's departure for Belton Park. The photograph shows Private Albert Hurst, 9311, of the 2nd City Battalion, with (left to right) his three brothers Winston, Walter and Joseph, his sister Dora and parents, Alice and Joseph.* Hurst

the Morecambe men. Their display of prowess included the attack and defence of numerous local farms, musketry, signalling, entrenching and bayonet exercises. General Dickson's whirlwind tour confirmed all was well. Arrangements were set in train for their joining with their Pals in the First City Brigade.

On Saturday, 24 April the First Brigade's men left for Belton Park.[4]

This was not the sort of parting which Manchester wanted. The men marched briskly, down from Heaton Park, in half battalions. In some places the streets were thinly lined with a ribbon of interested onlookers. In a few places a small huddle of work-mates, wives, girlfriends and children had gathered to wave good-bye, proud to see their men but unsure about the future. As the contingents came along Corporation Street, Market Street and on to London Road Station there was a marked absence of colour and enthusiasm.

> *Some of the contingents came down with brass bands gaily playing, and some with bugles and drums, those insistent bugles challenging the men on the kerb to come along and fall in. It was fine to watch, but it was certainly a broken display that the battalions*

*A section of men in the 2nd City Battalion form a Guard at Heaton Park in the summer of 1915. The four men with rifles are still using the Lee Metford model.* Hurst

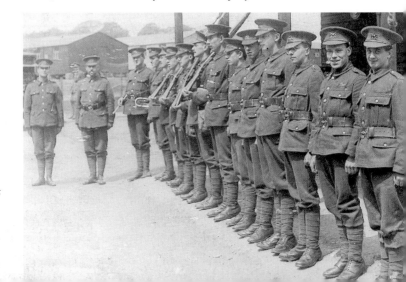

*Throughout Heaton Park many dozens of events were held in front of a crowd of over 20,000 spectators. Amongst those present were The Lord Mayor, Lord Derby, the Chief Constable and Brigadier General Westropp.*

*made, divided and isolated as they were, and the city's farewell was rather patchy. The lengths of street that were silent were greater than those that cheered, and the most favoured companies could not suppose that Manchester was demonstrative.* Manchester Guardian. 26 April 1915

The sense of disappointment continued at the railway station. Here the authorities had made every effort to ensure that the men and their families would be kept separate as the time for each train's departure drew near.

*Eventually the 17th Manchesters came into sight and we saw my father marching smartly. We stayed in the crowd until they had all passed on their way when mother and I made our way down to London Road station, to say our farewells. But to our*

**Mrs Westropp (wife of the Brigadier) presents prizes at the First Brigade's Sports Day, 21 April 1915.** Pawson

*The 1st City Battalion's machine-gun section, in smart step although very obviously still without its weapons!* MRA

*Abraham (Abie) Mosco. Photographed in the late spring of 1915 and clearly illustrating the new khaki and leather equipment which the Pals were issued with before Kitchener's review. Abie Mosco was one of many young Jewish men who served within Manchester's Pals. Before the war he had been a waterproof garment maker, his brother David served in a Manchester Territorial battalion and a further brother, Mendel, in the Royal Artillery. Possibly recorded as A. Moss, 17988, D Company, 5th City Battalion.* Moss

*disappointment high iron gates had been drawn across the entrances. We could see the soldiers and they could see us, but there was no contact. My father took his chance and climbed over the gates, they really were high, and said his goodbyes in person…* Len Riley

### Belton Park, Grantham

The Manchester Pals' hutments in Grantham were already well established, having previously served as accommodation for the 11th Division. It was three weeks since the 11th's men had left and the town of Grantham had reverted to its normal listless style, punctuated this and every Saturday with market day business. The first of the Great Central Railway company's special trains, drawn by the newly commissioned Sir Sam Fay, pulled into Grantham's goods yard at 1.30 pm. As a matter of course many towns-people came out to survey the arrival of the Pals from England's second city inquisitively. By early evening the remaining men had marched through the welcoming gaze of interest and were established in camp. Here the First City Brigade found the remainder of the newly formed 30th division assembling, under command of Major General W. Fry, C.V.O., C.B.[5] It was clear to every new arrival as he marched in that this was where the real training and preparation for war would take place. The contrast with Heaton Park was enormous and most of the men felt that they had 'Done Champion' with the Army's choice of venue. The umbilical cord with Manchester was severed.

All four of the camps were adjacent to each other and within sight of Belton Hall, home of Lord Brownlow. The weather had warmed appreciably. The fresh air, which contrasted pleasantly with their accustomed lot in Manchester, invigorated everyone. Rural tranquility and open countryside beckoned, revealing circumstances within which the men could now be honed and hardened into a fighting force.

*Grantham Village main street, 1914.*

*Belton Hall, home of Lord Brownlow and temporary landlord to the Manchester Pals at Grantham.* MRA

The worst of the winter's mud was now behind the men. This was fortunate since plenty of interest and laughter was generated on the first afternoon of their arrival. Within minutes of his entrance the unfortunate driver of Colonel Crawford's car watched in horror as his charge began to sink into deep bogland outside the 1st City Battalion's hutments. Within minutes the vehicle was down on its axles and a team of draught horses were unable to shift it. The situation and car was rescued by a company of men who dug and pulled a very bedraggled vehicle out of the quagmire.

During the coming weeks the sense of discipline and fierce determination was restored and increased. Quickly a number of the older instructing N.C.O's left the battalions, as did Brigadier-General Westropp, his place taken by Lieutenant Colonel C J Steavenson from the King's Liverpool Regiment. The process of weeding out those men whose health would prove unfit for service abroad went ahead relentlessly. In the 4th City Battalion, the 19th Manchesters, the departure of Lieutenant Colonel Kettlewell and the arrival of Lieutenant Colonel Sir H B Hill coincided with the deliberate redistribution of N.C.O's in order to dissipate the friendships which existed between the ranks and their immediate superiors.

The men were incensed. This did not square easily with the promises made to encourage their enlistment.

Manoeuvres at Harlaxton Park and trench digging at Willoughby Park began to familiarize the men with their anticipated roles in France. Route marches were extended to twenty-eight miles in full kit and packs as the processes of physical hardening were undertaken and progressively increased. In early June each battalion received a quantity of eighty Lee-Metford rifles, longer barreled and with a correspondingly shorter bayonet than their expected Lee-Enfields. Live firing practice with the Lee-Metford rifles began, platoons taking rotation to both complete part two of their musketry course and pose with the weapons for the numerous

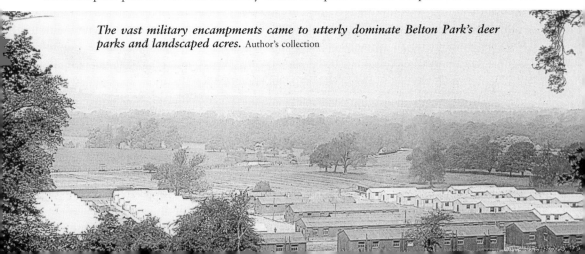

*The vast military encampments came to utterly dominate Belton Park's deer parks and landscaped acres.* Author's collection

Men of the 5th and 7th City Battalions at dinner, outside their huts at Grantham. Pawson

Below: Men of B Company of the 4th City Battalion resting during one of the increasingly lengthy route marches which were employed to harden the men's physique. This card, sent by Private Albert Andrews to his mother living in Gorton, is explained on the reverse. "A photo of us resting on the march coming from Ancaster after trench digging. We have fallen out for 10 minutes. You see I am having a smoke." Capper

The 'official' photographer, Tuson, was everywhere, never missing an opportunity to record any noteworthy event or group. Here the first prize of tinned fruit is proudly displayed by the winners of a battalion's wheelbarrow race. Although this was a time of intense physical preparation many such photographs reveal that a majority of the men persisted in smoking tobacco.

postcards which were sent home. The men were made very aware that their role was to kill or be killed. Bayonet technique and practice became an increasingly familiar art.

> After a week or two my father arranged, with a landlady in Grantham, for us to spend a few days there. This we did, and on the first day Mother and I walked to the camp, to see my father. Whilst she was waiting for him I wandered away for a 'look round' and saw and heard a sergeant shouting out orders at a line of soldiers with fixed bayonets. They were looking towards a line of large sandbags, swinging from a long horizontal wooden beam supported by two posts, either end, like extra wide goal posts. All of a sudden the sergeant gave an order. The soldiers with fixed bayonets charged, shouting, up to the suspended bags and proceeded to stick their bayonets into them, obviously German soldiers, withdrew their bayonets, carried on a few yards further and disappeared into a trench in the ground.
>
> This fascinated me and I waited, wondering what came next. But they stayed in the trench, out of my sight, so I went across to see where they were. The sergeant saw me, shouted at me, clouted me across the ear and pushed me away. That certainly taught me a lesson about minding my own business and I walked sadly back to my mother still waiting for my father. I was only five then but I remember it vividly. Len Riley.

It was into this far tougher atmosphere that the Second City Brigade would arrive on Tuesday, 4 May.[6] The previous evening was filled with the cheerful sounds of impromptu concerts. The

*Bayonet practise at Grantham, the scene so clearly remembered, almost eighty years later, by Len Riley.* Pawson

*Sergeant Philip Jenkins, 6th City Battalion, with his NCO colleagues. His promotions and the consequent welcome rise in income was furthered, soon after his arrival in Grantham, when he was promoted to the rank of Regimental Quarter Master Sergeant, for whom the rate of pay was very superior to that of the ordinary Tommy. 'In May 1915 we moved to Belton Park, Grantham, and were accomodated in huts. Lt Rowden, the Camp Commandant, held a parade of NCOs. He told us he had to appoint a RQMS for the 30th Division HQ which was being formed. As I seemed to be more familiar with the King's Regulations and Royal Warrant, on which he questioned us, I became a RQMS at 5s per day plus 6d field allowance when overseas.' RQMS P E Jenkins.* Hargreaves

Y.M.C.A. and soldiers' institutes had been the scenes of sincerest goodbyes. The many piers and parks saw more than their share of grief amongst the town's girls, many of whom had now spent their first springtime in love. Delicately, the town of Morecambe was awake and on its rather unsteady feet by six in the morning. For many of the young men, the last four months had provided much more than a military instruction and the leave-takings with newly won girlfriends were often difficult and tearful. For the normally imperturbable landladies of Morecambe, saying good-bye was not quite the same as summer's frequent departures.

From half past six the first trains began to move out. Throughout the morning the men were spirited away across the Pennine Hills. As the companies of men awaited their turn to board, officers allowed a little latitude to creep in. For a few this was the chance for one last kiss.

The two brigades stayed four months at Grantham.[7] During this time a notable magazine was prepared by members of the 1st City Pals, the 16th Battalion. Its title was *The Pull Through*. During mid July to August the penny publication gave voice to many of the men's proud feelings and worried concerns.

> *DON'T hit a man who says his battalion is better than yours. He may be a young recruit who has yet to learn that your battalion has pride of place in Belton Park. The Pull Through. 17 July, 1915.*

Grantham was also the scene of the first fatal casualty suffered by the Manchester Pals. He

*Men of the Reserve Company of the 1st City Battalion, No. XIX platoon. Front row next to the end on the left is Private N Fortune.* Fortune

'FALL OUT FOR 10 MINUTES REST'

The informal photographing of the men was an important task. This photograph shows Private A Morris, 20176, of the 7th City Battalion, third from the right of the seated row, with his friends in No. 3 platoon. Owen

*Church Parade, held in the open spaces of the Grantham parade ground area, showing men belonging to the 7th City Battalion, the 22nd Manchesters, and the 24th Manchesters Oldham's Comrades.* Pawson

was Private Harry Stromberg, 11935 of the 19th Battalion, who came from Urmston. Harry Stromberg frequently crossed the light railway which ran through the camp. On the afternoon of the 11th August he was seen playing with a puppy which had taken to the men who worked in the stables. The light railway line which ran nearby was used to move military materials but, without turntable and shunting facilities, it always proved necessary on some journeys to push the trucks by using a locomotive at the rear. Three days after his death the Grantham Journal reported the tragic circumstances. The first witness was Henry Stromberg, the dead man's father. In answer to the Coroner, 'who expressed the desire to clear up any misunderstanding, witness said he was born and bred an Englishman'! The main witness, James Walton, a pioneer with the Royal Engineers, stated that,

> *...at about 4.10 he was coming out of the Transport Stables near the level crossing on the Londonthorpe Road and about to make for his tent on the top of the hill when he heard the whistle of an engine. He looked round and saw the deceased had got his foot fastened in either the sleepers or the rails and was struggling to escape the approaching train composed of an engine and four trucks. He was unable to do so in time, and was caught by the front truck and knocked down between the metals...*
> Grantham Journal. 14 August 1915

In fact the engine driver never saw what happened and was unaware that anyone had been run over until his return to the scene sometime later, when he was stopped and told of the tragedy. On arrival at the camp's military hospital Harry Stromberg was pronounced dead, the cause his serious head injuries. The train driver, William Pryde of the Royal Engineers, was absolved of blame and a verdict of Accidental Death was returned.[8]

### The Plain

Salisbury Plain possessed a vast open skyline and ample space for the concentration of dozens of New Army units. Following their arrival, starting on 7 September, the two Manchester Brigades were able to embark on the brigade and divisional exercises which taxed the officers' powers of command and organization. During September the battalions received their full

*One of the few images which did emerge from Larkhill Camp on Salisbury Plain shows men of the 2nd City Battalion, fully equipped for their departure to France, carrying their service pattern Lee Enfield rifles, leather kit and wearing the distinctive ear warmers which are clipped above each man's cap.* Hurst

*Officers of the 1st City Battalion, the 16th Manchesters, photographed at Salisbury Plain in front of the Clerk's Office in October 1915, the last photograph of these officers before their departure to France in November.* Nash

*Officers who had served with the Pals before their departure. 2nd Lieutenant H de D Dyer and Lieutenant R O Philips, who had joined alongside many men from his family's business Lt. Philips soon rejoined the battalion in France.*

complement of Lee-Enfield service rifles together with four machine guns, provided in early October, enabling the men to complete their full musketry course. Transport and quartermastering were tested to their limits. Their departure date was set. Leave for men in the Manchester area proved impossible, an outbreak of measles in the city saw to it that there would be no final scenes of farewell at London Road Station.

Lord Derby made the final inspection on 4 November, in the enforced absence of the King who was still bedridden after a riding accident in France. The men looked forward to their imminent departure across the channel. Every one of them was confident that he was part of the finest battalion within the finest army the country had produced.

*The whole 30th Division was supremely fit, we were the finest Regiment in the British army, although I say it! They were. Because every man was so keen and so intelligent. For the man in the ordinary army I suppose it was just a job for them, but our men were really civilians turned into soldiers and every man was really each other's friend. There was no enmity at all whatsoever. Only sympathy. Relations between the officers and the ranks were supreme. It was a Pals battalion. That covers everything. You could say we were gentlemen who lived as gentlemen.* Scout Sgt. Bert Payne. 1st City Battalion

One final letter written by Private Burke confirmed such confidence. Writing on the Monday evening of 8 November Pat Burke, serving in the 5th City Battalion, already knew of his impending departure. During the final scramble he penned a few words to his family.

*Am delighted we are going out, and more so to think that I have so much to be thankful for, such strength and health that God has granted me to be able to take part in such an honourable war. You shall be hearing of great things very soon now – in fact it's a case of just going over to put the lid on it. Everything alive here – reveille is at 2 am tomorrow and according to how many things are at present, I can see little bed tonight for any of us.*

### Timetables for departure to France

Between 6 November and 12 November, 1915, the first seven battalions of the Manchester Pals left England to start their active military service abroad. In January of 1916 they were joined by their smaller counterparts, the 8th City Pals, who were serving in the 35th (Bantam) Division.

**16th Battalion.** 90th Brigade, 30th Division.
*6 November.* Left Larkhill. C.O. Lt. Col. C.L.R. Petrie. D.S.O. (Lt. Col. Crawford having left to command 1st Bn. in France.) By train from Amesbury to Southampton. Rest camp outside Boulogne, eve of 6 November. *7 November* by train to Pont Remy and march to St. Ricquier. Training in St. Ricquier until *17 November.* Thence on foot to Brucamps, St. Ouen, Flesselles, thence Villers Bocage until *27 November.* Thence Bonneville for training. Left Bonneville on *7 December* to Couin, near the lines at Hebuterne. *8 December,* into the lines at Hebuterne, where on arrival Lt. Behrens severely wounded. *5 January 1916* into the line at Maricourt.

**17th Battalion.** 90th Brigade, 30th Division.
*8 November,* left Larkhill. Via train from Amesbury to Folkestone. C.O. Lt. Col. H A Johnson. By ship to Boulogne. Left rest camp on *9th* by train to Pont Remy. Domqueur from *11-17 November,* training. *17 November* Vignacourt. *18–28 November,* Bertangles, training. Thence Montrelet until *7 December.* Thence Covin until *14 December,* trench routine instruction. Between the *9-11 December* the companies of the battalion alternated into the lines at Fonquevillers.

**18th Battalion.** 90th Brigade, 30th Division.
Departure on *8 November.* Train from Amesbury. C.O. Lt. Col. W A Fraser. Crossing, Ostrahove. March next day to Boulogne. (*9 November*). Following day by train to Pont Remy (*10 November*) and thence by foot to Coulonvillers. Remained there training until *17 November. 18 November,* Vignacourt. *19 November* Cardonette. Training. *28 November* to Canaples. Training. *6 December* to Puchevillers, thence into the lines in front of Engelbelmer and Mesnil for instruction in trench warfare routines. *16 December* back to Canaples. Jan 6th, took over front line trenches in Vaux sector (Somme marshes).

**19th Battalion.** 90th Brigade, 30th Division. (but on 21 December 1915 to 21st Brigade, 30th Division.)
Left Larkhill. *7 November,* C.O. Lt. Col. Sir H B Hill, Bart. Train from Amesbury to Southampton. Crossed Channel on SS *Queen Alexandra* with transport units aboard SS *Archimedes.* Le Havre at midnight on *8 November.* Train to Pont Remy. March to Beaumetz and stayed until *17 November.* Thence to Coisy, training, until *28 November.* Thence to Canaples until *8 December.* Halloy. Berles-au-bois on the *9 December.* Trench instruction under 6th Leicesters. *6 January* to Bray. *8 January* took over B3 sector trenches at Carnoy.

**20th Battalion.** 91st Brigade, 30th Division. (But on 20 December 1915 the 91st Brigade moved to 7th Division and the 20th Manchesters moved to the 22nd Brigade within the 7th Division.)
Left Larkhill to entrain for Folkestone on *9 November.* C.O. Lt. Col Spencer Mitchell. Left

same day for Boulogne on SS *Princess Victoria*. That night in rest camp at Ostrahove. Following day, *10 November*, to Pont Remy by train. On *11 November* on foot to Bouchon and Mouflers. One week in Mouflers training, thence to Flixecourt (*17th*), Belloy (*18th*) and finally Vaux-en-Amienois (*19th*). To Puchevillers on *26 November*. To Couin on *27 November*. To Hebuterne on *28 November* where it trained with 145th Brigade, 48th Division. Arrived front line area proper on *1 February 1916* at Morlancourt, the following day into reserve dug-outs south of Fricourt on the Fricourt-Bray road.

**21st Battalion**. 91st Brigade, 30th Division. (But on 20 December 1915 the 91st Brigade moved to 7th Division.)
*9 November*. Left Larkhill via Amesbury for Folkestone. C.O. Lt. Col. W W Norman D.S.O. Because of the terrible weather the 21st Bn were billeted in Folkestone Drill Hall that night. On *10 November* to Boulogne on HM Troopship *Atalanta*, that night at Ostrahove rest camp. On *11 November* by train to Pont Remy then on foot to Vanchelles-les-Domart. *17 November* on foot to Bertangles. On *18 November* to Pierregot, remained in billets until *26 November*, thence to Puchevillers. *27 November* to Couin. Attached to 143rd Brigade for trench instruction. *28 November* to Fonquevillers where they were instructed by 5th and 7th Warwicks until *4 December*. Final move towards front line proper on *2 February*, Bray-sur-Somme. *6 February* into front line, relieving 22nd Manchesters opposite Mametz.

**22nd Battalion**. 91st Brigade, 30th Division. (But on 20 December 1915 the 91st Brigade moved to the 7th Division. The Pioneer battalion to the 7th Division was the 24th Manchesters, the Oldham Comrades.)
Left Larkhill Wednesday, 12 November. Delayed at Folkestone. 13 November, departed Folkestone at 3.30 pm. Thursday night in rest shelters in Frange. Arrangements then similar to those made for the 21st Battalion. (See text for Alfred Bland's graphic account of his men's arrival and early experiences in France.)

**23rd Battalion**. (Bantams): 104th Brigade, 35th (Bantam) Division.
Left Salisbury Plain on 29 January 1916, under command of Lt. Col. R V Smith. Initial attempt to cross the channel foiled by mines. Eventually crossed on 30 January to Boulogne. 31 January by train to Blondeques, near St. Omer. Training and machine gun instruction. 11 February, inspection by Lord Kitchener. 18 February to Boeseghein. 19 February to Calonne. 20 February to Le Touret. Richebourg (St. Vaast) for trench instruction, until 24 February. Front line trenches in the Bethune area from 7 March.

### Notes:

1 Private Pat Burke. Monday 8 November, 1915.
2 Sergeant Bert Payne. Number 1 Platoon of the 1st City Battalion.
3 The two Brigadiers of Manchester's eight Pals battalions were later responsible for the compilation of the City's record of the initial volunteers in these battalions. See: Kempster. Brig. Gen. F. & Westropp. Brig. Gen. H C E (Eds.), *Manchester City Battalions of the 90th & 91st Infantry Brigades. Book of Honour.* (Pub. Sherratt & Hughes. Manchester. 1917.)
4 The Heaton Park camps were then used by many other battalions for training purposes. One of the first to be located there was the 24th Manchesters, another local Pals unit, the 'Oldham Comrades'.
5 The four battalions of the 1st City Brigade arrived in Belton Park under the command of Lieutenant Colonels J.C. Crawford, H A Johnson, W A Fraser and Kettlewell.
6 The 8th City, the 23rd Manchesters, going to Masham in Yorkshire to join other bantam units in the 104th Brigade, 35th Division. At this stage the 20th, 21st, 22nd Manchesters (5th, 6th and 7th City Bns) and 24th Manchesters (Oldham Comrades) formed the 91st Brigade, 30th Division.
7 Before departure to Salisbury Plain the CO of the 20th Bn, Lt. Col. Arnold, was replaced by Lt. Col. Spencer Mitchell.
8 Private Stromberg is buried in Manchester South Cemetery.

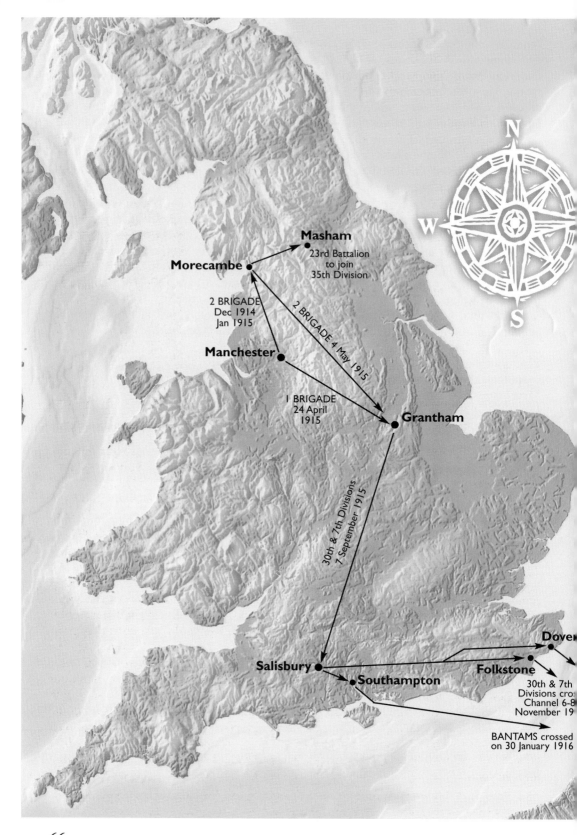

**Masham**
23rd Battalion
to join
35th Division

**Morecambe**

2 BRIGADE
Dec 1914
Jan 1915

2 BRIGADE 4 May 1915

**Manchester**

I BRIGADE
24 April
1915

**Grantham**

30th & 7th Divisions
7 September 1915

**Salisbury**

**Southampton**

**Dover**

**Folkstone**

30th & 7th
Divisions cros
Channel 6-8
November 19

BANTAMS crossed
on 30 January 1916

## Chapter Four

# The Calm Before the Storm

*'Dearest, I am entirely at ease with regard to the future.    I have no sort of premonitions, and I honestly believe it will continue to be an interesting picnic...'*[1]

Two days after Lord Derby's final inspection of the men, for whom he held the rank of Honorary Colonel, those first civilian soldiers from Manchester were in France. The 1st City Pals had been roused at 3.00 am, on the morning of 6 November and paraded in full kit at 4.00 am. It was still dark when they marched out of camp towards their trains drawn up at Amesbury station. From Southampton the channel had been crossed, en route for Boulogne. Whilst on board the men's interest and spirits had been sparked by the scene of Royal Navy vessels recovering a Zeppelin which had been downed during an air raid the previous night, its dark canvas partly submerged in the grey waters.

*The shoulder title of the 1st City Battalion, the 16th Manchesters.*

*When we got to Boulogne it rained cats and dogs. We went up the hill about two miles and it was waterlogged, the whole camp. We couldn't do a thing. It was really shocking and we stayed all night. There were tents for us but we just sat down in the water, soaked to the skin, but it didn't matter because we were always wet... the whole of November was terrible. On the second day we came down from [the rest camps on] the hill and got on a train to Pont Remy, everybody was quiet, told not to speak, no lights were shown passing through all the stations in cattle trucks, no ordinary carriages, thirty men to a truck. At Pont Remy we got out and marched from there. Scout Sgt. Bert Payne. 1st City Battalion.*

Their destination that day was St. Ricquier where they trained for a further ten days.

These first weeks in France were a period of unfolding and depressing reality. The constant foul weather, lousy billets, greasy estaminets and the men's introduction to the trenches combined to test the extraordinary enthusiasm of the Manchester Pals. However, in advance of any disillusion, the battalion's first appearance within the theatre of war often meant an unbridled optimism in many eyes. One such observer, Captain Alfred Bland, serving with the 7th City Battalion, the 22nd Manchesters, arrived in France on Thursday, 11 November. The weather was still atrocious. Within an hour of their arrival Bland's men were wet through, well before sighting their rest shelters for that night. On Friday morning the 22nd Manchesters had entrained south and then marched a considerable distance in continuing downpours. Later that filthy storm driven night Bland had been detailed to pick up the inevitable stragglers. Having commandeered three ambulances for lame and blistered men Bland came across further battalion stragglers in the dim arc of their headlights. The Medical Officer and another colleague, A Company commander Captain C C May, were helping keep the men going.

*They were willing to lie down anywhere and die, but May pushed them up and on, and up and on they went, staggering through the mud, desperate and lost souls. When*

*The shoulder title of Alfred Bland's 7th City Pals, the 22nd Manchesters.*

*I was full up we splashed and skidded past the battalion to our present Headquarters and then came right back again to the rear. The last of our merry troupe got in about 11.30 and just fell like logs in the stables and barns which constitute their billets... Nothing so fortunate could have happened as that our first day should be so thoroughly miserable, for everything subsequently pleasant will be damned pleasant, n'est ce pas?...*

*Dear, I am extraordinarily happy, simply bursting with riotous spirits. We are living like lords at the rate of one shilling a day. The one thing lacking is shellfire. I shall not achieve the real thrill till I get within sound of the guns and the phut-phut of the rifle and the glorious ping of the bullet that whirrs past like a singing whipcord. This is not blather. I mean it.* Captain Alfred Bland. 7th City Battalion. IWM. Department of Documents.

Before the war Alfred Bland had become established in an academic career as an economic historian. Now released from the cloistered atmosphere of that world Alfred Bland's letters, recording the Pals' progress, become enriched by the shared danger, sense of purpose and decision which many letters home now disclose. By 1915 Alfred Bland was in his mid thirties, yet his frequent letters reveal an enchantment with the harshness and challenge of his new circumstances. Such martial enthusiasm would eventually, inevitably, be dissipated. But in the meantime there was another round of billeting to be arranged, under the usual frenetic circumstances.

*The battalion receives orders at the last moment from Brigade, which receives orders at the last moment from the Division, which receives orders at the last moment from Headquarters, to*

*Captain Alfred Bland (left) with another unknown officer of the 22nd Manchesters.* Mace

*One of Captain Bland's men. Private Joseph Lamb, 21202, VII platoon, B Company, 22nd Manchesters. Before the war Joe Lamb had been a fine footballer with Newton Heath as well as an outstanding cricketer. He was destined to lose his right leg during actions east of Ypres in late 1917.* Lamb

*occupy a certain area. What is the result? The battalion marches into or nearly into its appointed village, the Interpreter follows exhausted on a bicycle, O.C. Companies ride on and around and do their best with no French on their tongue tips, while the battalion stands and shivers and pretends to be warm and happy. Then the various companies are marched by driblets to various cosy nooks or draughty corners, and after considerable adjustment, involving much marching and countermarching, settle down. Then the Officers look round for the said rooms in the said houses, and are quite glad to shed their packs in the first handy place that offers. By this time it is long past the appointed mealtime, but the cookers haven't yet come. They do come, in the end, and everybody is happy. One curious thing always happens. While the Officers are securing their own billets, the men clear the village of cigarettes and chocolate. They can always find enough French for that!* 23 November 1915*

The message of initial familiarization in the front lines was that survival of his men was the first responsibility for every platoon and company commander. The 22nd Manchester's first experience in the lines, under the tuition of the Royal Irish Fusiliers, would be memorable not only for the seeming proximity of the enemy but also for the pressing wetness of the winter's weather. Better than any other source the many letters which were scribbled by thousands of officers and men portray a vivid picture of life in the newly discovered excitement of the front lines.

*We've seen the trenches – carefully built up in the autumn – reduced to a horrible mess by the rain. We've been up and down in mud two feet deep and water deeper still. We've had rifle and machine-gun fire and shrapnel whizzing about our ears, and our own heavier shells shrieking high over our heads. We've been turned out at 3.00 a.m. to investigate a report of a German patrol cutting our wire, and I personally have been in a dug-out when a shrapnel shell fell on the roof and burst there... Life in the trenches is just like life in billets, only much more inconvenient. Rations have to be carried up from so great a distance, and all in the dark. It is frightfully difficult to get anybody anywhere, to collect your NCOs, to convey orders and organize work, and weather, weather, is a really terrible factor...* Captain Alfred Bland. 2 December 1915

The Private soldier's experience confirmed the difficulties and amazement at such grotesque mud and glutinous clay.

*...at stand to on Monday morning it commenced to rain – and then the trouble started. By the time we were relieved on Tuesday afternoon we had been through it, owing to continual rain the trenches had got into such a condition. I cannot explain the state I was in, but to give you an idea I had my greatcoat weighed and it pulled, owing to the quantity of muck there-on, 57 lbs. Wet thro' to the skin, and everything in a terrible mess we marched out to our billet in the nearest village feeling absolutely done up – but bear in mind in the best of spirits. Well if I wasn't then, I was when I found a parcel from you, Monty and Barney and lots of letters awaiting for me, it was a glorious reviver. A night's decent rest, was up at 6.30 following morning on ration fatigue, carrying grub to and fro from the trenches. Each journey the conditions were getting worse, the last journey was awful, too bad to walk along the fire trench, we had to climb on the parapet and walk along there. Wed. and Thursday was on working parties trying to mend the trenches, they were all falling in and inches deep in water, to speak precisely the average would be 2½ feet deep. One morning was watching the Germans doing their trenches up such as we were, so they must have been in the same state as we were. We went in again on Friday the rain never ceasing and that put the lid on it...* Private Pat Burke, 5th City Battalion, the 20th Manchesters, Sunday, 5 December, 1915

### The 30th Division's arrival on the Somme

On 8 December 1915 the 1st City Pals arrived in Hebuterne, a mere half mile behind the front line trenches and a mile south of the German occupied village of Gommecourt. Eight miles further to the south lay Albert, astride the River Ancre which flowed south westwards towards the River Somme. Hebuterne was to provide their introduction to trench warfare proper, under the direction of experienced Gloucesters and Worcesters of the 144th Brigade. The men were full of anticipation and pride, at last able to take their place alongside the veteran Tommies of whose exploits the men had heard so much.

*That's where all the stupidity came in, how ignorant we all were. We thought we were clever but we were just damned ignorant, from the top to the bottom, including me. First of all they should not have come through Hebuterne in daylight. They marched through with the bands playin' and the officers mounted on their horses. Jerry opened fire and I saw dud shells going along there. Captain Behrens lost his leg, he was shot off his horse. I saw dud shells thrown right through the square, what* would have happened if those shells had burst, there would have been carnage. We got through in the end to the trenches. It was the first time we had been under fire. Scout Sgt. Bert Payne. 1st City Battalion.[2]

*For the German Army, the early months of 1916 on the Somme brought the same rain and sucking mud which so fatigued Pat Burke and his comrades in the Manchester Pals during their first three months 'up the line'. If anything, conditions in the lower lying British trenches were even worse than those pictured here.*

A week later, having completed their very necessary course of familiarization in the front lines, the men were moved south, past Albert, towards the junction with the French Army.

In January of the new year, 1916, the whole of the 30th Division containing the first four of Manchester's Pals battalions came to the banks of the River Somme. The division consisted of three brigades, the 21st Brigade containing the 18th King's (a Liverpool Pals Battalion), 2nd Green Howards, 2nd Wiltshires and the 4th City Battalion, the 19th Manchesters. The 89th Brigade was composed entirely of the remaining Liverpool Pals, the 17th, 19th and 20th King's, stiffened with a regular battalion, the 2nd Bedfordshires. The 90th Brigade was the first three of Manchester's Pals, themselves stiffened by the 2nd Royal Scots Fusiliers. The Division's appointed place in the line was around Maricourt at the extreme right of the British held sector of the Western Front. Maricourt village occupied the centre of a shallow salient which pushed into the south of an upland area running from Guillemont, three miles north east of Maricourt, towards Thiepval, roughly seven miles north west of Guillemont. This upland, the Pozieres Ridge, protected the German railhead of Bapaume. A mile to the west of Maricourt lay the village of Carnoy, also in British hands and location for the 19th Manchester's tours of duty in the front lines with the 21st Brigade. On the other side of No Mans Land, in front of Carnoy to its north west and north east respectively, lay the three strongly fortified villages of Fricourt, Mametz and Montauban. Between Montauban and Guillemont villages lay two woodlands, Bernafay to the west with the tear drop shape of Trones to its east.

Two miles behind the 1st and 2nd City Battalion's lines, to the south, the men's billets were located at Suzanne, a quiet and comparatively undamaged village, above the River Somme, where French civilians were still to be found alongside the hundreds of French soldiers for whom Suzanne was also a billet and Headquarters. 90th Brigade's HQ were located in the

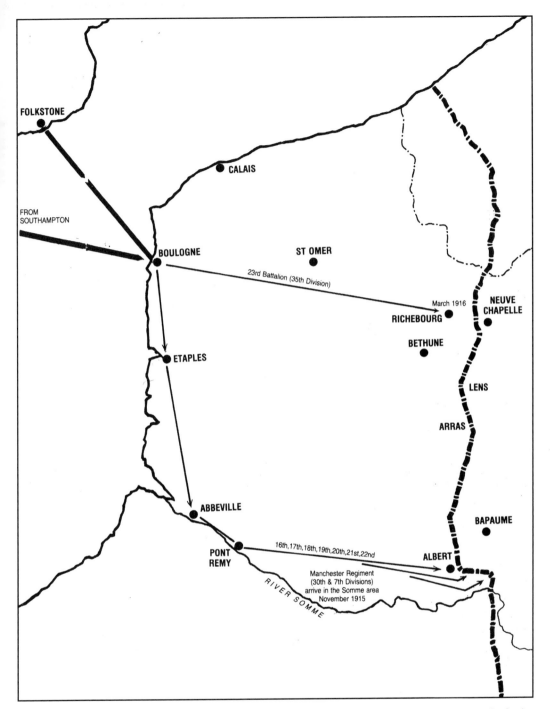

Chateau. From there the daily round of reliefs into the lines were planned during which the 16th and 17th Manchesters alternated into the front line trenches. Amongst the soldiers a constant round of rumour abounded that German spies signalled every relief and planned raid from the undamaged church tower in the centre of the village. Although they had already suffered casualties from shelling in the Suzanne area, the 17th Manchester's first relief of the 16th Battalion, on 10 January, was particularly distressing when 2nd Lieutenant William Tonge was later sniped in the front line trench just west of Maricourt. The mud here proved so

*Fricourt Chateau. Already showing the effects of damage and shelling in late 1915.* Reed

*By early 1916 the village of Mametz was already crumbling in the face of the shelling which its position, close behind the German front lined, attracted.*

*The village of Montauban before it was visited by the destruction wrought by occupation, fortification and bombardments during the period 1914-16.* Reed

impenetrable that the party sent to rescue his body was forced to bury him within the confines of the trench itself.

These trenches at Maricourt proved impossible to drain. The constant snow, frost, mud and rain of midwinter left the men filthied and sodden, without any anticipation of fresh clothing. Within days of their arrival both men and officers had cut the skirts from their greatcoats to prevent the glutinous knee-deep mud from attaching itself to the fabric. In the bottom of the trenches there were no duck-boards to give sound support. A footing of some sort was sometimes gained on the old French sand-bags which criss-crossed the deepest well of each trench, but the unwary were often caught in the sucking gaps between bags which made a decorous exit impossible.

*One man, 'Bunk' Mills, he was six foot four, I remember him saying 'Sergeant, I can't move.' So we got hold of him, pulled him out and left his shoes and trousers in the trench then walked him back to HQ and got him another pair... We were standing in that water for four days and four nights. No relief whatever. We were just there and we had to take it. The feet boiled up like puddings in gumboots, they were so soft they got trench feet. When we came out we chucked everything into a river or a pool and washed them, rifle as well, the whole damned lot! Then we dried them and put them on again, same shirts and everything. Still wet through. And so it went on for about eight weeks. Then we went back to Corbie. We had a bath there and they gave us a new outfit of clothing, new underwear, new shirt. At night time they were just as lousy with lice as though you hadn't bothered. They gave us an*

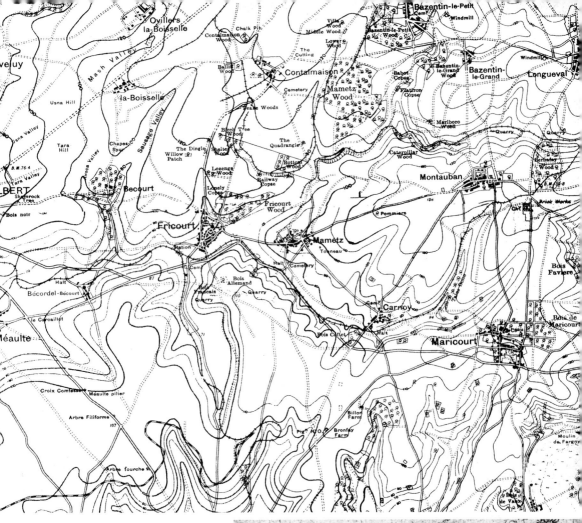

Map 1 from the **Official History of Military Operations in France and Belgium, 1916,** *showing the area into which Manchester's Pals arrived during January 1916.*

*This sketch of his farm billet, in the area of Bray-Sur-Somme, was made in June 1916 by Pte John Anderson, 20606, 7th City Pals.* Everitt

*ointment called 'Blue Unction' to put on our bodies. The doctor gave me some of this saying, 'You've got enough there to kill all the lice in England.' I said, 'I've got 'em.' Of course we laughed about it, but we were desperate. You couldn't keep the lice down, you had to live with it. Scout Sgt. Bert Payne. 1st City Battalion.*

A myriad smells and the pungent intrusion of decay were ever present. It was possible to become inured to the foulness of trench life, but some platoon and company commanders made unusual attempts to combat the unremitting unpleasantness. Hubert Worthington's attempts with the 1st City Battalion had started with a visit to a church in the Suzanne area where he had obtained a quantity of incense which was regularly burned in the braziers in A Company's section of the line. Although sometimes debated, the aroma was generally believed to be a small improvement. Most impressed of all was the Divisional Commander, General Shea, the successor to Major General Fry as 30th Divisional Commander, who on visiting this stretch in front of Maricourt was moved to say 'Good Lord, Worthington, what an awfully good idea'! The end product of making such an impression was an immediate invitation to dinner at the Divisional Chateau for the bemused A Company commander. The fine meal was served on sparkling silver by skilled mess waiters and accompanied by the best wine and spirits. The contrast could not have been more marked.[3]

Gradually the amateur soldiers learned the need for care and self discipline as part of the fight for self preservation inside the front lines. Within one post facing east, in Maricourt Wood, an incident in January 1916 proved to all who witnessed it the need for the greatest caution. The weather had dried and the ground become hard with frost. In the half

*Maricourt Chateau, one of the many postcards purchased by the Pals showing 'their' home opposite Montauban.* Hurst

*The trenches at Maricourt.*

*2nd Lieutenant R.K. Knowles, of C Company, 1st City Battalion and the transport officer to the battalion, Lieutenant L.F. Wilson.* MRA

greyness before dawn,

> We were looking through the bottom of the trees round this wood and Lieutenant [P J ] Mead came into the trench with a pair of binoculars and he said, 'This'll make it easier for you fellas. I don't know who's going to have them.' We were only lads of twenty. I were twenty one. He gave them to a middle aged fella. So he says, 'Just be careful how you use them.' He put them to his eyes and within twenty seconds he was dead flesh. He never heard it. They'd glinted in the sun because we were facing the east you see and the sun glittered on these and of course, you know what snipers are, crack, straight through, you never feel anything, too quick. He just slid down. His heart might take a few seconds to pump itself out and then you're finished. Whereas a few of us said, 'You lucky so and so, you're bloody lucky to get those.' Nobody wanted 'em after!
> Private Charlie Heaton. 6254. II Platoon, A Coy. 1st City Pals.

In fact the art of camouflage was only learned by experience. When an observation post was 'marked' by the enemy its value was less than useless. Any attempt to make use of such an OP by a sniper often resulted in an accurate round back through the loophole. To maintain the illusion of normality, rubbish and detritus was never moved from near an OP. Scouts and snipers went to the greatest lengths to prevent other soldiers and units from using 'their' posts, becoming familiar with every blade of grass, corn and weed, past which they built up a picture by compass bearing of every location in front of themselves. Gradually, over many weeks, the deception opposite would reveal itself, perhaps a false tree, sometimes movements around a hidden gun, sometimes the sound of men breathing, listening. Tension was ever-present.

The men spent many nights during the coming three months improving, draining, revetting and strengthening the trench system here. Amongst those at ease, once work parties and fatigues had finished their imposition upon the men's time, the sweet smell of tobacco hung limply in the air. Concerned mothers had abandoned their normal caution and cigarettes abounded. The men almost invariably found it impossible to sleep. The cold, creeping damp

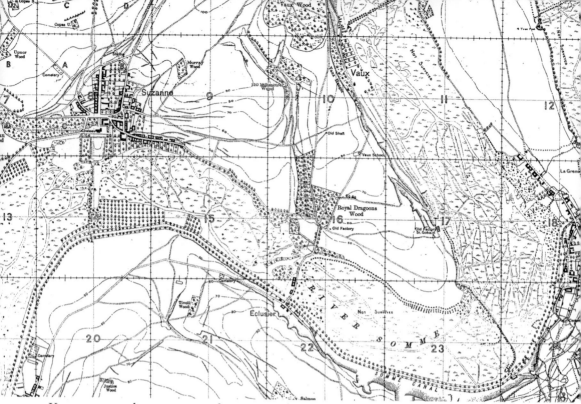

*Vaux area trench map, corrected to spring of 1916. Sheet 62c NW3. The 3rd City Battalion occupied trenches toward Vaux. To the west lies Suzanne where the 1st and 2nd City Battalions were billeted during early 1916. A number of the first men to be killed are buried in the Military Cemetery which lies next to the village cemetery on the road leading north west from Suzanne.*

and ever present lice always saw to that. Much ire was initially heaped upon the previous occupants who were often blamed for the presence of the avaricious insects. Before the arrival of Manchester's sons the trenches had previously been occupied by the French Poilus who were universally regarded as having had slovenly habits. However, contact behind the lines sometimes gave rise to good deals when surplus English tobacco and cigarette papers could be bartered for superior French bread. Baguettes and gross pain were very much in demand since the rations available to Manchester's Tommies often left a lot to be desired.

> *In the morning I'd send four men to the cookhouse in the brewery yard in Maricourt where the field kitchens were. The men came back with a dixie of tea and on top of that was a tray with bacon and a lid on top of that. They put that on top of a stretcher and two men carried it the mile and a half from Maricourt to the front lines. Another two men brought sand-bags full of food. We should have had twenty loaves for the men. If we were lucky we got two. Two loaves between twenty men! By the time they got to the trench you peeled a piece of bacon off and put it on a piece of bread. That was your breakfast. The tea had gone cold, that didn't matter, you never had hot meals excepting when we made it ourselves. We were given a lot of corned beef, Fray Bentos, but it was so salty the men just couldn't eat it so we buried it in the trenches to make a firm foundation to walk on. They're still there, thousands of tins. Scout Sergeant Bert Payne. 1st City Battalion.*

Much prized were the solid fuel tablets, sent from home, which enabled men to brew an individual tea or coffee with the dried cubes which accompanied the fuel. Less valued were the Oxo cubes, subject of a successful advertising campaign at home and now thought of by

Manchester's mothers as the soldiers' delight. In truth the men had been sent so many that even the field kitchens were overflowing with Oxo! They usually joined the Fray Bentos.

Away from these trenches, the village of Suzanne provided welcome hot douche baths and the opportunity to dig innumerable dug-outs within the chalk embankments, an occupation which took a disproportionate amount of the men's rest time. However, on 13 January Suzanne was registered and shelled by the German artillery. Within hours an intermittent file of families carrying bundles of possessions was leaving the area and the Manchester's contact with the civilian world was broken. It was a preliminary to the further, and much more intense, series of bombardments which took place a fortnight later, between 24 and 28 January. The village of Suzanne now stood empty, the properties exposed to the vicissitudes of war.

*In the North Street houses, they had all been farm labourers I presume, each garden had a grave with a cross on it as though one of their lads had been killed. But it was so regular, everybody having one, that it couldn't be true. Our men dug them up and found jars of wine and all sorts of things in there, family ornaments, of course we didn't want those but we took all the wine and lots of potatoes which we took to cook. That was the graves in all the gardens. Of course they were all peasants, they made their own patches where they grew their own potatoes and hid them. Their cupboards were sealed but I didn't undo those, but somebody else must have done later because other people came, not us, took over and they'd open up and steal whatever might have been in. The Manchester boys, the Pals, were gentlemen, they wouldn't steal anything. You could leave your money on your bed. I but you couldn't leave a cake on your bed. You could leave your cigarettes and they wouldn't touch those but not food, that was understood. Anybody got a cake from home they shared it out if somebody else hadn't got one.* Scout Sgt. Bert Payne. 6310. No 1 Platoon, 1st City Battalion.

During this mid-winter period the 3rd City Battalion, the 18th Manchesters, occupied a hazardously exposed position along the Somme marshes on the extreme right of the British line near the village of Vaux. The location was one of scattered posts, duckboard walkways and squelching marshland. Their constant occupation of this sector put the 3rd City's men in daily contact with the French and Senegalese troops whose trenches and defences abutted those of the Manchesters. On 11 January the battalion suffered its first casualty, Private

*The shoulder title of the 3rd City Pals, the 18th Manchesters.*

*The marshlands which characterized the slow meanderings of the Somme at Vaux. It was an impossible area in which to dig trenches and casualties were heavy during the 3rd City battalions tour here in early 1916.*

Brown (11005) being killed by a sniper. During the coming weeks the battalion both made and suffered a succession of raids, pressing for possession of outposts and pockets of firm land among the reed-beds and rivulets of water. These raids, and a series of shellings, gradually took their toll in casualties killed, wounded and missing. These were added to when, on 7 March, Lieutenant Powell was seriously wounded by the accidental discharge of another officer's revolver and a day later by the death of 2nd Lieutenant J L Nelson who was killed by an accidental rifle discharge. By mid March when the battalion was relieved from its vigil at Vaux the casualty figures amounted to over one hundred men. At this time Lieutenant Colonel Fraser was replaced, as a consequence of ill health, by Major W A Smith, 20th King's Liverpool Regiment.

The 4th City Battalion, the 19th Manchesters, were billeted during this period with other 21st Brigade units at Bray-sur-Somme and occupied the front line trenches at Carnoy. Being rather more distant from the junction of the two armies made life less threatening and between January and March the 19th Battalion were able to effect considerable improvement to the security and comfort of their trenches.

Between the middle of March and early May the 16th, 17th, 18th and 19th Battalions all worked on fatigues behind the lines, followed by brief periods of training and more fatigues. Since mid February the Somme had been designated as the location for the 'Big Push'. With virtually no labour battalions available behind Fourth Army, the material preparation for battle fell to the men. These Manchesters were engaged on railway track laying, road widening and strengthening. One hated task resulted from the decision to bury all cables, forward of Divisional Command, to a depth of six feet to make them proof against German medium howitzer shells. In many ways this woefully detracted from the men's already sketchy training. The constant effort exhausted the men.

There was, quite simply, almost no time to train, rest and prepare for the forthcoming cauldron of battle that was destined for the Somme.

On 2 May the 90th Brigade were back in the trenches around Maricourt and Carnoy, bracing themselves for the usual round of shelling and raids which accompanied any relief into the lines by new units. On 8 May the 3rd City Battalion took over a sector of the front line, just outside Maricourt, from the 1st City Battalion, the 16th Manchesters. Five days later, on 13th May, whilst C and D Companies were in the front line, the heat of conflict became intense. After launching a considerable bombardment the enemy attacked the entirety of 30th Division's frontage, intent on capturing prisoners and causing maximum damage and disruption to the defences. Although the 3rd City Battalion's frontage held, a foothold was gained to the south of the battalion's trenches. Within minutes enemy bombing parties began to work their way along into the 18th's trenches, but after close fighting the German raiders were dispersed and driven off. During that fighting Private C E Brooke of D Company won the DCM for his gallant actions in rescuing a number of wounded Lewis Gun team colleagues in the face of a great deal of hostile fire. However, it was during these events that an unfortunate and substantial number of deaths occurred amongst the 18th Manchesters. During the bombardment a trench mortar shell fell into the shaft of a mine which was being dug northwards, fifteen men sheltering in its entrance all being buried. Although four were pulled clear, eleven men were lost as the soft soil defeated every attempt to dig towards those buried men.

Retaliation by the 30th Division's artillery was often marred by the poor quality of the ammunition whose explosive qualities were, at best, dubious. On the 21 May a bombardment of 'Y Wood', an important German front line position just south east of Maricourt on the Peronne Road, showed just how disastrous the position had become. The shoot was undertaken by 25th Siege Battery equipped with 8″ howitzers.

*Private George Greatbanks, 11215, 18th Manchesters (1st left on the back row). George Greatbanks enlisted in September 1914 along with his friends shown here from the Johnson's Wireworks in Manchester. Private Greatbanks was awarded the Military Medal for his bravery during the German raid on the 13 May and was later promoted to the rank of Sergeant.* Jones

*21 rounds were fired on the Co. H.Q. at A.23.a.25.55, but no direct hit was scored, the nearest round being over by 8 yards.*

*40 rounds were fired on trench from A.23. a.70.21 to A.23.a.75.05. 12 rounds struck the trench. A large explosion followed one of the rounds. Between A.23. a.70.23 and A.23.a.95.30 about 30 yards of parapet were knocked down.*

*40 rounds were fired on trench between A.23.a.90.23 to A.23.a.80.05. One good hit on dugout at 90.77 and trench was badly damaged. The possible effect of the shoot was much reduced by 20 blinds and about 30 very poor bursts. Report by Brigade Major Heavy Artillery. XIII Corps. 25/5/1916.* Public Record Office Ref. No. WO95/2316.

Quite incredibly as many as fifty per cent of the shells used in this action had proved to be faulty.

On 1 June a more complex relief was carried out when 90th Brigade's trenches were taken over by the French XXth Corps. This relief ensured the presence of French troops north of the river Somme and, therefore, a point of real contact between the two armies in their forthcoming joint offensive towards Bapaume and Peronne. From now on the French lines had moved north and west, the dividing line between the two armies now bisecting what little was left of the village of Maricourt.

*Sergeant John Farrow, 8138, 2nd City Battalion, 17th Manchesters. Sergeant Farrow had been born in 1894. After taking a special Law course at Manchester University, he graduated to work in the firm of Richard Haworth & Co Ltd., of which his father was a director. The company was one of the contributors to the Pals' Guarantee Fund, giving £200. He died, on 5 May, 1916, as a result of wounds received in action.* Guest

By 10 June the 1st City Battalion were back in the front line, but this time just to the west of Maricourt around the area of Tallus Boise, a long slender finger of woodland whose northern tip pointed past Glatz Redoubt towards Montauban. During the coming week the men began to familiarize themselves with the area and discuss the inevitable rumours that the 'Big Push' was soon to be underway. In the trenches around Oxford Copse, Cambridge Copse, Machine-Gun Wood and Talus Boise itself, the scene was of unremitting preparation. Such obvious activity was impossible to disguise. On the night of 13 June a new 'jumping off' trench was under construction by men of the 1st and 3rd City Battalions, the 16th and 18th Manchesters, when the digging parties were surprised by a brutal and systematic German barrage which preceded a raid on the trenches at the junction of the British and French armies.

On 16 June the 1st City Battalion began to move out towards the village of Heilly, from where they moved on towards Le Mesge via Ailly-sur-Somme and Picquigny. Under the direction of General Shea, the assault units from the 30th Division began final preparations for their part in the forthcoming Battle of the Somme. Nearby to Le Mesge, at Briquemesnil, the whole of the Montauban area had been reproduced in great detail. Here 'a complete system of trenches, reproduced exactly from air photographs, was constructed representing the whole of the objectives to be attacked by each brigade."[4] North of the facsimile of the village the final objective of Montauban Alley was identified, hidden beyond the yards of tape and dummy hedgerows which replicated Montauban. After five days of continuous rehearsal here the 1st City Battalion moved into billets at Oissy where, on the evening of 24th, the first of the Manchester Pals battalions held their final concert within the grounds of the village chateau. Here, and in dozens of similar venues, barns and halls, the men were reassured in pierrot and picture shows that the German war effort was faltering and that the coming events would presage imminent victory. Meanwhile the 3rd City Battalion's assault rehearsals went ahead at Saisseval and the 4th City Battalion's at Reincourt. During those preparations the 3rd City Battalion's D Company were detailed to place the enormous quantities of forward ammunition and stores to be used by 90 Brigade in their forthcoming assault on Montauban. During the six days allotted for this task these two hundred men dug pits and shelters to house 10,000 Mills grenades and 4,300 rifle grenades all of which required to be primed with their detonators, almost half a million rounds of rifle ammunition (S.A.A.), 6,000 rounds of revolver ammunition, 2,000 Very lights, 1,120 flares, 300 rockets, 4,000 Stokes Mortar bombs, 600 water cannisters, 400 trench ladders, 400 trench bridges, 700 iron pickets for entanglements, 150 wiring tools and 95 coils of barbed wire. Having dug the pits the men then manhandled every item of the munitions and equipment into their allotted locations, all without casualty.

### The 7th Division's arrival on the Somme
In the February of 1916 the reformed 7th Division had arrived on the Somme. Within their ranks were the 5th, 6th and 7th City Battalions, the 20th, 21st and 22nd Manchesters, very much the juniors in what had, until the previous December, been an all regular Division until its dilution by the three Manchester Pals battalions and some other New Army units. The 22nd Brigade now consisted of the 5th City Battalion (the 20th Manchesters), 2nd Royal Warwicks, 2nd Royal Irish and the 1st Royal Welch Fusiliers. The 7th Division's Pioneer Battalion was the 24th Manchesters, the Oldham Comrades. As part of the 22nd Brigade, the 5th City Battalion found themselves opposite the village of Fricourt. These battered farms and tumbled houses hid the fortifications which made the position one of considerable tactical importance to the German Army. From a point just half a mile south of the village of Fricourt (F9d7/7) the front line trenches ran northwards, past La Boisselle, towards Thiepval and the River Ancre. However, from that same point those trenches turned eastwards, running past Mametz in the direction of Hardecourt. That shift in direction took place within the Bois Francais where the front line trenches were less than fifty yards apart. Here the area had been turned into a tottering lunar landscape by the constant mining and counter mining which was employed by both sides in their desperate attempts to win control over this high ground. The

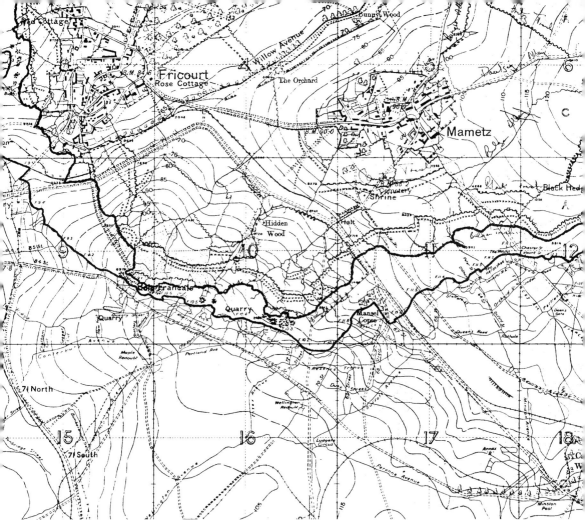

*Sheet 62dNE2. Showing the locations of Fricourt and Mametz, including Bois Franeais at F9d7/7. The trenches are corrected to the 15 June 1916.*

reason was simple; from here superior artillery observation was possible across Fricourt towards the higher ground rising to the rear of that village.

During the spring and early summer of 1916 the 5th City Battalion would often be found in the chaotic confines of Bois Francais, in front of Maple Redoubt, engaged in the constant revetting, carrying, digging and preparing which were the men's lot at this time. When out of the lines the men's rest billets were at Morlancourt, but the constant drafting of men into Tunneling Companies meant that 'rest' was only a figment, conjured by the imagination of HQ staff struggling to organize the preparation and logistics of forthcoming battle. This preparation included the construction of new jumping off trenches and the process attracted considerable attention from the German artillery located behind Mametz Wood and in the shelter of Caterpillar Valley.

*Here's the excitement, we are digging a new trench in front of our own line – now you know what that means. Well, our last night in reserve was our turn to do the job, and as there had only been two parties on the job previously you can guess we hadn't much cover. A shiver came down our backs when we knew we were for it. Everything was prepared, a dozen stretchers or so, motor Red Cross vans – the sight of these*

German trenches at Point 110 – the high ground at Bois Francais – which commanded an uninterrupted view over the surrounding terrain. It was from their trenches that the 5th City Battalion's preparations were viewed during the early summer of 1916.

improved our taste. However, of course Fritz had heard us coming so he began giving us a warm time before we got started and you know you cannot dig without making a noise, so when we did start our friend over the way didn't half get his wind up. We were dodging and digging from 11 to 2.30 am and wasn't we glad when time was up – and our luck again, nobody was hurt – except a chap who Tom Stevenson cut his eye open with a spade. The following day we moved into the line, and with that new trench and other things happening [the German] has fairly got his back up, it's so hot these days it shall be catching fire 'ere long. Our first night's [duty] in there was to provide a screen to cover the working party – ten of number four platoon volunteered for that, and this is what happened. Owing to bad arrangements they got out of touch with one another – owing to being heavily shelled some of them had gone forward for safety and got too far. Our Sergt. and two of the boys came in contact with a bombing party of the Germs [sic], who intended no doubt to pay the working party a visit. Our boys got surrounded but bombed their way back again, loosing sight of one another. When the roll was called after they retired the Sergt. was missing and not until daybreak was he sighted, laying very near their lines. There and then some brave chums of his volunteered to go and fetch him in – that would have been suicide so they were prevented until the following evening At 7.15 pm they set out but came across a German patrol so retired for a few minutes and returned when they cleared away. Alas, the body was there no longer, evidently they had taken him in and no doubt would find plenty of information in his pockets. This same night another screen had to be found and it was our platoon's turn to provide same. Our Sergt. came round and asked for volunteers so nine of us and a L/C said we would take it on. After what happened the night before you can guess it wasn't a pleasant job – however it had to be done. We set out at 10 o'clock... It was a lovely moonlight night and we went over the bags at 10.30 and were posted in couples 25 yards apart. A chum and I got into a shell hole and tried to dig (with our hands) cover, at any rate enough for our heads. We hadn't been out many minutes when the shells were bursting right and left of us. It's a sensation Reg you will never imagine, you hear the gun fired and the shell comes whistling over gradually falling and then you trust in the Lord. Putting up with this for four hours and never knowing what was going to happen next minute. Apart from the danger it was starvation – thank goodness Fritz had nobody crawling about. So, at 2.30 am we got the word to retire. As soon as I got up, up went a Very light – I ducked – machine gun set on me – so when it finishes I was back in to that trench in three strides and we were all there untouched to answer the roll, but it was a night I shall never forget. Enclosed is a picture of what it really is like... Private Pat Burke, 5th City Battalion, 10 April, 1916.

*Pat Burke, 5th City Battalion, with four of his friends outside a trench dug-out opposite Fricourt in the spring of 1916. This photograph was included by Pat Burke with his letter dated 10 April, 1916, in which he says, 'Enclosed is a picture of what it really is like.'* Burke

*The Scouts of the 5th City Battalion, the 20th Manchesters, photographed in the May of 1916. Harry Westerman is seated on the ground on the right of the photograph. The Scouts were the eyes and ears of a battalion and as such were kept busy in the struggle for supremacy and observation in the area of Bois Francais.* Westerman

*Panorama showing the southern part of the Somme battlefield and its fortified villages including Montauban photographed from behind the British lines opposite. These photographs were almost certainly taken during the early summer of 1916 before the intense bombardment of late June had destroyed the woodlands and hedgerows which were such prominent features of these locations.*

Unfortunately the good luck with which Pat Burke's 5th City Battalion had, so far, often been blessed then deserted the unit. The following tour within the forward trenches saw a number of men fall victim to the awful, impersonal hazards of trench existence. Private Burke was fortunate to escape with his life on 17 April.

> *We were doing our afternoon shift yesterday, seven of us working together, when a rifle grenade fell amongst us. What a sight, two of the chaps died in our arms whilst another chum and myself were doing all we could for them, but it was almost instantaneously. One of the boys you could have put your fist inside his head, the other had a similar wound over the heart and his nose blown off. A third of the party got his face, head, arm and leg severely wounded, no doubt he will be on his way to Blighty now. The fourth victim got a wound in the shoulder blade but was not detained. The remainder of us, three, got off Scott free, remarkable.* Private Pat Burke, 18 April, 1916

The 91st Brigade of the 7th Division now consisted of the 6th and 7th City Battalions (the 21st and 22nd Manchesters), the 2nd Queen's and the 1st S.Staffordshires. The 21st and 22nd Manchesters, within this 91st Brigade, found their section of line to be opposite another fortified German held village, Mametz, just a mile due east of Fricourt. Mametz stood at the foot of one spur of slowly rising ground, running in an easterly direction past Montauban towards Guillemont. Between Fricourt and Mametz, the Willow Stream exited from Caterpillar Valley which ran north easterly, to the north of Montauban. To the north of Caterpillar Valley itself lay four areas of woodland, Mametz Wood, the two Bazentin Woods and Delville Wood. All these canopies of still upright beech, ash and oak trees stood on the high ground of the Pozieres ridge, sheltering imposing German fortifications and observation positions.

### The Raid

Whilst in the line many opportunities were presented to the battalion's chroniclers to record the consequences and progressive impact of the attrition which leeched at every unit. The raid by A Company of the 22nd Manchesters, undertaken on Bulgar Point at 11.00 pm on 2 June, was just one such occasion. Bulgar Point was a German listening post located in a sap jutting out into No Man's Land south of Mametz. As the forthcoming battle approached it became imperative to have up to date information about the enemy's dispositions, the nature of his defences and the strength of his protection. For five weeks prior to their raid the men had rehearsed on a model of the German trenches dug behind the British lines, south of Bronfay

Farm. The raiding party consisted of sixty men, twenty in a covering party and forty who would enter the German trenches with the intention of wreaking havoc and taking prisoners. Lieutenant Oldham was in command, the covering party being led by 2nd Lieutenant Joshua Cansino. Before the raid a substantial bombardment took place, lasting for forty minutes, using howitzers, 60-pounders, 18-pounders and trench mortars. The assembly of the men and their entry into the German trench was undertaken without real difficulty apart from the need to force gaps in the wire. Five large dugouts containing an unknown number of men were bombed and fifteen further Germans were killed in the nearby trenches. Lieutenant Oldham remained at the point of entry just west of Bulgar Point whilst his second in command, 2nd Lieutenant Street, went further forward with the bombers. These men took four prisoners belonging to the 23rd Silesian Regiment, two of whom were killed because they offered resistance. Everything was going according to plan.

Unfortunately the withdrawal was less successful. Considerable delay was experienced as the men searched for the gaps in the wire. Within seconds the Germans were able to bring a machine gun to bear and bombs began to fall around the men. 2nd Lieutenant Edmund Street was seen to be stuck fast on the wire. Alfred Bland, A Company commander, was devastated when his returning men brought news of what had happened.

> I have borrowed two B Coy Officers. It's extraordinary. All the original A Coy Officers are gone, and I alone am left. Yes, at one blow we have lost four officers, three killed and Oldham wounded. Street, Burchill and Cansino are dead. Oldham, Street and Cansino with sixty NCO's and men raided the German trenches opposite on Friday night last. They had been practising the show for three weeks and all was arranged, every man to his task, perfect in every detail. As a show it was a success. They did considerable damage, secured two prisoners and dealt destruction to a great many more. The only hitch was the enemy wire, which had not been cut by the Artillery preparation. Street, as last to leave the Bosche trench, ran greatest risks, and got fast

*2nd Lieutenant Joshua Cansino. Killed in Action on 2 June 1916 during a raid on the German positions opposite the 7th City Battalion's trenches. Cansino was a graduate of Manchester University. He had spent a year in Berlin researching and teaching during progress towards his M.Sc degree but when war broke out he was living in Paris, returning to England to enlist as a private in the Royal Sussex Regiment. Having quickly reached the rank of sergeant he was commissioned into the 7th City Battalion, in November 1915, and posted to France in March 1916. As his great friend Alfred Bland says in his letter, Joshua Cansino's body was not recovered and his name is therefore commemorated on the Thiepval memorial.* Guest

*on the wire. Burchill went across to help him and received a fatal stomach wound, and Cansino did likewise and, so far as we know, was killed in attempting to save Street. The two latter have not been recovered. Oldham is all right, with a 'blighty' in the shoulder. Six men are missing. The Officer casualties are appallingly heavy, but the task attempted was magnificently accomplished We mourn our three beyond speech. Street leaves a widow and three children. Cansino a widow and an unborn babe...* Captain Alfred Bland. 4 June 1916

The battalion commander made no reference to the significance of the deep dugouts which had withstood the raid's preliminary bombardment.

When out of the lines the 6th and 7th City Battalions found themselves at Bray-sur-Somme. Whilst here their rest days were not taken as labour for the tunneling companies labouring at Bois Francais, as were the 5th City Battalion's men. However, the 6th and 7th Pals' men were, more often than not, put to work on the new narrow gauge railway lines being prepared behind their lines, in readiness for the 'Big Push'.

### The Genesis of Battle

Since early 1916 plans for Franco-British offensives had been evolving. Initially these had been devised as geographically separate, although strategically supportive. By mid February General Joffre, the French Army Commander in Chief, and Haig had agreed that the Franco-British offensive would be a joint assault 'astride the Somme about the 1 July'.[5] However, the catastrophic impact of Germany's attack at Verdun, beginning on 21 February, meant that all planning would be influenced by and, to a degree, subjugated to the need to sustain the French Army in its life and death struggle here with the Germans. One of the first actions by the British had been the taking over of a longer section of line, the decision which brought the Fourth Army, under the command of General Sir Henry Rawlinson, to the rolling landscape just north of the River Somme. Rawlinson's command then stretched from Fonquevillers on his left to Maricourt on his right.[6]

Through his reconnaissances here Rawlinson had become aware of the complexity, strength and depth of the German defences opposite. He knew the significance of the series of front line fortified villages, Gommecourt, Serre, Beaumont Hamel, Thiepval, la Boisselle, Fricourt and Mametz, and the depth of barbed wire which protected the whole. Further back, some 2-3000 yards to the rear, a second line of defences were known to have been established on reverse slopes with similarly strong protection. Between the two positions airborne reconnaissance showed a number of intermediate positions, the villages of Beaucourt, Pozieres, Contalmaison and Montauban. Further work was also being undertaken some 3,000 yards to the rear on the construction of a third German line, behind High Wood in front of Pys, le Sars and Flers, although at this point in time Rawlinson was not aware of that work.

In view of such strength in depth Rawlinson initially decided upon a step-by-step attack, utilizing massive artillery preparations to neutralize the defences and limit the infantry casualties which battles like Loos in 1915 had witnessed. Whilst hoping that his artillery could deal with the German defences to a depth of 4-5000 yards, Rawlinson hesitated to commit his infantry to making such a deep penetration. His concerns lay in the inexperience of the New Army battalions and his early planning suggested only the occupation of first line defences well short of the high ground on the Pozieres ridge. His plan was to bite into German held territory, under the protection of his artillery. His hope was that German counter-attacks would be devastated by the strong positions his Divisions would then hold. In the south of the battlefield, around Mametz and Montauban, the territory gained would be held fast whilst further advances towards Contalmaison would force the German Army to give up their intermediate positions around Mametz Wood.

In short, by April 1916, Rawlinson had devised a battle plan in which his strategic objective was to put his Fourth Army in a position to kill as many German soldiers as possible. Rawlinson had decided that gas was not to be used to saturate the deep dug-outs which protected the German defenders; German gas helmets were efficient and the consequent need to use their own helmets would hamper Rawlinson's advancing men considerably. Cover and surprise would be best achieved by the use of smoke discharges. Haig was unimpressed.

Haig wanted to break down the German Army's ability to defend on the Somme. He instructed Rawlinson to plan for a more substantial advance, now in conjunction with the French on their right, behind a 'hurricane bombardment' lasting just five to six hours. The centre of gravity of this would be along the Albert to Bapaume road. Behind the town of Albert, Haig was creating a Reserve Army whose purpose would be to burst through past Ovillers and La Boisselle towards Bapaume before swinging north eastwards to roll up the German positions north of the Somme towards Arras. Haig was reluctant to appreciate that insufficient

*General Sir Henry Rawlinson, the meticulous planner whose historical misfortune is to be tarred with a degree of responsibility for the catastrophe which many politicians, historians and ordinary people believed the Somme battles were.*

quantities of heavy howitzers and longer range field artillery were available to provide a hurricane bombardment over the wide frontage being planned for. On this point of the artillery preparation Rawlinson stood firm. A long bombardment was essential. However, Haig's intention to capture the German second line and open up the nature of the warfare was insistent. As Commander-in-Chief his wishes were complied with. The unfortunate outcome was that Haig, in his understandable hope of forcing breakthrough and victory, forced Rawlinson to dilute his artillery preparation into a much wider area, of necessity including wire cutting in front of the German second line defences. But above all considerations, throughout the spring and early summer of 1916, the spectre of Verdun continued to determine what should be aimed at during the forthcoming Somme offensive. The German offensive there had made the launching of Kitchener's New Armies into a massive attack imperative, irrespective of their state of readiness. And on their right the weight of the French assault would be weakened by the ever present need to rotate virtually every French division through the battlefields of Verdun, across which France had determined that the enemy would not pass.

Of course, as the final weeks of preparation ticked away, the strategic direction of the forthcoming battle gave way to the need to delegate tactical decisions about artillery, smoke and troop deployments towards Corps and Divisional command levels. In this respect the Manchesters, like almost all the assaulting units, were already frustrated and hampered by lack of time to train and prepare in their facsimile trenches. XIII Corps was concerned. *'Brigades of the [neighbouring] 18th Division were enabled to get an average of ten days practice over these model trenches, those of the 30th Division an average of six days.'* A bare minimum of time had thus been allotted to effect these, Manchester's final preparations around Picquigny. The 7th Division's facsimile trenches were mostly in the Corbie area. At

*Private Charles Price, 7180, 1st City Battalion. Killed in Action on 15 June 1916. Charles Price was an ex-student of Manchester Grammar School. He had later been articled to the Town Clerk of Hyde, passing his final Law examinations in June of 1914 and enlisting in the 1st of Manchester's Pals in September. The Battalion War Diary on the day of his death simply states, 'Quiet day. 1 O.R. killed.' Guest*

this stage there were frequent moments of doubt about the ability of the 30th Division's Major General Shea to control the attack on Montauban, the 30th not being regarded in early 1916 as either experienced or well led.

Nevertheless, as these final weeks ticked away, the Manchesters were constantly engaged in constructing many miles of new fire trenches, dug in front of their existing front lines trenches, to bring the departure trenches as far as possible within assaulting distance and parallel to the enemy trenches, as well as many new assembly positions behind the front lines. Dozens of deep emplacements for the $2''$ and Stokes trench mortars were dug with the intention of accommodating the extra weapons which would be available for the attack. The in and out communication trenches for the attack were dug, enabling troops to cross all ground under German observation unseen. The average length of these communication trenches was 2,500 yards to the rear. To facilitate the expected advance, Russian Saps were constructed forward into No Man's Land, the hope being that these would be linked to any convenient German communication trenches as soon as sufficient advance had been made. Beyond these preparations which would directly affect their own circumstances on the morning of the attack, the men were also engaged in the construction of Divisional, Brigade and Battalion battle headquarters, as well as similar posts for all nearby Corps and Divisional artillery groups. On any suitable higher ground the observation posts for Forward Observation Officers (F.O.O.s) were built. Ammunition, ration, water and R.E. dumps proliferated. Prisoner cages were erected. Their parts in the construction of regimental aid posts, advanced dressing stations, main dressing stations and clearing posts reminded the men that the forthcoming battle, the Battle of Albert on the River Ancre, would be the severest test of their resolve and courage.

### Final Plans for 30th Division's attack

The final plans issued to the 1st, 2nd and 3rd Manchester Pals Battalions on 25 June, from 90th Brigade HQ, left no doubt about what would be the main thrust of their assault as part of 30th Division's operations. Units of the 90th Brigade were to assemble in front of Oxford Copse within assembly trenches either side and behind Cambridge Copse, at A.15.a. One hour after the commencement of the Battle of the Somme the 1st and 2nd Pals were to attack, side by side, in a frontal assault on the village of Montauban, lying 1500 yards behind the German front line positions. On their left would be men of the 55th Brigade of the 18th Division, in the area of Breslau Alley. The dividing line between the 30th and 18th divisions was the track running north from the tip of Talus Boise. The German front line positions were expected to have been already overrun by leading battalions from the 21st Brigade of 30th Division, the 18th King's Liverpool Regiment and the 4th Manchester Pals. On the right of the 21st Brigade battalions from the 89th Brigade of 30th Division would also attack the

German front lines before pressing on towards the east of Glatz Redoubt and Dublin trench.[8] The 21st Brigade would therefore be expected to hold the west of Glatz Redoubt and thence westwards towards the junction between Train Alley and the track which ran northwards out of Talus Boise (at A.3.c.8.6).

Brigadier General Steavenson's orders for his 90 Brigade were precise. One hour after the opening of battle, and the assault on the German front lines and positions through to Train Alley, Glatz Redoubt and Dublin Trench, the 2nd Manchester Pals would leave their assembly positions, moving forward with their right on the track running thirty yards west of sap A.9.2. in the British front line, through the west edge of Glatz redoubt, passing through the men of the 21st Brigade. The men were then expected to face due north to attack and take Montauban itself. The 1st Manchester Pals would attack on the left of the 2nd Pals. The 1st Pals' left would be on Talus Boise and the track which left the wood's tip towards the west of Montauban. In support would be the 2nd Royal Scots Fusiliers with two companies in support of each Manchester

*The German positions had an air of permanence. Each trench was fully equipped with deep shell-proof protection as well as many personal comforts for the men. Behind the front positions the many derelict farms provided opportunities for photographers to record the presence of a well equipped and determined army of occupation.* Taylor

battalion. Three platoons of the 2nd Royal Scots were to act as nettoyeurs, moving into Montauban behind the Manchester Pals with orders to clear the enemy out of communication trenches, dug-outs and cellars. Two companies of the 3rd Manchester Pals, the 18th Manchesters, were designated as the 90th Brigade's tactical reserve. The other two companies were to operate as carrying parties, moving ammunition, trench bridges, water and supplies forward to the leading units.

Whilst the assault by the 21st Brigade was being completed, the artillery supporting this attack would be expected to fire on a line just north of Train Alley (on the line A4a41/38—A3b65/30 – A3c83/94) until two hours after zero when it would lift onto Montauban village, Southern Trench which lay two hundred yards south of the village, and Montauban Alley two hundred yards to the north of the village. At two hours and twenty six minutes past zero that barrage would lift off those locations to form a protective barrage north of Montauban just

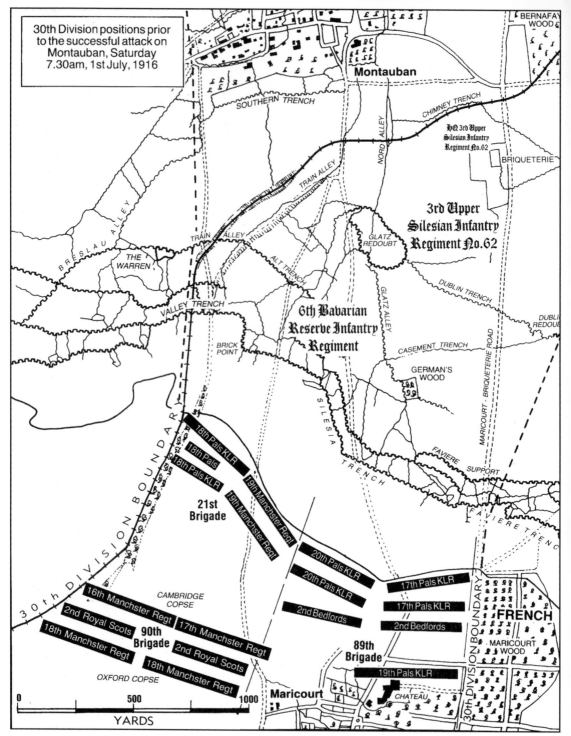

30th Division positions prior to the successful attack on Montauban, Saturday 7.30am, 1st July, 1916

beyond Montauban Alley. The troops were told that if their advance were to get ahead of the schedule, 'infantry must wait there until the barrage in front lifts'.[9] Once the barrage was correctly located to the north of the village the 1st and 2nd Manchester Pals would then attack and take Montauban. These two battalions, the 16th and 17th Manchesters, would then advance to and clear Montauban Alley trench, sending forward parties including

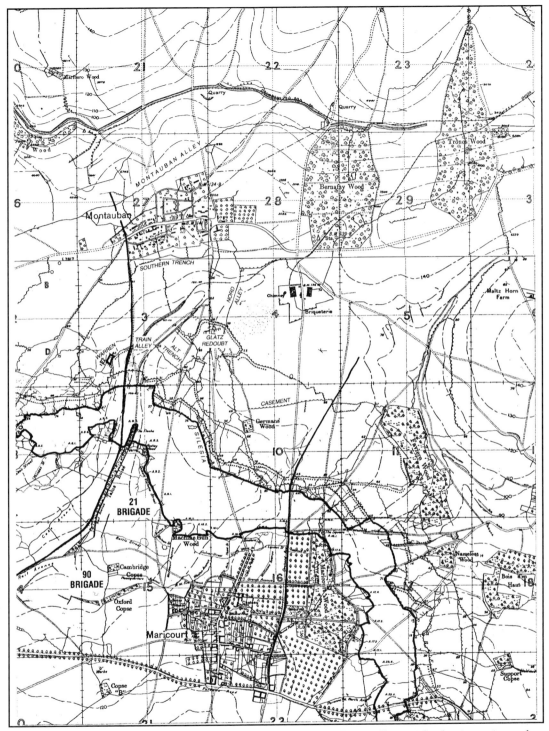

Lewis gunners to the positions overlooking Caterpillar Valley with the intention of preventing effective counter attacks from the north and east, as well as preventing the withdrawal of artillery from Caterpillar Valley. Whilst there the Manchesters would reverse the parados for defensive fire and put out wire to secure the village.

On the appointed day, as they crossed No Man's Land to join battle in front of Maricourt

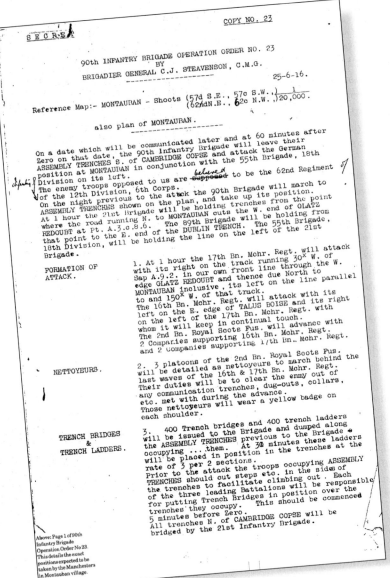

COPY NO. 23

90th INFANTRY BRIGADE OPERATION ORDER NO. 23
BY
BRIGADIER GENERAL C.J. STEAVENSON, C.M.G.

25-6-16.

Reference Map:- MONTAUBAN - Shoots (57d S.E., 57c S.W.,) 1
(62dN.E., 62c N.W.,)20,000.

also plan of MONTAUBAN.

On a date which will be communicated later and at 60 minutes after Zero on that date, the 90th Infantry Brigade will leave their ASSEMBLY TRENCHES S. of CAMBRIDGE COPSE and attack the German position at MONTAUBAN in conjunction with the 55th Brigade, 18th Division on its left. The enemy troops opposed to us are *believed* to be the 62nd Regiment of the 12th Division, 6th Corps.

On the night previous to the attack the 90th Brigade will march to ASSEMBLY TRENCHES shown on the plan, and take up its position.

At 1 hour the 21st Brigade will be holding trenches from the point where the road running N. to MONTAUBAN cuts the W. end of GLATZ REDOUBT at Pt. A.3.c.8.6. The 89th Brigade will be holding from that point to the E. end of the DUBLIN TRENCH. The 55th Brigade, 18th Division, will be holding the line on the left of the 21st Brigade.

FORMATION OF
ATTACK.

1. At 1 hour the 17th Bn. Mchr. Regt. will attack with its right on the track running 30° W. of Sap A.9.2. in our own front line through the W. edge GLATZ REDOUBT and thence due North to MONTAUBAN inclusive, its left on the line parallel to and 150° W. of that track.
The 16th Bn. Mchr. Regt. will attack with its left on the E. edge of TALUS BOISE and its right on the left of the 17th Bn. Mchr. Regt. with whom it will keep in continual touch.
The 2nd Bn. Royal Scots Fus. will advance with 2 Companies supporting 16th Bn. Mchr. Regt. and 2 Companies supporting 17th Bn. Mchr. Regt.

NETTOYEURS.

2. 3 platoons of the 2nd Bn. Royal Scots Fus. will be detailed as nettoyeurs to march behind the last waves of the 16th & 17th Bn. Mchr. Regt. Their duties will be to clear the enmy out of any communication trenches, dug-outs, collars, etc. met with during the advance.
Those nettoyeurs will wear a yellow badge on each shoulder.

TRENCH BRIDGES
&
TRENCH LADDERS.

3. 400 Trench bridges and 400 trench ladders will be issued to the Brigade and dumped along the ASSEMBLY TRENCHES previous to the Brigade occupying ...them. At 30 minutes these ladders will be placed in position in the trenches at the rate of 3 per 2 sections.
Prior to the attack the troops occupying ASSEMBLY TRENCHES should cut steps etc. in the sides of the trenches to facilitate climbing out. Each of the three leading Battalions will be responsible for putting Trench Bridges in position over the trenches they occupy. This should be commenced 5 minutes before Zero.
All trenches N. of CAMBRIDGE COPSE will be bridged by the 21st Infantry Brigade.

Above: Page 1 of 90th Infantry Brigade Operation Order No 23. This details the exact positions expected to be taken by the Manchesters in Montauban village. MRA

*Page 1 of 90th Infantry Brigade Operation Order No. 23. This details the exact positions expected to be taken by the Manchesters in Montrauban village. MRA*

and Talus Boise, the Manchester men, here as elsewhere, would be burdened by at least 66 lbs of kit and equipment.[10] The advance across this shell cratered wasteland from Cambridge Copse assembly trenches to Montauban would be 3,000 yards. It would be no push over.

### Final Plans for 7th Division's attack

In front of Montauban the 30th Division formed part of XIII Corps, commanded by Lieutenant General W N Congreve, VC. Further west the villages of Mametz and Fricourt would be attacked by XV Corps, commanded by Lieutenant General H S Horne. The Corps plans accepted that Fricourt village, with its massive and complex defences, was an almost impossibly hard nut to crack. As a consequence it had been decided to launch an attack around both flanks of the village, leaving its defenders effectively surrounded and forced to withdraw, surrender or be overrun. 21st Division would attack north of Fricourt. 7th Division would

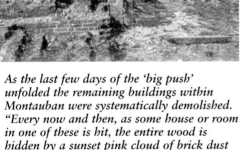

*As the last few days of the 'big push'
unfolded the remaining buildings within
Montauban were systematically demolished.
"Every now and then, as some house or room
in one of these is hit, the entire wood is
hidden by a sunset pink cloud of brick dust
and one after another old familiar buildings
disappear."*

attack the southern flank of the Fricourt
salient, towards Mametz and the Willow
Stream which exited from Caterpillar Valley
between Mametz and Fricourt.

The initial pincer movement around
Fricourt would involve the right hand
brigade of 7th Division, the 91st Brigade
including the 6th and 7th Manchester Pals,
in an attack past the east of Mametz
towards their first objective, Danzig Alley
trench. Their second and third objectives were Fritz Trench and then on towards White
Trench on the spur overlooking Caterpillar Valley.

On their right would be 18th Division of XIII Corps, attacking just west of Montauban.
On the left of 91st Brigade the 20th Brigade would also attack towards the west of Mametz
village, then forming a line facing west and threatening the Fricourt defences. However, the
inner Brigades of both 7th and 21st Divisions would stand to in their front lines until it was
clear that the time was ripe for a determined assault on a helpless Fricourt. The hour at which
that attack would be launched would be determined by Horne himself. Therefore the 5th
Manchester Pals, as part of 22nd Brigade, were destined to start the day in waiting.

### The Final Days

The last days of June 1916 were a watershed in the British Army's perception of war in France. It was now clear to all that a moment of great significance was soon to unfold. Some men were spared the ordeal which awaited their Pals here on the Somme. Behind the village of Carnoy Taylor Chapman, serving with the 4th City Battalion, was struck down by illness on 20 June.

> As it happened I got an infection in the glands of my neck and they operated on me at Corbie, then they sent me down the line to Boulogne where word came through that this big attack was to take place and to clear the hospitals. So, before I knew where I was, I was sent home to England and I finished up at Royds Hall at Huddersfield. Private Taylor Chapman. 4th City Battalion.

Among the junior officers an overwhelming spirit of optimism was about.

> The Valley of Death behind us is white with chalk trenches and roads, pocked with shell holes, pimpled with gun pits. The woods and copses are full of mighty mounds of shell, 15″ to 18-pounders; the air is patrolled by a restless fleet of planes successfully keeping off the Bosche; this morning early I saw two of them drive a Bosche down in his own lines; we soared high above him and dived down like a hawk, peppering him with machine gun fire. He dropped steeply out of sight.
>
> Rhumor [sic] says all four of our armies and the French are going to push. Cavalry is behind us; the Greys are at Amiens I hear. Rhumor also says we have given Germany four days to declare peace or to take the consequences. I am not addicted to boasting, but I think that if he could see all the guns behind, all the grenades, trench mortars and other stores in front, if he knew how thoroughly ready we are with communication trenches run out to his front line with only a crust of turf on top, ready to knock in; mines under their wire and loaded pipes bored across no man's land ready to blow up and so form trenches; and if he could conceive how we are longing for 'the day' – I think if he knew the Kaiser would cut his losses and – take poison. 2nd Lieutenant Kenneth Callan-Macardle. 2nd City Battalion. Mancourt 23 June 1916.[11]

The enormous bombardment of the trenches around Mametz and Montauban, the reverberations from which ran back into the very earth, chalk and fortifications within which the Manchester men lived, carried all of these civic soldier's hopes and aspirations. The huge dumps of ammunition which surrounded each gun pit at the start of the barrage seemed impressive enough to the infantryman. Behind the 7th Division these dumps amounted to 1,100 rounds for each 18-pounder, 1,010 for each 4.5″ howitzer and hundreds for each of the short range mortars. They made success seem, if not a formality, then at least a good each way bet.

> We stand on the fire step; the abused, over-worked, underpaid infantry come into its own at last; now that the push is in sight and dirty work to do we have the front row of the stalls in the theatre of war, and the gunners, working hard behind the scenes can't ever see the show they are putting on. But they do it uncommonly well. All along the Boche front line, black and yellow, white and grey puffs of smoke dance in mighty cruel glee; fountains of brown sand or black clay shoot up high carrying with them a bunch of stakes all tangled up with wire. That's the 18-pounders, aerial torpedoes from the French, Stokes guns and mortars from us. Our 2″ footballs, huge iron balls with steel rods 2″ by about 2 feet long, roar high into the air from just behind our line, sail slowly up and fall with a rush from a great height, exploding with a crash that slaps one softly in the face. Much further back on the sky line 9″ shells are pounding the Bricketery [sic] and Montauban, both of which are surrounded by little woods. Every now and then, as some

*Taylor Chapman was an original Manchester Pal, although this photograph was taken after his return to active service in 1917. Taylor. Chapman was one of the men for whom severe illness in June 1916 ensured that they would be spared and therefore survive the ordeal of the fighting on the Somme the following month. Right up until the end of his long life (he died in 1992) Taylor Chapman knew that this illness excused his participation in the assault on Montauban and felt that he had been cheated of taking his place in the line with his Pals. In the very last hours before the assault many men were ill, as a consequence of the unwavering tension, wetness and poverty of food. Nevertheless, very few reported as sick because of their fear of missing 'the great day'.*

Chapman

house or room in one of these is hit, the entire wood is hidden by a sunset pink cloud of brick dust and one after another old familiar buildings disappear. The heavy shells throw black volumes of smoke some 300 feet into the air, salvos of them obliterate the village with dense, rolling clouds in the heart of which red flames flash and disappear. Over the whole stretch of country in front a thin pall of smoke is hanging. 2nd Lieutenant Kenneth Callan-Macardle. Maricourt. 26 June 1916.

The men were, of necessity, optimistic and preoccupied with final preparations, coping with and carrying the organizational and physical demands of assembling the material and munitions required for their assault. That Monday, 26 June, Alfred Bland was also confident, writing that:

*The whole of the German line has been named by us – every blessed trench – and is as familiar to us, each in our own sector, on the map, as is our own system ... Our Manchester lads are in good form today, burnt brown, eager and keen. I love 'em.* Captain Alfred Bland 7th City Battalion. 26 June 1916.

Two days later, by Wednesday, 28 June, Alfred Bland felt philosophical about the enormity and complexity of the events he was caught up in.

*What does it feel like to be on the edge of what may prove to be the mightiest battle waged in the history of the world? Like all romance, it is most unromantic to the participators at the time of participation. The spirit cannot grasp either the facts or the issues, the imagination is at work with the practical possibilities, and the brain is busy with the overload of detail, immediate and prospective. We are all like ants, as they appear to a disturber in their nests, terrifically busy in an apparently purposeless orgy of chaos.* Captain Alfred Bland. 7th City Battalion. 28 June 1916.

The possibility of failure was not even entertained within the Operation Orders which abounded on every officer's desk, pad or dug-out card table. Under the heading of 'Enemy Ruses' the 17th Battalion made plain to its commissioned staff that,

*Officers must impress most carefully on all ranks that the use of the word 'retire' is absolutely forbidden, and if heard, can only be a ruse of the enemy, and must be ignored.* 90th Br. Supplement to O.O. No.23. 29 June 1916

During those last hours Private Pat Burke of the 20th Manchesters knew that matters had come to a head. His battalion were expecting to attack the tip of the Fricourt salient, just south of that village.

*Whilst we were out on that last rest the bombardment started which lasted for six days gradually getting hotter and hotter. When we got back to our billets near the line – what a change in the village [Morlancourt], everything was made into hospitals, all the cafes were closed, and great preparations had been made for the great day. We went up to the line on the Wednesday, expecting to go over the following morning, but the weather was so bad we were brought back to the village – sadly disappointed. However, Friday soon came round, and we went up again, the boys were in wonderful spirits. That day I helped to carry rations up the line to them, and such a job it was, it was killing. Our trenches were blown to hell, it was a case of going over the top nearly all the way, but those lads must have their rations, and thought I, and all of us, beggar the consequences. After going up and down six times with rations, bombs etc, on my last journey I left them absolutely happy, and in the best of spirits…*

Private Pat Burke. 5th City Battalion.

In fact the destruction in the British front lines which Pat Burke had seen was problematic. The 7th Division's front line trenches were so severely damaged that in many places new jumping off trenches were being constructed behind the front lines. In other locations the men would go over the top from their support trenches or the narrow confines of their assembly trenches.

The delay announced at 11.00 am on Wednesday, 28th brought about by inclement weather conditions, meant something of an anticlimax for the infantrymen and their officers. Battalions due to lead the attack were taken back to damp and muddy bivouacs or rest billets, having come up to the line in a state of high anticipation. At airfields behind the lines pilots fretted in frustration, unable to observe with any consistency the impact of the artillery barrage which still thundered, unseen, to the east. Quartermasters' staff were apprehensive about the impact of delay on ration supplies. Pioneer battalions watched in dismay as carefully dug emplacements and assembly trenches became slimy with treacly chalk and mud. Transport sections wondered if the tracks and roads so meticulously identified as ready for the advance would still be passable when the rain stopped.

During these two extra days, Y1 and Y2, the British artillery continued to maintain its pressure. Economies in the use of shells were forced on the heavy gun teams, but each morning the eighty minute concentrated bombardment was maintained. Throughout the days and nights a sustained bombardment continued, adding to the torment and apprehension of the men opposite. The 7th Division were heartened when a deserter from the 109th Reserve Infantry Regiment, stationed opposite just outside Mametz, admitted that although no signal of an impending attack had been received, all of his friends predicted one and hoped that it would arrive soon and, thus, be over all the sooner. In that man's case no supplies had reached his unit for three days and the men had been compelled to eat their iron rations, contrary to orders.

Nevertheless, the Manchesters were also waiting in trying circumstances. The men had now spent seven months in frustrating waiting, exhausting carrying fatigues, digging and preparation. This had not dulled the men's enthusiasm for their cause. Everyone was keyed up and full of determination. On the occasions when companies had visited their own front line trenches the men could see and hear what, to all intents and purposes, seemed like a systematic and unanswerable destruction of a massive area of enemy entrenchments and wire. The men little knew, however, that the weight of artillery shells thrown against the defences in front of Fourth Army was unlikely to have shaken the resolve and destroyed the protective dug-outs of all those experienced soldiers who opposed them, especially positions within the confines of Mametz and Montauban. Facing the Manchester Pals were the 12th German Division in the Montauban area, their troops holding the lines opposite the British 30th

Division being the (3rd Upper Silesian Infantry) 62nd Regiment with two extra battalions from the 6th Bavarian Reserve Infantry Regiment (who would be in the front lines on the morning of the attack). The 23rd German Regiment had its battalions split between the 62nd Regiment in the Montauban sector and the 109th Reserve Infantry Regiment in the Mametz sector, with its HQ in Mametz village. The 28th German Reserve Division were in the Mametz and Fricourt area, opposite the British 7th Division, the German front lines there being held by the 109th and 111th Reserve Infantry Regiments respectively.

Fourth Army was clearly wrongly and overly optimistic about the devastation of German dug-outs located along many of the trenches opposite which were due to be attacked. This was not surprising in view of the fact that 'the bombardment, in terms of weight of shell per yard of trench attacked, possessed only half the intensity of that delivered at Neuve Chapelle'.[13] Nor had that bombardment in any way dimmed the clear observation which German-held positions in Mametz Wood and the Bazentin woods gave of the gargantuan preparations which were now all too clearly underway in the southern part of Fourth Army sector.

> We could just as well 'ave shouted to the Germans what we were doing. They took ladders in, unpainted new wood, fixed up days before on the jumping off trenches. Well, you would have thought they would have painted the wood brown, not leave it in the brilliant weather that we had. Private Charlie Heaton. 1st City Battalion.

However, in front of 30th Division the position did look genuinely optimistic for the Lancashire soldiers due to assemble in front of Montauban. The artillery reports for the 27 and 28 June were unambiguous on this point.

> 27 June. Fine – All wire cut in front line and progressing satisfactorily in second and third lines.

> 28 June. Wet – Bombardment continues – Observation very difficult – more retaliation on our front trench than usual – 'Z' day put off 48 hours – Rather unfortunate as from our point of view everything ready.[14]

A raid carried out on the night of 29 June by men of the 19th Manchesters had confirmed the state of the parapets opposite.

> Lt B Higgins and 2nd Lt Craston with 37 OR undertook a raid on the German front line with the object of getting a prisoner. Party left our trenches at 11.20 pm, after fifteen minutes bombardment and left German front line at 11.40 pm. No enemy were seen, and their front line had been practically levelled by our bombardment. One man was wounded slightly on the way out & one killed as party were returning.[15]

Rawlinson's expectations were clear. With less than twenty-four hours to go his Fourth Army HQ had reliable evidence that the German wire in the southern sector had been better cut than that further north towards Thiepval and Serre. He was optimistic that the French bombardment towards Bois Faviere had been effective and that the right flank of his advance would be secure. To the left of the French XXth Corps the 30th Division were expected to take Glatz Redoubt and Montauban. The impetus of the Manchester's attack towards Montauban would thus be greatly helped by the Pals' proximity to the French Army's attack towards Maurepas and Clery. On 30th Division's left the 18th Division would fight their way past the Loop and Pommiers Redoubt to stand on a line overlooking Caterpillar Valley. Mametz and Fricourt would be taken by 7th and 21st Divisions, ending the first day of battle on a line 500 yards short of Mametz Wood. All along the British battle-front, from Montauban north to Serre, Rawlinson expected an advance averaging two miles on the first day of battle, Z day.

Haig's wider aspirations were also considerable and optimistic. The Commander-in-Chief expected Fourth Army to take the Pozieres Ridge quickly as the second phase of battle unfolded. North of Serre the diversionary attack by Third Army's VII Corps would give impetus and help to the initial attack by VIII Corps towards Beaumont Hamel and Serre. Having secured the localities of Serre on the first day, Fourth Army would then press past its other first day objectives to take the Ginchy-Bapaume line. This position was expected to be achieved two days to a week after the commencement of the battle. Haig anticipated that the attack would then focus northwards towards objectives in front of Third Army.

With just hours to go the men who would turn these aspirations into fact or fiction were already preparing to depart for their assembly trenches. Some were writing letters. Some made entries in their log books, diaries or wills. Some talked nervously. Some felt the chill of premonition. Some were optimistic and full of anticipation.

> *Tonights the night. Tomorrow is der Tag!*
>
> *Only four officers per company go over but although I missed all the wonderful training the other seven had, still I am to go in with the Coy. O blessed, blessed Adjutant Macdonald; if you get hurt I shall weep over you. The others have done it over and over again; stormed the trenches, taken Montauban and Glats [sic] redoubt a dozen times, down by Picquigny – where it was all marked out with flags and shallow trenches exactly to scale. They know every house (as it was before we bombarded the village with 12 inch shells). They know every yard where every man is to go and they have passed most of it on to me. Tonight in the dark we assemble – brigades and brigades and more and more brigades – tomorrow in the pale dawn we go over the lid.* 2nd Lieutenant Kenneth Callan-Macardle, 2nd City Battalion, the 17th Manchesters, Montauban. 30 June, 1916.

The historic watershed had arrived. The Battle of the Somme was about to start.

### Notes:

1 Captain Alfred Bland, 7th City Battalion, writing three days after his arrival in France.

2 Frank Behrens. Later to become the greatly respected President of the 16th Manchester's Old Comrades Association.

3 General Shea was by all accounts a respected soldier and very competent Divisional Commander. The story about the incense became a favourite amongst members of the Worthington family for whom, in later life, Hubert Worthington would often adopt his best 'brass hat' accent to recount the tale.

4 *XIII Corps, Operations of the Somme. 1 July to 15 August.* Manchester Regiment Archives.

5 *Military Operations France and Belgium. 1916. Vol 1.* This Official History and its appendices, compiled by Br. Gen. Sir J E Edmonds, carries exhaustive analysis of the genesis of the Battles of the Somme in 1916.

6 Thus, whilst Rawlinson took command over that area which became known in Britain as the Somme battlefield, the reality was that the British sector was astride the River Ancre.

7 *XIII Corps, Operations of the Somme. 1 July to 15 August.* Manchester Regimental Archives. Because of its relatively high number the 30th Division had not been well treated during the share out of regular officers and NCOs, thus contributing to an initially rather poor reputation of both the Division and its Major General.

8 For an excellent description of what happened to the four Liverpool Pals battalions see *Liverpool Pals,* Graham Maddocks. Published by Leo Cooper, 1991.

9 *XIII Corps, Operations of the Somme. 1 July to 15 August.* Manchester Regiment Archives.

10 See Edmonds. pp 313

11 Typescript copies of papers available in the Manchester Regiment Archives, located in the Tameside Local Studies Library, ref Manchester Regiment, MR1/3/2/6. The original manuscript is in the Imperial War Museum's department of Documents.

12 Private Burke's letters held in the Department of Documents. Imperial War Museum.

13 *Command on the Western Front.* Prior and Wilson. pp 174. Neuve Chapelle had been fought on the 10, 11, and 12 of March, 1915, at a cost of 11,652 casualties to the British and Indian troops who took part.

14 Br. Major's report on 30th Division artillery preparation. Public Record Office Ref. No. W095/2316.

15 P.R.O. Ref. No. W095/2329.

## Chapter Five

# 'Our path is set; we've but to follow.'

*'We trailed out wearily and crossed the battle field down trenches choked with the dead of ourselves and our enemies, stiff, yellow, stinking – the agony of a violent death in their twisted fingers and drawn faces.'[1]*

Already, on 28 June, there had been one false start. Now there could be no turning back. In these last few hours the soldiers knew very well what such heavy artillery bombardment and obvious material preparations meant. Quite apart from the confidence born of camerarderie, and hope, there was also realism and a fear that the massive forthcoming offensive might be effectively countered by their opponents opposite. The unanswered question in everyone's minds was whether, along the ruins and chalk spoil which marked those opponent's parapets, the artillery's shells had done their work completely. If any German soldiers survived they also would know, very well, what to expect.

At 7.00 pm on the 30 June, the 1st City Battalion had been marched from Etinehem camp, through Billon Wood, to their assembly trenches just west of Cambridge Copse. The men arrived at fifteen minutes past midnight. To their right, within the copse, stood the 17th Manchesters, the 2nd City Battalion, who had arrived two and a quarter hours earlier. Behind them were the 2nd Royal Scots Fusiliers, in support, and behind the Fusiliers were the 18th Manchesters, the 3rd City Pals, in reserve, occupying their assembly trenches in front of Oxford Copse. Each battalion's sounds of movement were hidden in the rumble of shelling which rolled along the entirety of the forthcoming battle-front. Momentarily each man's

*Fourth Army hoped its massive artillery barrage would clear a path through the dense thickets of barbed wire which protected the German positions. In front of Montauban that hope was well founded. Further north, past Fricourt, the cutting of the wire proved to be far less effective.*

*General Sir John Shea, G.C.B., K.C.M.G., D.S.O., commanding 30th Division.* Nash

anxiety was illuminated to his friends in the flicker of light which every shell's explosion shed on the scene. The 90th Brigade was assembled. The battle, for which the largest portion of Manchester's youth and manhood had been prepared, was now only hours away. In these last few hours the pals of many years standing from the city's work-places and offices were packed together, leaving precious little space for comfort. As time wore on the stench of apprehensive men became stronger.

*We had a comfortless night in the assembly trenches for they were very crowded and there was no room to sit down, it was cold and the morning broke with a chill white mist on the ground over which the sun shone turning the white and yellow balls of schrapnell [sic] smoke all pink.* 2nd Lieutenant Kenneth Callan-Macardle. 2nd City Battalion, the 17th Manchesters.

With two hours to go a last opportunity to scribble a few lines was offered to the men. One who passed his note into the sandbag offered by the post corporal was twenty-two year old Alick Howells, 7121, of the 1st City Battalion. His message to his mother, living in Chorlton on Medlock, was concise.

*Our path is set; we've but to follow.*[2]

It would have been impossible to encapsulate the men's hopes more accurately.

In front of those men lay an advance of 3,000 yards. Apart from their standard equipment each Manchester soldier here in front of Montauban carried 250 further rounds of rifle ammunition, two Mills bombs, extra rations, a pick and shovel, and a canvas bucket with ten extra Mills bombs. Some men were excused from the need to carry these extra grenades, their burdens were a trench ladder or further rolls of barbed wire. On their backs the Manchesters wore a bright yellow patch for the benefit of Forward Observation Officers. Just in case this proved insufficient every tenth man wore a polished square of metal to reflect the sunlight and make surveillance of their progress more certain.

In their assembly trenches behind the front line the 1st and 2nd City Battalions, the 16th and 17th Manchesters' had placed their A and B companies in the first line of advance. With eight minutes to go before zero the Stokes mortar batteries opened a hurricane bombardment and observation of the German front lines became impossible as dust and smoke filled the air. From behind the Manchester's assembly trenches sixteen Vickers guns poured an unbroken stream of overhead fire in the direction of Montauban. With moments to go, the ends of the Russian Saps within yards of the German front lines were opened.[3] At 7.30 am, the Manchester Pals in the 16th and 17th battalions watched as the first waves of khaki-clad soldiers swept out into view. On their right the blue uniforms of French soldiers could be seen working quickly towards Bois Faviere. To the left of the 30th Division things did not immediately go as well. Here, in front of Carnoy village, the leading battalions of the right brigade of the 18th Division, the 55th Brigade, came under very heavy rifle and machine gun fire as soon as the men crossed the British front line trenches. From their assembly trenches behind Talus Boise the Manchesters could already see many casualties lying out in No Man's Land between the Casino Point craters and Breslau Trench in front of the Warren (62cNW1.A2d/A3c).[4] The tension was almost unbearable, only broken by the issue of rum during those final minutes before Manchester's 1st and 2nd City Pals battalions stood up to advance.

### 19th Battalion's attack[5]

As part of the 21st Brigade, the 19th Manchesters, the 4th City Battalion, had been ready for many hours in the front line, their attack timed to go in at zero. The 19th Manchester's objective was the north face of Glatz Redoubt (62cNW1.A4c2/9). On their left were the 18th King's Liverpool Regiment, the 2nd Liverpool Pals. On the Manchester's right were the 20th King's Liverpools of the 89th Brigade, the 4th Liverpool Pals. The advance of these units would prepare the way for the following battalions who would move through to assault Montauban itself. During the final minutes of the bombardment the ground on which the 4th City Battalion's men stood had begun shaking as brutal salvoes of shells were hurled at the positions opposite. At 7.30 am the men went over the top, many casually smoking a 'woody'. The 4th City Battalion were led by C Company on the left and A Company on the right. In support were B Company with D in reserve. Overhead machine gun bullets crackled northwards. Four further machine guns were moved forward with the rear company of each attacking battalion.

*As we got nearer dozens of Germans were running through us towards our lines with their hands up, others stopped there, throwing bombs, firing machine guns and rifle but they will fire no more what stayed until we got there, well very few. I jumped into the German trench, what was left of it, near a dugout door. In the doorway there was a big barrel. As soon as I jumped in a German jumped from behind this barrel. I was already on guard and had my bayonet on his chest, he was trembling and looked half mad with his hands above his head saying something to me which I did not understand at all. I could make out that he did not want me to kill him. It was here that I noticed my bayonet was broken, I could not have stuck him. Of course I had one 'up the chimney' as we call it, you only have to press the trigger the bullet being in the breach. I pointed to his belt and bayonet, he took these off, his hat, water bottle, emptied his pockets offering them all to me. Just then one of my mates was coming up the trench, 'Get out of the way Andy, leave him to me. I'll give him one to himself', meaning that he would*

**In the front line trenches protecting Montauban the artillery preparation had been devastating. As the 4th City men poured forward 'dozens of Germans were running through us towards our lines with their hands up.' Those who stayed in their trenches were overwhelmed and the 4th City men moved confidently towards Glatz redoubt.**

*The shoulder title of the 4th City Pals, the 19th Manchesters.*

*Behind the front lines signallers and Observation officers watch the early events intently.*

throw a bomb at him which would have blew him to pieces. I said, 'Come here.' He was on his knees in front of me now, fairly pleading I said, 'He's an old man.' He looked 60 at the finish. I pointed my thumb towards our lines never taking my bayonet off his chest. He jumped up and with his hands above his head run out of the trench towards our lines calling out all the time. He was trembling from head to foot, frightened to death. This was the only German I ever let off and have never regretted it, because I believe he could have done me quite easily as I jumped into the trench.

Well, him away, we both bombed the dugout and turned round to go along the trench when three fine Germans came running towards us with their hands up. They would be about twenty yards away. We both fired. Two fell, my mate saying, 'That's for my brother in the Dardanelles' and he fired a second. The other fell. 'That's for my winter in the trenches.' We walked up to them. One moved. My mate kicked him and pushed his bayonet in him. That finished him. This kind of thing was going on all along the line. No Germans being spared, wounded were killed by us all, we having been told 'No prisoners'. Private Albert Andrews. 19th Manchesters

The first and second lines of German trenches, consisting of Silesia and Silesia Support Trench defended by men of 6th Bavarian RIR, fell easily, the prolonged British artillery bombardment having wreaked a terrible toll. Some opposition was met from scattered groups of German defenders who threw bombs, but these men were quickly overwhelmed. All eight of the mobile machine guns reached the German support positions with very few casualties amongst their crews. North of Silesia Support trench the Manchester men crept close to their own barrage which was pounding Alt trench. The men waited here until 7.45 am, when the barrage lifted forward onto the gorge of Glatz Redoubt and the waves moved forward with great purpose to take Alt Trench. Within moments the barrage enabled the men to press on to the gorge in front of Glatz whilst the barrage itself moved further forward onto the north face of the redoubt. Casualties amongst the Liverpools to the left of the 19th Manchesters had been considerable, some hundreds being caused by machine gun fire coming from the direction of the Warren. The same fate was suffered by many men in the 2nd Yorkshires who were in support for the attack being made by the 21st Brigade. Of the left company of the 2nd Yorkshires only one corporal and thirty men reached the German front line. Nevertheless, by 8.26 am the 19th Manchesters began to enter Glatz Redoubt and had gained their objective. En route the battalion had captured two machine guns, three trench mortars and many prisoners. They occupied the north eastern portion of the redoubt with men of the

18th KLR on their left. Immediately the redoubt was gained, consolidation and re-entrenching work began, T saps being dug to house Lewis guns in advance of the arrival of Vickers guns. The communication trenches, running south to the old German front line, were deepened and Nord Alley, leading towards Montauban, was blocked. By 8.30 am, the Battalion had an advanced HQ in Alt Trench where men of D Company were busy reversing the fire-step and where the battalion's four machine guns were in place to provide support for the imminent assault of the 90th Brigade upon Montauban. Further forward, A, B and C Companies of the 4th City Battalion were now busily engaged in deepening trenches, reversing fire steps and sand bagging the new parapets to the north and east of Glatz Redoubt. At 8.38 am the 19th Battalion's men lit smoke candles and flares with the intention of concealing the advance of the 90th Brigade. The conditions for a successful attack on Montauban itself had been laid.

Casualties had been, in the context of other battalions' experience this day, relatively light. Forty men and one officer killed, eleven men and one officer missing as well as one officer and one hundred and thirty six men wounded. By contrast, the 18th King's who had advanced to the left of the 19th Manchesters, would suffer nearly 500 casualties this day, almost all of them during the first hour of the assault, and almost all of those as a consequence of the initial difficulties and repulse of the 55th Brigade's attack towards the west of Montauban, beyond the western side of Talus Boise.[6]

### The 1st and 2nd City Battalion's Attack

No one who was there could ever exaggerate the anticipation and sense of high expectation which surrounded this attack. The 1st City Battalion, the 16th Manchesters, were the closest of all the Pals units to the city's heart. Although the Liverpool Pals and the 19th Manchesters had prepared the way, there was a terrible and exposed haul in front of these men, almost two miles across a landscape littered with bodies, pocked by shellfire and periodically swept by the random and unexpected bursts of shrapnel shells and the snap of machine gun fire.

At 8.30 am the first two of the Manchester City Battalions climbed out of the protection afforded by their assembly trenches and moved forward. To their front the pall of smoke, lit by the assault battalions of the 21st and 89th Brigades, obscured the men's view of Montauban. For the first hundred yards of their advance the lie of the land meant that almost no hostile fire was seen. On their left the men of the 18th Division were held up by fighting in the vicinity of Pommiers Redoubt. The 18th Division's men appeared to be keeping to the trenches whilst in front of them German soldiers could be plainly observed, aiming rifle fire on the advancing British south of Montauban. From the north the machine guns in that village could be heard, already active, and from the direction of Pommiers Redoubt, to the north west of the men, machine guns firing in enfilade now began to get the range of the 1st City Battalion as they advanced into the open, north of Talus Boise. To observers on the Peronne Road it was clear that the worst of this fire was coming from

*Although this photograph shows their Maxim gun arranged for air defence. The image clearly illustrates the equipment which caused terrible carnage amongst the Manchesters on the Somme.* Taylor

the direction of the Warren, near to where Train Alley joined Breslau Alley. However, the proximity of the 18th Division's men meant that XIIIth Corp's artillery was not turned onto this location. Along with the guns in Pommiers Redoubt this one machine gun had already taken a heavy toll of the 18th Division's men and had now swung round to enfilade the 30th Division's attack. Having advanced less than a quarter of a mile from his assembly position, the commanding officer of the 2nd Pals, Lieutenant Colonel Johnson, was hit and command passed to his adjutant and second in command, Major Macdonald. Nor were machine guns the only deadly hazard. Without warning the burst of overhead shrapnel shells would cut gaps in the ranks of men.

> The German shells littered the battle field with dead and wounded; all around us and in front men dropped or staggered about; a yellow mass of Lydite schrapnel would burst high up and a section in two deep formation would crumple up and be gone. 'A' Coy was in front of us, advancing in sections with about twenty paces between blobs in perfect order at a slow walk... 2nd Lieutenant Kenneth Callan-Macardle. 6 July 1916

The scenes of carnage left indelible imagery on the memories of those men who passed this way. Sometimes the wounds were terrible and the maimed begged to be relieved of their suffering. One such,

> ...was an old soldier of the Borders, attached to the 16th Manchesters, who had about fifteen years service in and who was about 46years of age. I saw him in a shell hole just outside the German wire and he asked me to shoot him but I couldn't although his back was a hellish sight. A huge piece of shell had ripped his back open.
>
> Do you know what that man did? He cursed me to blazes and then deliberately cursing all the while stuck his bayonet right through his neck and his jugular vein, pierced – finished the poor fellow. He died kicking though and I felt as if a good cry would give me more satisfaction just then than anything else. He left a wife and four youngsters, two older lads (one wounded and at home). Of course hundreds of gallant deeds passed unnoticed. CQMS C F Warren. 6444. 1st City Battalion.[7]

The impact of the British artillery barrage had also been immense in this sector of the line. On crossing No Man's Land,

> It was impossible even to locate the German front line, his second was a great irregular ditch, all craters and fresh earth.
>
> We advanced in artillery formation at a slow walk. We led our sections in and out of the stricken men who were beyond help or whom we could not stop to help; it seemed callous but it was splendid war. Men crawling back smiled ruefully or tried to keep back blood with leaky fingers. We would call a cheery word or fix our eyes on Montauban – some were not good to see. 2nd Lieutenant Kenneth Callan-Macardle. 6 July 1916.

As part of A Company's attack with the 1st City Battalion, Charlie Heaton's party of six men were all designated to carry bombing supplies into Montauban. Their passage along the communication trenches towards Montauban village was to be protected by a rifleman with bayonet fixed. So great was Charlie Heaton's load that he was unable to carry arms.

> I'd got five men with supplies, and me, and a bayonet man in front of me, he happened to be a German, Louis Alban [6202], who lived at Ardwick. He was supposed to go round these trenches where these German dugouts were. He had a map on him of where the water supply was, and we'd got to look after it if we got there. I'd got six men who were carrying supplies who would follow me up this trench. My job, and others, was to bomb them out, but I couldn't go round a trench because I couldn't carry a rifle with all I'd got. Alban's job was to go round a trench [bay] first and if there was

*a man there he was to shoot them and warn me, and then we'd throw the Mills Bombs into that trench. He'd just stood up on top of the trench when they came round with their fire. As soon as he got on top and flexed his knees he went down, clean through the head. Well, all my other five were down, howling like cats and horses, screaming they'd been hit with this fire. I couldn't do anything. You're not supposed to give any help to wounded, 'somebody else 'll do that', so they said. The sergeant of the platoon, he was shot, straight away as soon as he got on top, shot through the liver. I don't know who it was said, 'You'd better push on.' There was a drop from the trench where we started from until you come to Jerry's communication trench. Well, I'd no men. They were all out. Hundreds of 'em. On the parados of the communication trench sit two officers. One's Captain Worthington and the other's Captain Elstob, who shouted, 'Get some men and work along this communication trench.' And I thought to myself, 'How the so and so can I get men. They're all dead.' There was nobody followin' either! So, anyway I started up this trench and the first [dugout] I came to had about seven in who were bloody glad to give themselves up...* Private Charlie Heaton. 6254. 1st City Battalion.*

*Charles Heaton, photographed during 1915 and in 1988.*

Having cleared his section of trench in the vicinity of Brick Lane, Charlie Heaton then set off north towards Montauban. Before he had gone many yards he was hit in the arm, a decent 'Blighty One'. For some time he lay in the nearest shell hole, recovering his strength. The first man to see him was Tommy Dawson [6232], who, ignoring orders, stopped to cut away the battledress tunic around the wound and applied a field dressing. Within minutes Private Heaton was making his way back across the wreckage of the German front line to the crowded confines of the old British front line. Once there he was amazed to discover dozens of men, some badly wounded and all without medical support, their wounds undressed. Even here, in what was developing into a relatively successful assault, the numbers of casualties were beginning to mount alarmingly.

Meanwhile the 1st and 2nd Manchester City Battalions, the 16th and 17th Manchesters, continued to press forward. As the ground here in front of Silesia Trench and Brick Lane had been smashed and churned by the continuous shellfire of previous days, there was no problem with any uncut

wire. The 16th and 17th Manchesters passed Alt Trench by 9.10 am. Minutes later, as their leading waves began arriving at Train Alley, it was becoming clear from where the enemy machine gun, on the left of the 16th Battalion, was firing. The 16th Manchesters here were taking casualties caused by machine gun fire both in enfilade and reverse. The location of the offending gun had, so far, withstood the attack of the 55th Brigade on the left of the Manchesters. By 9.30 am, however, the gun and its team were engaged and destroyed by a Lewis gun team of the 16th Manchesters, the German gunners staying at their posts until the end. Now less troubled by fire from their left, the 1st and 2nd City Pals entered Glatz Redoubt where the scene was still one of utter devastation. Papers and burnt bodies littered the ground. Those trenches not required by men of the l9th Manchesters and 18th King's lay flattened and bloodied. Men were searching for documents, and often the souvenirs and trophies which could later be sold to others to the rear. Many Germans had already escaped to the north. Some had remained, often to be bayonetted, sometimes to be taken prisoner. Private Gregory of the 18th King's Liverpools had a lucky escape as Manchester's 1st and 2nd City Battalions approached.

*When we got to the Glatz Redoubt it was in a right mess. There were bodies everywhere, in all kinds of attitudes, some on fire and burning from the British bombardment. Debris and deserted equipment littered the area, and papers were fluttering round in the breeze. There were only two of us at the start, and then we met with others coming in. Then a German came up, we thought out of the ground, but he was coming up some steps, proper wooden steps, about twelve or thirteen. They led down to a huge dugout, with wire beds in three tiers, with enough beds to take about one hundred people. This little German came out and put his hands in the air, and I couldn't shoot him. I just indicated for him to go over the top to our lines, and he just scampered off. I'll always remember that little lad, he had a little pork pie hat. I couldn't face the shooting.*

*Then we went down into the dugout to do a bit of 'souveniring'. The Germans must have left pretty quickly because they hadn't even taken their coats, so we went through the pockets. I got a German soldier's pay book, some buttons and a spiked helmet. One other souvenir I collected from a German officer's tunic was a diary, which I later handed over to an officer at a dressing station. The remainder of the 'loot', like tunic buttons, I found a ready market for, at the base at Rouen, where the Army Service Corps blokes who were on 7s a day pay, ours was only 1s, would pay any thing for these small souvenirs. I hung on to the pay book and the officer's helmet, which my mother later threw out, because it had bloodstains on the inside!*

*Another of our lads also got a spiked helmet which he put on his head. He was still wearing it when we went back up to the trench, and he was larking around with it. Just then, one of the Manchesters who were coming up behind us, came round the traverse, and seeing him with this helmet on, must have thought he was a German, and shot him dead. It couldn't be helped, it was just one of those things that happens in war.* Private W. Gregory. 17122, 18th Bn. KLR.[8]

All around here the scene was of frenetic preparation. Trenches were being reversed. Prisoners were being sent back and their comrades bodies cleared. During this period the 30th Division hesitated. On the left the 55th Brigade, 18th Division, were clearly in trouble. However, the decision was made to order the advance towards Montauban in order to relieve pressure on the 18th Division's men. For many minutes the Manchester men had waited, taking what cover they could find.

*The ground was so rough and broken with shell holes that when I lay down under our barrage I found myself ahead of the first line – I had four men left. The 17th had advanced too quickly. We had done it all at the slowest walk and been quite unchequed [sic] – so we lay down for forty minutes, under the shells, waiting. Waiting is hard. We were to rush the village at 9.56.*

*The time came. I was watching A Coy to see them rise but the seconds ticked on. I haled a sergeant and asked him, shouting in his ear, where his officers were. 'All gone Sir,' he shouted back.*

*I caught a glimpse of young Wain, his face haggard with pain, one leg soaked with blood smoking a cigarette and pushing himself forward with a stick. His voice was full of sobs and tears of pain and rage. 'Get up you ————-s. Blast your souls – get up'. I waved to him and he smiled and dropped – he knew it was not absolutely up to him any longer. We of 'B' Coy, took over, for he was the last of 'A' Coys officers and their Sgt Major also was killed. We were enfiladed from our left (where another battalion had failed to advance), by machine gun and rifle fire...*
2nd Lieutenant Kenneth Callan-Macardle.

*Private Percy Wade, 8317, 2nd City Battalion. Like very many of the Pals who had enlisted together into the first Brigade of Manchester's Pals, Percy Wade was a well educated and self confident man. His father was an Oldham headmaster and Justice of the Peace in Middleton. After leaving Manchester Grammar School Percy Wade's qualifications and contacts enabled him to become the Deputy Town Clerk of Middleton. He refused the offer of a commission, preferring to stay in the ranks with his friends. He was one of the 17th Battalion's men killed in action on 1 July, 1916.* Guest

From Glatz Redoubt a screening barrage was raised by 4″ Stokes mortars, throwing smoke on the right towards the Briqueterie and Maltz Horn Ridge. This effectively confused the German Forward Artillery Observation, bringing wasted shellfire down on the billowing clouds to the right of the Manchester's advance. This was fortuitous as the crossing of Southern Trench, proved difficult. The trench was wide and could only be crossed at one or two points. Traffic within the trench was obstructed by the flow of prisoners and casualties. As the groups of soldiers emerged from Southern Trench the men of the 2nd Royal Scots were intermingled with the rear of what had now become two broad attacking waves of Manchesters. At 10.05 the 16th and 17th Manchesters finally moved on through as the leading troops from the 18th Division arrived on their left. Although the pace was slow, at best a deliberate methodical walk, the men were well up with their own barrage. Gradually succeeding platoons became mixed with those in front and the attack by the 90th Brigade came to resemble one dense mass of soldiers. As the 16th and 17th Manchesters with their supports moved northwards, Nord Alley was occupied by infantrymen and a Lewis gun team from the 19th Manchesters who pushed forwards as far as Chimney Trench, where they began the construction of one of a number of strong-points.

Above them the occasional and indiscriminate shrapnel shells continued to do their deadly work amongst the men now desperate to take the sheltering confines of Montauban village in front.

The seemingly interminable British barrage which had played on the village of Montauban and the trenches to its south now lifted to the north of the village. Beyond Montauban Alley the earth was being ruptured into great spouts of chalk, clay and torn equipment which marked the limit of the protective barrage. Beyond, some few German survivors were already fleeing from the continued ferocity unleashed by the British Artillery here. Within the

*Private Frederick Harry Waldron, 8949, No VIII platoon, B Coy, 2nd City Battalion. Harry Waldron was a bugler within the Battalion Band, and therefore a stretcher bearer in action on 1 July. Harry died of wounds received during his battalion's attack on Montauban that day. He was just twenty years old. The photograph shows him with his fiancee, Miss Cox of Withington in Manchester. He has no known grave and is commemorated on the Thiepval memorial to the missing. Harry was one of three Waldron brothers from the suburb of Withington who served within the First Manchester Pals Brigade. His eldest brother, Lance Corporal Benson Waldron, was also severely wounded this day, but recovered from his wounds.* Westerman

wreckage small groups of German troops still remained, but proved unable to bring any concentrated rifle or machine gun fire on the mass of men now advancing in front of them. Whilst still taking casualties from enfilade to their left, the combined 1st and 2nd City Battalions, the 16th and 17th Manchesters, now advanced quickly through the village to occupy the secure confines of Montauban Alley and Triangle Point, soon after 10.30 a.m. Although their training at Picquigny had familiarized the Pals with the layout of the streets in the village, the effect of the bombardment had been terrible, making the tangled confines almost unintelligible. There was very little fight left in Montauban's garrison and upwards of one hundred dazed and dusty German soldiers surrendered immediately.

The 90th Brigade's telephone line had been taken up by men belonging to the 1st City Battalion, although they had moved forward behind the third wave of the 17th Manchesters attack.

*I had made up my mind that when once having proceeded over the top, on no account would I hesitate unless compelled by bullets or shratnel, and so on we went till the halt for the barrage to lift. Callous I may have been, but I certainly had no eyes for those who fell around me. To my front was the village of Montauban, on which my whole thoughts were concentrated, along with visions of the Victoria Cross, Blighty and death.*

*I and my load of wiring apparatus were fortunate enough to reach the grand objective. Following the completion of our proud capture, a bottle or two of soda water and a cigar the Bosche had so kindly left were enjoyed by way of well earned refreshment. Lance Corporal W Aukland. 6210. 1st City Battalion*

Across the scene of devastation through which the 1st and 2nd City Battalions had advanced, two platoons of the 4th City Battalion, the 19th Manchesters, now moved into Train Alley facing east, just south of Montauban, where they also began the construction of a further strong-point. On route they had passed the bodies of many men, almost all the clerks and warehousemen of Manchester's pre-war commercial life. Within the village of Montauban itself the 2nd Royal Scots now leant their weight to the process of consolidating more strong-points. Major Macdonald of the 2nd City Battalion recorded that,

*There was no opposition to the entry. Bombing parties proceeded to clear NORD and TRAIN ALLE Y & C T in orchard NE of B strong point, the enemy met with in these places surrendered without opposition and the leading waves pushed on through the town. The rear waves consisting partly of carrying parties arrived in rather an exhausted*

*Montauban 'was practically deserted and was completely in ruins. It was almost impossible to trace the run of the streets.'* Taylor

*state, due chiefly to their desire to be 'in at the finish'. The town was practically deserted and was completely in ruins. It was almost impossible to trace the run of the streets.[9]*

The whole atmosphere was still foul with choking cordite fumes and orange brick dust. However, it was more than fortunate that the artillery had been so effective in reducing the defences of Montauban. Had it been possible to mount an effective defence by one or two well sited machine guns in front of the open ground across which the Manchester Pals had advanced, the carnage would certainly have been as terrible as elsewhere on the battle-front this morning.

However, disaster had been averted. The men's throats were now parched with the electrifying terror of what they had seen and done. Emotions were running high after making their attack.

> *Inside all was wreck and ruin, a monstrous garbage heap stinking of dead men and high explosive. Down in deep dugouts, a few of which had survived our heavy shells, (for the hun builds perfect dugouts), cowering men in grey were captured, living with old corpses. A Brigadier Colonel [sic] and staff of six officers were captured in one which was fitted with electric light and a push bell; large parties laughing and dancing like demented things full of mad joy went streaming back to Maricourt unguarded, holding their hands up and calling 'Mercy Cammerard', they had thrown away their equipment and arms and looked utterly demoralized in filthy and stinking grey uniforms. The village was full of the terrors and horrors of war; dying Germans among the brick dust and rubble, horrible wounds and reeking corpses.* 2nd Lieutenant Kenneth Callan-Macardle.

Those members of the 16th and 17th Manchesters who had survived the machine gun fire and shrapnel shells which had stalked their advance now took cover within the crumpled but

*One of the German 77mm field guns captured near Montaubanon 1 July.*

*Published in the* Illustrated London News, *on 22 July 1916, this artist's impression conveys a stylised image of the Manchester's success at Montauban on 1 July.*

welcoming heaps of dereliction which marked the site of the village, and within the deep confines of Montauban Alley, to the north of Montauban. Once established north of the village, Forward Observation Officers equipped with squared and lettered panoramic maps and sketches were able to bring a devastatingly accurate rain of artillery shells onto desperate groups of men, fleeing across Caterpillar Valley along the road towards Bazentin le Grand. A small party of soldiers from the 1st City Pals went even further than their objectives. Privates 6232 Dawson and 6203 Aldcroft ran down the hill beyond the protective confines of Montauban's trenches, rushing the gun pits below just north of Spur Point and shooting the fleeing gunners. Although they quickly chalked their own names and the Battalion's title on these two 77mm guns, it was an impossible position to hold and the men withdrew southwards to their positions in Montauban Alley, having captured the first pieces of artillery taken during the day.[10] In many places Montauban Alley was almost untouched. Its depth and untroubled dugouts amazed the men. Their days spent in rehearsal for this attack would now pay dividends since the number of officer casualties was already high. An initial counter attack was launched on the positions held by the 1st City Pals almost as soon as they had occupied Montauban Alley. It proved possible to repel this attack by Lewis gun and rifle fire alone, and within fifteen minutes all was quiet apart from the intermittent crumps of incoming shells from the north and east. By 11.00 am the whole of 30th Division's final objectives had been taken, although this could not yet be said of the 18th Division to their left. Every company commander in the 1st City Battalion had been wounded this day, although Wilfrith Elstob commanding C Company was able to stay. All the officers of A and B Companies were either dead or wounded. The officers commanding the front line by 10.30 am were Captain Morten Johnson and Lieutenant Tony Nash. On their left flank everything was in the air where the attack by the 18th Division had not been able to keep pace.[11] On their right the 17th Manchesters were in touch, although Captain Ford of the 17th's A Company was dead, as was Captain Vaudrey of B Company and Captain Kenworthy of D Company. The battalion commander was already hospitalized. The positions occupied by the 17th Battalion, to the right of the Church and towards the orchard on the east of the village, began to attract considerable shellfire from early afternoon as the Manchester's consolidation and new trench construction was observed from the direction of Bernafay Wood, due east of Montauban. Most of this was 77mm and 15cm shelling and was to continue with unnerving accuracy and almost without cessation throughout the next forty-eight hours. Adequate trenches were proving impossible to construct given the soft and shattered nature of the subsoil.

> *Practically no dug-out shelters were available for the men and casualties were heavy from the commencement of the bombardment. The enemy was making accurate observation of the village during the whole of our tenancy of it and his shooting was extraordinarily good. No sooner did a working party commence to work on a new bit of trench than shells rained on them.*[12]

Having come through the advance to Montauban with relatively light casualties fate had now dealt the 2nd Pals a poor hand.

> *Consolidation was started everywhere without delay and fair progress made, but in MONTAUBAN the enemy's artillery fire rendered the proper carrying out of the scheme impossible, from about 1.45 pm when his guns commenced a systematic bombardment of the village, which has never ceased since. The Scots Fusiliers, the supporting battalion of the 90th [Brigade], were however able to do good work on the trench parallel to and S. of MONTAUBAN.*

The prearranged scheme for consolidation had to be considerably modified owing to the state of pulp to which the enemy's trenches and the village of Montauban had been reduced.

> The carrying parties [the 18th Manchesters], always rather small in numbers and reduced by casualties, did really good work, but there was a tendency to bring them up exhausted – largely due to their anxiety to be 'in the fun' as soon as possible. [Narrative report on these operations by 30th Division][13]

*Men of the 1st City Battalion shelter in the depths of Montauban Alley after their successful assault on the village earlier that day.*

*2nd Lieutenant Harvey in Montauban Alley. This snapshot was taken with great presence of mind, at about 12.00 p.m. on 1 July, by Tony Nash. To the left of the duckboarded trench floor are the deep dugouts under the south face of the trench.* MRA

*Scout Sergeant 'Bert' Payne. Also shown is the scouting badge which he wore proudly throughout his service.* Pickstone

In mid-afternoon Sergeant Bert Payne came to. Hours before, as Montauban was being rushed, he had arrived at a shell hole, clustered within which were many dead and blinded men. As his section had rushed on, Payne himself was hit in the face, a bullet from the left smashing through his cheek and into his teeth. Spitting blood and bone he sank towards unconsciousness, thinking gratefully that he could still breathe.

*About 4 o'clock I must have come round. My left eye was closed. My mouth was round to the left and I couldn't talk. I could breath, that was all. I got my field dressing out and bound it round my face and my left eye. I could see through my right eye... One of my Corporals, Corporal Bill Brock, had been shot through the foot. I took his boot off, bandaged it up and put his boot on again and gave him his rifle to use as a crutch. I brought him back. It was here that I met our Chaplain and Doctor [Captain] Fletcher. I said to them, 'You shoun't be out here, go back to the dressing stations Mr Balleine [the Chaplain], don't come out here, you're useless here, you'll only get killed! There's nothing you can do.' They didn't know what to do. There was nobody there, only dead. I saw one man, a shell had come over and hit this man, it knocked off his left arm and his left leg, his left eye was hanging on his cheek. He was calling out 'Annie'. It always gets to me that does. I shot him. I had to. He couldn't have done anything and it put him out of his misery. It hurt me. I didn't know who he was, he could have been anybody, he was just anybody's boy but he was calling out for 'Annie, Annie', his cheeks were bleeding and his eye was hanging there, pulsing I had to shoot him. He was sitting down there, but he couldn't have moved, he'd have died in any case, but I had the courage to do it.*

*Then I said, 'Now Bill, we've got to get you back somehow.' We were just walking along when Jerry opened fire again and one shell exploded near us and it lifted us up over the barbed wire, we cleared it, Bill Brock with a bullet through his foot! I tore my bottom on the wire. That's what you can do when you've got to! Then I came to a trench with a German doctor in and some German prisoners. I asked this doctor to bind Corporal Brock's foot but he wouldn't. I said, 'You'll bind his foot up or I'll shoot you.' He said, 'Blame your own Government.' He spoke that in English. So I shot him. Then I picked up Bill and walked on 'till we came to another dressing station...* Scout Sgt. James Albert Payne. 6310. 1st City Battalion.

Throughout the day the men of the 18th Manchesters, the brigade reserve, were enthusiastically engaged in the processes of clearing the connecting communication trenches, sending back the wounded comrades and foes who had made

*Thomas Anthony Havelock 'Beau' Nash*

*Montauban had become 'a monstrous garbage heap stinking of dead men and high explosive.'
Yet below the surface pulp evidence still remained of many deep positions which had been created
to ensure the security and well being of the German troops who occupied this sector of the front.*

it into the respite of a trench, dealing with prisoners, and bringing forward water, supplies and ammunition. Unfortunately, the persistent and accurate German shelling of the area between Montauban and the Alley, since mid-day, meant that very little of these supplies proved capable of being taken forward to the foremost front line positions. The men of the 1st and 2nd Pals in those front line positions were parched, having had no opportunity of filling their water bottles on the previous evening. Behind them, scattered in the open spaces between the maze of shattered trenches, many more severely wounded and dying men lay out, hoping for attention and feeling the cold onset of nightfall. Although they had not directly engaged in the initial attack and subsequent defence of the new front positions, the 18th Battalion, the 3rd Pals, suffered five officer casualties and one hundred and seventy three further casualties amongst the men, mostly within C Company.

It would only be a matter of time before further counter attacks were launched against the Manchesters in the front line positions in Montauban Alley and to the north east of the village.

The Pals' resolve to repel these counter attacks was undoubted, their preparedness sketchy, their numbers thin. In front of Montauban Alley it had proved impossible to occupy a number of prominent positions overlooking Caterpillar Valley because of persistent shellfire from the British artillery. From Montauban Alley the field of fire northwards, for riflemen, was limited, as little as one hundred yards in places. Hardly any mills bombs had survived the journey

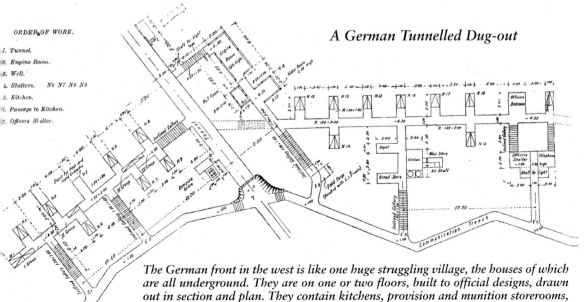

*A German Tunnelled Dug-out*

*The German front in the west is like one huge struggling village, the houses of which
are all underground. They are on one or two floors, built to official designs, drawn
out in section and plan. They contain kitchens, provision and munition storerooms,
a well, a forge riveted with sheets of cast iron, an engine-room and a motor-room.
Many of the captured dug-outs were thus lighted by electricity.*

*Two of Harry Waldron's brothers who survived the events of 1st July. On the left is Ernest Percy Waldron, 3rd City Battalion, the 18th Manchesters, and on the right is Benson Waldron, 6568, 1st City Battalion. In front is the mother of all three brothers, Clara Waldron, and her youngest son, Hugh, aged six. Lance Corporal Benson Waldron, the eldest brother, was severely wounded in the leg during the attacks through Montauban towards Montauban Alley. His wound was staunched by a tourniquet made from 2nd Lieutenant Nash's puttees. Hospitalized at home, Benson convalesced with others from his unit within the ranks of the 3rd Battalion of the Manchester Regiment who were stationed at Cleethorpes. Benson Waldron then underwent officer training and was Commissioned into the 19th Manchesters as an officer in C Company. He was destined to be killed at the Battle of Paschendaele in 1917. Harry's other brother, Ernest, was unscathed and survived the war, later to serve in Egypt during the Second World War.* Westerman

across from the Maricourt dumps. No Very lights were available because of the casualties amongst the officers and communication with the artillery was therefore, at best, doubtful.

However, before returning to the story of these men's defence of Montauban on the night of 1/2 July, it is essential to consider what was happening further west along the southern arm of the Somme battlefield. The initial assault by the Rawlinson's Army had taken place along a gigantic 'L' shaped front, the bottom right of which was now secured by the 16th and 17th Manchesters and other men from the 30th Division. At the crook of the 'L' the village of Fricourt was due to be enclosed in the advance towards Mametz and, further north, towards Contalmaison.

## 7th Division's Attack on Mametz

The 6th City Battalion, the 21st Manchesters, had left Bois des Tailles at midnight. Their strength was twenty officers and 796 men.

As dawn broke, south of Fricourt in the vicinity of Bois Francais, the 5th City Battalion, the 20th Manchesters, were already stood to in their support trenches, awaiting orders to attack Fricourt. To their right, further east, stood Mansel Copse. Mametz itself was roughly 1000 yards from the

*The shoulder title of the 6th City Pals, the 21st Manchesters.*

British front line trenches, protected by a well sited defensive position, Cemetery Trench, which ran through the graveyard in front of the village's ruins. 1500 yards east of the village stood the Pommiers Redoubt, a strong-point on the Montauban road whose machine guns enfiladed the slopes in front of Mametz.

The two assault battalions of the 91st Brigade were the 7th City Battalion, the 22nd Manchesters, on the right and the 1st South Staffordshires on the left, due to assault from positions east of Mansel Copse facing Bulgar Trench. Here, as elsewhere along parts of XV Corp's frontage, the men were to be assembled prior to their attack in new trenches dug just behind their battered front lines. The 21st Manchesters were part of the 91st Brigade's reserve. The objectives of the 91st Brigade were Bunny Alley and Fritz Trench, north and east of Mametz. No Man's Land here was roughly 150 yards in width. In support were the 2nd Queen's and in reserve the 21st Manchesters. Opposite were men of the 109th RIR, whose Headquarters were in Mametz itself, and a company of men from the 23rd RIR. To the right of these men, from Hidden Wood to positions north of Fricourt, were men of the 111th RIR. The German artillery had been extensively beaten in counter battery exchanges and was incapable of producing a really effective defensive barrage to protect No Man's Land here. By contrast XV Corps' artillery was well prepared and the 7th Division's assault troops were to move forward behind a creeping barrage, consisting of shrapnel shells fired by the Divisional 18-pounders, a system which was to become progressively more widely used as the war continued.

> During the advance of the infantry a barrage of artillery fire will be formed in front of the infantry according to the timings shown on the tracings issued to those concerned. The lines shown on the tracings indicate the nearest points on which guns will fire up to the hour indicated. At the times shown heavy guns will lift their fire direct to the next barrage line. The divisional artillery will move their fire progressively at the rate of 50 yards a minute. Should the infantry arrive at any point before the time fixed for the barrage to lift, they will wait under the best cover available and be prepared to assault directly the lift takes place. 7th Div. Artillery orders, issued on 18 June by Br. General J G Rotten.

At 6.25 am the intensive bombardment had begun. With fifteen minutes to go gas was released in front of Fricourt, its purpose to confuse and mislead the village's defenders that an attack from

*This map from the Official History identifies the positions assaulted by the 5th, 6th and 7th City Battalions during the events of 1st July, 1916.*

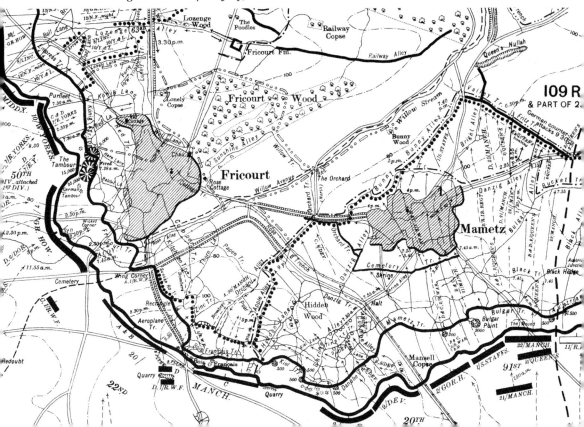

*Tiny figures can be clearly seen against the chalk spoil as the 7th Divisions assault battalions, the 7th City Battalion, the 22nd Manchesters, and the 1st South Staffordshires move forwards towards Mametz.*

*The wreckage of Mametz village soon after its capture on 1 July.*

*Below: The fragile ruins of Mametz after the British attacks had cleared the village on 1 July.*

the thinly held trenches opposite was imminent. With eight minutes to go the Stokes mortars joined in. With four minutes to go smoke was discharged in order to obscure the moves of the brigades either side of Fricourt, whose flanks would be otherwise exposed. With two minutes to go three massive mines were blown at the Tambour, west of Fricourt. Simultaneously a series of smaller mines were detonated in front of Mametz, the largest being under Bulgar Point. Already the assault battalions were on the move. At 7.30, as the 7th City Battalion, the 22nd Manchesters, passed through their old front lines, the air was still thick with debris and choking chalk dust, thrown up by the detonation of the Bulgar Point mine. B Company were on the right and D on the left. One man's experience with D Company illustrates the severity of the fire which, even close to the British lines, was intense and accurate. His squad of bombers had been detailed to go over with D Company's second line, bombing out the German front lines just east of Bulgar Point.

> I'm afraid I disobeyed orders that day, because instead of following the squad, I took up first Bomber's position with Private Clarke, who was an athlete, as my bayonet man. Leaving D Coy's line we proceeded in extended order along the new trench and just as Clarke turned round and shouted to me that the cross trenches were just in front of us I stopped my fourth hit, which proved to be a bullet just under my left nostril, and as this shattered my right jaw, I decided to go back, which I did after a brief respite on the ground, which I think was spent spitting out. Anyway, it was then that I found out that I had only three men left, Clarke in front and Gleave and Greenhalgh following up. The latter two paused on their way to see where I had stopped one and as I raised my head to them one of them said, 'Oh, he's got it in the neck, he's done for'. So I waved them to carry on and then started off back. How I managed to get back to our front line without stopping another one goodness only knows... L/Corporal Sidney McCoy, 21371, 22nd Manchesters

Of Sidney McCoy's 11 man bombing squad, six were killed that morning.[14]

Although a number of German front line posts had been blown in by the detonation of the mines, the defence of Mametz village and Danzig Alley was still capable of being undertaken by the machine gunners whose deep dugouts, further back, had protected them during the barrage. At the last moment they emerged, shaken but unscathed. Nevertheless, the German front line was carried with relatively few casualties since No Man's Land here was narrow and few German shells fell to impede the men's progress. Immediately A Company of the 21st Manchesters followed the assault to begin the process of clearing German dugouts and sending back prisoners. However, as the attacking waves drove forward, the toll on their lives increased and casualties became heavy. After fifteen minutes Black Trench had fallen to the 22nd Manchesters. Despite the creeping barrage the machine guns in Mametz and Danzig Alley cut many more men down as they moved on northwards. The speed of the barrage now proved marginally too fast for the infantry. Their pace slowed. Nevertheless, within thirty minutes of the attack starting, small parties of the 22nd Manchesters were entering Bucket Trench, and the South Staffs were in Mametz. For the 22nd Manchesters their first objective had been taken in twenty five minutes. A great many of the casualties, suffered by both the Manchesters and the South Staffs, had been caused by a machine gun placed in a house in the south west corner of the village, its loopholes protected by 4" armour plate!

By now the advance had clearly lost contact with the creeping barrage. Many of the South Staffs were forced to withdraw to Cemetery Trench, south of the village, leaving small detachments cut off in its ruins. After taking Bucket Trench, the 22nd Manchesters moved on Danzig Alley, entering it by 8.15. Their objective was Fritz Trench. However, it proved impossible even to hold onto Danzig Alley and the 22nd's men fell back, having found many determined defenders emerging from unscathed dug-outs there and in the face of a German counter attack from the direction of Fritz Trench. By 9.30 parts of the supporting battalions were sent forward and men of the 2nd Queen's arrived at Bucket Trench with the 22nd Manchesters. On their left B and C Companies of the 21st Manchesters arrived in Cemetery Trench but also found it impossible to advance immediately. At 10.00 am a further bombardment of the Danzig Alley, Fritz Trench, Bunny Alley triangle was ordered, but to little effect, the few men managing to get into Danzig Alley being quickly repulsed by counter attacks.

By 11.15 am it was known that the Pommiers Redoubt, on the right of the 22nd Manchesters, had fallen and that German soldiers had been seen in full retreat north of Montauban. Just before 12.30 a further bombardment took place, with the same objectives as designated in the 10.00 a.m. orders. In Mametz the German communications with the Montauban area were now severed and by 1.00 pm the defenders of Danzig Alley to the east of Mametz were falling back, north westwards along Fritz Trench or back into Mametz. By 1.30 the 22nd Manchesters, reinforced by D Company of the 21st Manchesters were in occupation of Danzig Alley. Ten minutes later, by 1.40, the 2nd Queen's were in Fritz Trench and bombers of this battalion and the 22nd Manchesters began to clear west and north towards Bright Alley and Valley Trench, taking more than 75 prisoners in the process. Simultaneously B and C Companies of the 21st Manchesters along with the 1st South Staffs had advanced into the southern end of Mametz and captured the remaining parts of Danzig Alley still in German hands. It was now, at 2.30 pm, that the attack on Fricourt itself began. This distraction to the west undermined much of the German resistance in Mametz and the 21st Manchesters had been able to move through the village. An attack at 3.30 pm by two companies of the 2nd Warwickshires caused panic among the remaining defenders south of the village, in the area of Shrine Alley, south of the village cemetery. At this point many of the objectives allotted to the abortive attack made by the 9th Devons in front of Mansel Copse were able to be taken. D Company of the 21st Manchesters were then sent up from their positions in Danzig Alley, just east of Mametz, to reinforce attacks being made by the 2nd Queen's towards Valley Trench and Queen's Nullah.

*Lieutenant Roy Mellor who was killed in action at Mametz on 1 July, 1916. On the outbreak of war Roy Mellor was only nineteen years of age. He had been a pupil at Macclesfield Grammar School and a member of the O.T.C from where he was commissioned into the 7th City Battalion, the 22nd Manchesters. By the time he arrived in France with the battalion in November 1915 he was already a Lieutenant and would serve as Musketry Officer, Acting Adjutant and Intelligence Officer before his death.* Guest

Soon after 4.00 pm the whole village of Mametz was clear and Bunny Trench to the north occupied. The attack of the 91st Brigade east of Mametz had succeeded and, in tactical terms, compensated for the horrendous casualties suffered by 20th Brigade directly in front of the village. Fritz Trench was clear, as was the communication trench, Bright Alley, which ran from Danzig Alley to Fritz Trench. In the front line overlooking Caterpillar Valley, men of the 2nd Queen's, 21st Manchesters and 1st South Staffs were making preparations to fend off counter attacks. Lieutenant Colonel Norman of the 21st Manchesters was placed in charge

*The shoulder title of the 24th Battalion of the Manchester Regiment, the 'Oldham Comrades'. This battalion were the pioneers of the 7th Division and therefore served throughout much of the Great War side by side with the men of the 5th, 6th and 7th Manchester Pals who also served within that division.*

*The attack on Danzig Alley left the 7th City Battalion with more casualties than any other Manchester Pals unit on 1 July.* Taylor

*Alfred Bland and his beloved wife, 'Letty'.* Mace

of the Mametz defences, having taken command of the 1st South Staffordshires as well as his own battalion. Wells were cleared and a wireless relay station erected in the village. To the rear the divisional services were able to effect road repairs in almost unchallenged quiet. The Oldham Comrades moved up to engage in wiring the 7th Division's front. Unfortunately, the atmosphere here was one of untroubled defensive preparation, when unremitting aggression was what was required. All along the front of the XIII Corps and 7th Division the men overlooked Caterpillar Valley, Mametz Wood and other positions which could, at much less cost than was later incurred, have been taken. Unfortunately the Corps commanders remained moribund. It was to prove a terribly costly missed opportunity.

Behind the British lines the military post was moving many thousands of letters. Alfred Bland's latest letter was already on its way home. Its writer lay dead in front of Danzig Alley trench. Inside the folds of paper were the petals of a small flower, a forget-me-knot. The words were brief and poignant:

> *My Darling*
> *All my love for ever.*
> *Alfred.* Captain Alfred Bland. 30 June 1916

His battalion had suffered almost 500 casualties this day. The battalion's diary records that eighteen of the officers were casualties, ten being killed. Amongst the men 472 were casualties, 241 wounded, 111 missing and 120 killed. The 7th Manchester City battalion had ceased to exist in any recognizable form.[15]

### The 20th Manchesters in front of Fricourt

On the morning of 1 July the 5th City Battalion, the 20th Manchesters, held half a mile of front line between the quarry, three hundred yards south east of Bois Francais, to the cross roads south of Fricourt on the Mametz-Becordel road. The entirety of the 22nd Brigade's attack would therefore be carried out by just this one battalion. Initially anticipated at 10.30 am, the attack had then been postponed for four hours. On the afternoon of their attack the battalion fighting strength was 20 officers and 670 men. At a crucial point in the battle-front

Alfred Bland's grave in Danzig Alley cemetery. **Author**

The important German salient of Fricourt—south of when the 5th City Battalion attacked on 1 July. Above shows the British bombardment and the bottom photograph was taken by a German unit in March 1915.

it was an injudicious decision to leave such a long frontage to so few men, the reason being the use of the 2nd Royal Warwickshires and 2nd Royal Irish as Divisional Reserve. By the time XV Corps' commander, Lieutenant General Horne, had made his decision to implement their attack the 20th Manchesters' men had waited fully seven hours, knowing that their assault was anticipated and would be undertaken in the full glare of daylight.

At 2.30 pm the 20th Manchester's attack went in. On their left the attack by the 7th Green Howards between Wing Corner and the Tambour mines foundered in the face of terrible machine gun fire in No Man's Land.

> All those weary hours the lads remained calm, but very eager to get it over. They did not go over after a strong ration of rum as some people imagine these affairs are carried out, no, they went over feeling themselves. The Colonel watched them mount the steps, and his last words were 'Isn't it wonderful?' The way they extended to six paces, and walked over at the slope one would have thought they were at Belton Park or our other training quarters. Our reserves were calling out 'Bravo Manchesters' 'Good Luck' 'Cheer Oh' and every word of praise that such calmness could bring to their minds. Down they fell one by one, but no excitement occurred until they closed on the German front line... Private Pat Burke. 7 July 1916.

C Company moved forward over the quite incredible cratered terrain at Bois Francais. A and B Companies advanced towards the sunken road which ran from Wing Corner, near Fricourt, up the hill towards the wood. D Company provided support, Battalion HQ moving forward with the platoons supporting A and B Companies. As Pat Burke witnessed, machine guns in the areas of Zinc Trench and Wing Corner played havoc with the men of A and B Companies, together with the supports from D, as the men approached the exposed ground in front of the sunken road. One of those killed was the commanding officer, Lieutenant Colonel Lewis, leaving the Adjutant, Captain F. Bryant, in command just fifteen minutes after the start of the

The shoulder title of the 5th City Pals, the 20th Manchesters.

attack. Bryant entered the trench with one other officer, Lieutenant Denton-Thompson, and just nine men who were now the left hand of the 22nd Brigade's force south of Fricourt, a mere handful of men. After engaging snipers firing from within Rectangle Support and from Fricourt Bryant established his HQ in Sunken Road trench. Unfortunately almost all the bombers whose task had been to clear Sunken Road trench towards Fricourt had been shot down. To their right 2nd Lieutenant A G N Dixey and Lieutenant H S Bagshaw managed to make their way further forward into the area of German support trench known as the Rectangle, only to find they had no men left to command. Unknown to Bryant's party in Sunken Lane these two officers then moved further right collecting small parties of men and bombers to make contact with the men of C Company who were into Bois Francais support without serious opposition or casualties. At this moment the HQ of the 5th City Battalion was totally surrounded and without support in Sunken Lane trench. Denton-Thompson was wounded and four of the nine other men there had also been shot.

The men of C Company now continued their attack, climbing out of Bois Francais support in the face of heavy machine gun fire, to advance a further 150 yards northwards towards Orchard Alley trench, during which move very many casualties occurred. During the afternoon

*2nd Lieutenant Frank Brooks. Killed in action during the 20th Manchesters' attack at Bois Francais on 1 July 1916. Before the war Frank Brooks had been a law student at Manchester University. On the outbreak of war he was commissioned into the North Staffordshire Regiment, but later transferred to the 20th Manchesters, departing for France with them in November 1915. He is buried at Danzig Alley.* Guest

the bombers from A Company worked their way northwards along Orchard Alley trench, although their efforts here proved in vain. Many were shot down by a machine gun, still operating in Zinc Trench, which was later put out of action by men of the 1st Royal Welch Fusiliers. Nevertheless these bombers were able to block Orchard Alley at its junction with Zinc Trench and then to proceed as far as Papen Trench. Forced to retrace their steps, these few men then met with a group of the 1st R.W.F.

*Pte Thomas Bryan, 18082, B Company, 5th City Battalion. Unusually, for the men whose fate it was to be killed in action on the 1st July, Private Bryan had already been identified as a very courageous and deserving soldier. For the bravery referred to in the newspaper's notification of death Thomas Bryan was granted a Military Medal (awarded after his subsequent death on 1st July), scant compensation for the wife and seven children he left at Dingle Fold in Astley. Many such notifications were printed in the local newspapers which abounded in the Manchester area. On request from the bereaved relatives the newspaper would print the notification details onto a postcard which could then be sent to family and friends as a permanent record of the man.* Potter

**ASTLEY HERO KILLED.**

Last week Mrs. Bryan, of 3, Dingle Fold, Astley, received word from an Army chaplain that her husband, Pte. Thomas Bryan, of the Manchester Pals Regt. had been killed. He met his death at the beginning of the big push. It will be remembered that Pte. Bryan was some time ago recommended for the D.C.M. In a letter which he wrote at that time he said: "You will be very pleased to hear that I have been recommended for military honours and that in all probability I shall receive the D.C.M. We had been rather heavily shelled, and there was quite a number of wounded lying in the open. To get these men to the doctor it was necessary to expose oneself and take them to the doctors' dug-out. I managed to get one of them there and also two other poor fellows who had been badly hurt. Whilst I was doing this the Germans were shelling our line very heavily. God only knows how I escaped alive. For this the doctor and our officer, both recommended me, and I have been told I shall receive the D.C.M." Pte. Bryan, who leaves a wife and seven children, before the war worked at the Nook Pit.

**PTE. T. BRYAN.**

who were then organized to bomb down Zinc trench from its south end.

Pat Burke's anger at seeing so many of his comrades lost was understandable. Written within hours of his leaving the area of the attack, his account is full of the animosity and bitterness which warfare brings.

> We thro' bombs of every description down, smoke bombs especially, and as the hounds came up, crawling half dead, we stuck the blighters, and put them out of time. In one dugout there were about 25 in, and we set the place on fire, we spared them no mercy, they don't deserve it. They continued sniping as we were advancing until we reached them, and then they thro' up the hands. 'Merci [sic] Kamerade,' we gave them mercy, I dont think. We took far too many prisoners they numbered about a thousand, and they didnt deserve being spared. What tales they told us, and they would give us anything for souvenirs to spare their lives. Private Pat Burke. 7 July 1916.

During the mid afternoon Lance Corporal F. Barnes (18417) volunteered to go over the top in the face of heavy machine gun fire to report the seriousness of his unit's position to the Officer Commanding the 1st R.W.F. Incredibly he survived to deliver the message and return to the Sunken Lane. Just after 5.00 pm telephone communication with Brigade HQ was established and the seriousness of the Brigade's position on its left flank realized. Two hours later, at 7.15 pm, two bombing sections of the R.W.F. arrived and secured the left flank of Sunken Road trench, enabling Captain Bryant and his group of five effective men to feel a little more secure! Battalion HQ was then moved to Bois Francais support where it was realized that only five of the battalion's officers, two of whom were wounded, remained. The work of reversing the parapet was put in hand and as twilight settled on the scene the men stood to on their gains, running from Apple Alley north westwards to Zinc Trench. By now the 5th Manchester City Battalion were down to an organized strength of 150 men. Their attack, along a Brigade frontage, marked the end of progress along the southern arm of Fourth Army's attack north of the Somme. Whilst they had not made great progress, enough had been achieved to secure the left flank of the 20th Brigade. Within twenty-four hours Fricourt itself was occupied and the disintegration of the 5th Manchester Pals justified in the eyes of the divisional and higher commands.

The 5th Manchester City Battalion's casualties were by no means the highest suffered by any of the Manchester Pals this day. Nevertheless, they had lost their Commanding Officer, together with four Captains killed, six of their subalterns killed, six other officer casualties, 110 men killed, 29 missing and 171 wounded. During the coming ten days the battalion required drafts of more than five hundred men to make good their losses.

### Nightfall on 1 July, from Montauban to Fricourt

As daylight withered towards nightfall, the German position on the Somme battlefield was still advantageous after twelve hours of the most brutal and momentous warfare ever waged. On the right of the British assault the French had made gains towards Hardecourt and Curlu. The impetus of those attacks and the bravery and sacrifice of the 30th, 18th and 7th Division's men had carried the British attack northwards along the southern arm of the British front. However north of Fricourt many of the British attacks had been repulsed, often amidst scenes of the most horrendous slaughter. By contrast German losses were comparatively slight. It was clear, therefore, that attempts to recover the ground which had been lost around Montauban and Mametz would be made, and that the relatively secure position of the German Army facing much of the British attack elsewhere on the battlefield would allow those counter attacks to be developed in strength.

In front of Montauban the men of the 1st and 2nd City Battalions were still desperate for

*Within twenty-four hours of the attack on Fricourt the village was abandoned by the German Army. During their abortive attack the 5th City Battalion lost their C.O. killed, four captains killed, six subalterns killed, six other officer casualties, 110 men killed, 29 missing and 171 wounded.*

water. Each man had laid out his remaining ammunition on the parapet. With the onset of darkness many exhausted men found it almost impossible to resist sleep. They had been awake for thirty six hours. Many of the men had not drunk water for twenty four hours. The position was exposed and accurately registered by the German artillery. Since the initial counter attack that morning the men had been ordered to stand to and expect a further attack at any time. Since then the hours had slid by, stretched to a seemingly interminable length by the men's thirst and the anxiety of the moment. Once darkness shrouded their work, the men made further attempts to construct and revet more effective trenches, especially those facing to the east of the village. However, the whole area was searched by German artillery, systematically from north to south, in a very thorough fashion. It was clear that the most methodical arrangements had been made by the departing Germans to make the village almost uninhabitable to its new occupants.

> *The trench became littered with dead and wounded. The dying called for water, but there was none; those in agony asked pitiably for stretchers but eight stretcher bearers had been killed, three stretchers out of the four destroyed and the doctor was overwhelmed with work. It was of course impossible to spare a sound man to help along a broken one...* 2nd Lieutenant Kenneth Callan-Macardle.

At 3.00 am the men were anticipating the order to 'stand down'. The first pale light of dawn had already started to relieve the darkness. Just at that moment, when remission seemed imminent, the whistle of incoming shells and the crash of high explosive was everywhere. Lines of grey clad figures moved into sight, across the ridge. These were men of the 16th Bavarian Regiment (10th Bavarian Division).[16] Their attack was launched in very close packed waves of infantrymen. From their unsteady gait it looked as if some of these German troops were drunk. Opposing them, in Montauban Alley,

*The cap badge worn by all of the Manchester Pals, together with the shoulder title unique to the 17th Battalion, the 2nd City.*

were roughly 150 men of the 1st City Battalion on whose right were an equally small number of the 2nd City's men, the 17th Manchesters. Some of the 16th Manchester's men climbed out of the protection of the trench to get a better field of fire. Immediately their SOS rockets were sent up requesting a protective barrage but for fifteen long minutes no artillery response materialized. In the absence of artillery four waves of infantry were broken up by rapid rifle fire alone. A number of the German soldiers who had massed on the west side of the Montauban – Bazentin-le-Grand road managed to dash into an unoccupied section of Montauban Alley to the west of Triangle Point. However, at this moment the protective artillery reply began to fall and the impetus of the attack wavered. Those few brave Germans who had entered the Alley now became demoralized as the heavies searched their trench, parties of them dashing back across the road towards the dead ground towards Longueval. However east of the junction between the 16th and 17th Manchester Battalions, a lodgement in advance of the front lines was made by a party of German soldiers who occupied the detached post held near Triangle Point. The defenders, from A Company of the 17th Manchesters, held out until their small supply of grenades gave out, only then attempting to retire. Of that group just three got back, two of whom were wounded. This was the last counter attack launched during the 2nd July on the Manchesters holding the village of Montauban.

During the preceding twenty four hours the 1st City Battalion had lost heavily.[17] Even after the second German counter attack, the remaining men were able to get little respite as arrangements began to withdraw the 16th's men, who were to be relieved by two companies of the 2nd Wiltshires. By early morning the remnants of the 1st City Battalion were able to file down the communication trenches back past Talus Boise towards Cambridge Copse. For the 2nd City Pals that relief would take a further twenty four hours. In the meantime the Scots Fusiliers and men of the 18th Manchesters were drafted in to garrison parts of the village and secure its defences.

*All day and night the shriek of shells like a hurricane among the telephone wires and in narrow streets; the last scream and then the all powerful thud and rending crash of them went on ceaselessly. We got tired of the shock of their explosions making us reel and feel dizzy and numbed; we got sick of the reek of high explosives which is synonymous with dead and broken men; Our cheery triumphant treatment of this most unpleasant situation changed. When the first day & night were gone, when the second night began we were silent and grim and – yes – a little afraid. At least we had got to longing for a relief – to hating the endless shattering of the shells – to receiving news of more casualties among our dwindling force (no longer very much a force) with a weary shrug. Of course we knew Montauban was safe – we would keep Montauban – but every time a pallid runner came down the trench or over the top & handed one a note, one wondered was it to say; 'Lt Humphreys is Killed, You are in command of the 'Coy' ' or 'The enemy are in Montauban'...* 2nd Lieutenant Kenneth Callan-Macardle.

Early on the 3 July the 2nd Manchester Pals' hard won place in the line was taken over by the 12th Royal Scots of the 9th Division. For the moment the tension and anxiety were dissipated. The surviving vestige of the 2nd Pals had been on their feet for sixty hours. They had also suffered extensive losses, 8 officer casualties and 350 men leaving a battalion

*A dead German photographed 'during the British advance.' The British cameramen and cinematographers took virtually no images showing the carnage which had occurred throughout the British Army.* Taylor

strength amounting to 450 of all ranks.

*We were relieved in a hurricane of shells.*

*We trailed out wearily and crossed the battle field down trenches choked with the dead of ourselves and our enemies, stiff, yellow, stinking – the agony of a violent death in their twisted fingers and drawn faces. There were arms and things on the parapets and in trees; shell holes with heaps of three or four in them. The dawn came as we reached again the assembly trenches in Cambridge Copse... A molten sun slid up over a plum coloured wood on a mauve hill shading down to grey; in a vivid flaming sky topaz clouds with golden edges floated, the tips of shell-shocked bare trees stood out over a sea of billowing white mist; the morning light was golden.*

*We trudged wearily up the hill, but not unhappy. All this world was for ever dead to Vaudrey & Kenworthy, Clesham, Sproat, Ford and of the other ranks we did not know how many... On Peron[ne] Rd. we met McGregor Whitton of the Royal Scots Fusiliers. He had been wounded in the hand early in the push but had carried on. He was looking for a lost company and very fed up. I asked after Godfery. Young Victor was killed – his problem of marriage to a woman six years senior to him finally settled. Towers Clark too was dead and Capt. Law of County Down and others I did not know so well.*

*In Billon Wood we got water from the gunners – they had moved heavies up there and 18-pounders into Montauban. We had our rendezvous at Bronfay Farm. At Happy Valley a bivouac was arranged for us and breakfast. We ate enormously, washed the worst of the grime away and slept for hours.* 2nd Lieutenant Kenneth Callan-Macardle.

*Left to right: Lieutenant G.P. Morris; Captain F. Walker, who was blinded in both eyes at Montauban, and Captain Hubert Worthington of A Coy, an architect who had worked with Lutyens before the war and who would supervise the rebuilding of Manchester Cathedral after the blitz during WWII. All three were officers serving with the 1st City Battalion.* MRA

Here at the most inappropriately named Happy Valley, just off the Bray-Albert road, the 1st and 2nd Manchester Pals met. It was a sorrowful time for all of these men as they searched, all too frequently in vain, for the welcome of a friendly face belonging to members of their work-place, family or friends. Everyone who had trudged into the camp knew that the original Manchester Pals, those first to enlist in the City's first flush of civic enthusiasm, had effectively ceased to exist. Talking amongst themselves the sections and platoons considered the forfeiture, swopped stories and tried to come to terms with their personal loss.

> *...one had sufficient leisure time to think it all over and count the cost. Four popular members of the Section had been killed – Johnny Chaters, whose body was never found, smiling Danny Maher, the irrepressible Ross and his pal Rolly Ashton, who was last seen tending Ross or someone else who had been severely wounded. Cpl Heywood, 'Toc Esses' Campbell, and 'Erb Peel, three excellent signallers, left the section through wounds, and one cannot but remember that L/Cpl. Palmer was shot through the hand, and carried on for the greater part of the day, before he casually reported to the Sergeant that he was afraid he would have to go down to the C.C.S.* Sergeant Pennington. 1st City Battalion's Signal Section

Such men already knew that Manchester did indeed have something to be proud of. Lance Corporal Palmer's water bottle had also been pierced by a bullet, yet, ravaged by thirst and pain his maintenance of forward communication throughout the 1st July would win him the Military Medal. Of course very few other survivors of these days had won anything, but the bonds forged in such circumstances would stay with all of these men for the rest of their lifetimes.

Further west the positions at Mametz and Fricourt fought for by the Manchesters in the

7th Division had also been held successfully throughout that first night of the Somme battles. In the early hours of 2nd July it had become clear that Fricourt was no longer strongly defended. The 1st Royal Welch and 20th Manchesters were able to push patrols into the area east of Sunken Road trench and north towards Rose Alley and the village of Fricourt itself. Once these men had linked up with the 17th Division, who had now pushed into Fricourt, the 22nd Brigade were progressively withdrawn as divisional reserve to a position between Carnoy and Mansel Copse. The 20th Manchesters themselves were relieved from the front line at 5.45 am on the morning of the 3 July. It proved impossible to use the 20th Manchesters in action during the coming days until drafts had restored their numbers.

On the right of the 22nd Brigade, the 91st Brigade had also been able to improve their positions. Patrols by groups from the 22nd Manchesters had found Queen's Nullah unoccupied. The 2nd Queens had moved forward at 11.00 am along Beetle Alley, to occupy White Trench and Cliff Trench, south of Mametz Wood. During that afternoon, of 2 July, the 21st Manchesters came forward at 12.40 pm to deepen and reverse the defences of White Trench, with the aid of a Durham Field Company. Whilst this work was undertaken their positions were persistently shelled. Nevertheless, a small counter attack, delivered at 10.30 pm, was easily stalled by the battalion's rifle fire and an effective artillery barrage. During the next twenty four hours the 21st Manchesters stayed in the area of White Trench and Bottom Wood as plans for the capture of Mametz Wood unfolded and units of the 7th Division continued to secure this position. Throughout this period the few

*Private Fred Wood, 10294, 1st City Battalion, who survived the events of 1 July 1916, and the war.* Flaherty

remaining men of the 22nd Manchesters occupied Bright Alley, consolidating and strengthening the defences. It was not until 5.00 pm on the evening of 5th July that the remnants of the 22nd Manchesters were relieved, by 13th Royal Welch Fusiliers, marching back to their billets at Buire.

Certainly the capture and holding of Mametz had been a remarkable achievement for the 7th Division. The Division boasted a fine history since 1914 when their regular soldiers had landed in France only to be terribly thinned in number as the battles of First Ypres, Neuve Chapelle, Festubert, Givenchy and Loos had taken their terrible toll. The loss of a regular

Brigade in December 1915 had been clearly regretted by the established Battalions and their Brigade and Divisional staffs. However, by July of 1916 the Manchesters, and the other battalions who had joined the 7th Division, had forged their place as an integral part of an experienced and determined unit. That determination had been reflected in the casualty lists. During the first five days of July the 7th Division's casualties around Mametz had been heavy, a total of 151 officers and 3,673 men. By compensation the 7th Division had captured about 1600 other ranks as prisoners, as well as twenty-three officers, four field guns, one naval gun, ten machine guns, six trench mortars and four *Minenwerfers* as well as the village of Mametz.

## Notes:

1 2nd Lieutenant Kenneth Callan Macardle. 2nd City Battalion, the 17th Manchesters.

2 Alick Howells was killed soon after the attack got underway that morning.

3 Throughout the day these covered saps were used as tunnels leading towards the German front line, saving many casualties among the support units' carrying parties.

4 Map references in the Maricourt area are taken from Maricourt, Edition 3.A, corrected to 2-6-1916. Sheet 62C.NW1.

5 See Narrative of operations carried out by the 19th Battalion Manchester Regiment, in the offensive beginning 1 July 1916. P.R.O. ref W095/2329.

6 Noting the disparity between the casualties suffered by its left and right leading battalions, 91st Brigade's recorded casualties for the period 1-4 July are as follows:

|  | Officers | Men |
|---|---|---|
| 2 Yorks | 11 | 246 |
| 2 Wilts | 1 | 49 |
| 18th KLR | 16 | 477 |
| 19th M/cr | 3 | 191 |

7 Writing in a letter to his wounded Company Commander, Captain J H Worthington.

8 I am grateful to Graham Maddocks for his permission to quote from his interviews with Private Gregory. See pp 87/88, *Liverpool Pals*, Published by Leo Cooper, 1991.

9 *Report on Operations of 17th Manchester Regiment on 1 and 2 July 1916*. P.R.O. ref W095/2339.

10 It proved impossible to bring these guns in for some days owing to the heavy machine gun fire in this locality.

11 The 18th Division had met with difficulty from the very start of their attack and throughout the morning. '*By 12 noon after considerable opposition, assisted by the successful advance of the 30th Division on their right, the right of this brigade [55th] had secured its final objective and was in touch with the 30th Division: the left, however, was unable to make much progress and was completely out of touch with the right of the 53rd Brigade on its left. It was not until 6.45 pm after very heavy fighting (casualties just over 2,200) that the left of the [55th] Brigade finally reached its objective and gained touch with the right of the 53rd Brigade.*' [XIII Corps. Operations on the Somme.]

12 *Report on Operations of 17th Manchester Regiment on 1 and 2 July 1916*. P.R.O. ref W095/2339.

13 The 'pulp' which the 30th Division's Operational Reports refer to had been induced by 102,000 18-pounder rounds, 18,000 4.5″ howitzer rounds and over 4,500 trench mortar rounds of various calibres fired by its own artillery. All this on top of the thousands of larger calibre shells fired by XIIIth Corps' artillery during the same period. During the infantry assault, '*as it happened only about 10,000 Mills grenades have been expended.*' [30th Div Operation Report P.R.O. ref WO95/2310]

14 Pte William Bruton 21390, Pte Harry Hudson 20362, Pte Norman Gleave 21147, Pte James Dunscombe 21476, Pte Thomas Greenhalgh 21333 and Pte Fred Hilton 20495. [See letter from L/Cpl McCoy to Lt Colonel Darling, 30/6/1935. MRA]

15 The officer's names recorded in the 22nd Manchester's War Diary showed that virtually every officer who had gone over the top had become a casualty. The officers who were killed were Captain C C May, Captain A E Bland, Lt R Mellor, Lt W E Gommersall, 2/Lt N Peak, 2/LtW E Brunt, 2/Lt G G Swann, 2/Lt J Nanson, 2/Lt J E Price and 2/Lt C T Gill. The wounded officers were Captain C M Lloyd, Captain T R Worthington, Lt J F Prince, 2/Lt H S Cotton, 2/Lt J P H Wood, 2/Lt G Ryall, 2/Lt M L Woodhouse and 2/Lt E L Riley who was slightly wounded but remained at duty.

16 From the direction of Bernafay Wood, attacking simultaneously towards the east of the village, came men of the 51st RIR.

17 Two officers killed, 13 wounded. Among the men – 38 killed, 257 wounded and 30 missing.

## Chapter Six

# 'You will attack again soon'

*'To me now, everything seems like an impossible nightmare...
how I wish I had a Blighty.'*[1]

At Happy Valley, the reception given to the first two battalions of Manchester's Pals was enthusiastic, but the many messages of congratulation swung a double edged sword. Casualties had reduced most of the battalions engaged to little more than a third of their establishment. The few officers and men who had survived physically unscathed were exhausted and battle weary. Even though these men had taken part in what was, by any Great War standard, a successful attack, many were shocked and tortured by what they had seen. They both expected and deserved a substantial period of rest and reorganization. The words of their honorary Colonel were succinct and to the point.

> *Convey to the 30th Division my best congratulations on their splendid work. Lancashire will indeed be proud of them.* Derby.

At home however, the people who inhabited the communities from which the Pals had been drawn had, as yet, very little idea of the reality of battle. The veils of secrecy and censorship were still tightly drawn. Few in Manchester knew what losses they would have to come to terms with. However, Lieutenant General Congreve commanding XIII Corps and General Rawlinson commanding Fourth Army understood what had been given and had even greater reason to be proud of 30th Division's work. Drawn predominantly from industrial Lancashire the 30th had made the most substantial penetration into the German defences above the Somme of any of the New Army units, and had held their ground. Within the terrible context of the British Army's experience on 1 July here was a success to be applauded. Unfortunately for Rawlinson's aspirations, these accomplishments of the 30th Division had not been matched elsewhere. As a consequence, and unfortunately for the Manchester battalions, the very fact of their advance meant that attempts would soon be made to capitalize upon that success. It would not be long before the seemingly irresistible tide of the Somme battles would suck these men back into the Montauban area and the further terrors which awaited them there.

> *The Brigadier had wired General Shay [sic] of the Division, '90th Brigade has taken Montauban in drill formation,' the highest possible praise. We were flattered and praised and our hands were crushed in welcoming handshakes – and the sun kissed away the ravages of our ordeal. That was the 3rd and today is the 6 [July] but we are still in Happy Valley in bivouac. Happy Valley is soaked with rain and sloppy with mud.*

*Once the central axis of the Somme offensive had moved from the Albert-Bapaume road to the Mametz-Montauban area it was essential to clear these villages and make good the roads. This photograph shows Mametz village after the front had passed to the northeast of the village. The road has now been repaired, debris cleared and water supply pipes brought through.* Whippy

*Captured German artillery found in the area north of Montauban, which had been overwhelmed by the British and French bombardment prior to the 1 July.*

> *We have had about half rations issued so that after sixty hours of fighting with only biscuits to eat none of us have had anything like one square meal since, or a bath or a bed or a moment of comfort. And Shay has wired, 'Well done 90th Bgd. You will attack again soon.'* 2nd Lieutenant Kenneth Callan-Macardle.[2]

The men's feelings upon hearing of the probability of further imminent action can be only imagined. Within days the General's prediction would come true. Shea knew, of course, that the centre of gravity of the Somme battle had already shifted. Bapaume could no longer be regarded as somewhere to be reached within forty eight hours. Now the rolling countryside northeast of Montauban with its great horseshoe of woodlands would become the focus of battle.

In the meantime drafts of men were placed within the depleted ranks of each platoon and the battalions were brought up to something approaching their nominal strength. Very often this meant cutting the umbilical link between the City of Manchester and its own Pals battalions. The 22nd Manchesters, for example, received a draft of 434 reinforcements in early July. Although 105 of these came from the Manchester Regiment, including twenty men drawn from the Regiment's 23rd (bantam) battalion, 121 came from the Middlesex Regiment, 119 from the Royal West Kents, 77 from the Royal Sussex Regiment, ten from the Royal Fusiliers and two from the Border Regiment. Immediately there was tension between the experienced, battle hardened men and the drafts who were forced to take the place of dead and wounded friends in the ranks. Surviving experienced officers initially felt that the gulf between the Manchester originals and the men from the south of England was both marked and regrettable in that it denoted an end to the uniquely localized character of Manchester's Pals.

However, the war would not wait for a leisurely assimilation of these drafts. Within days those many woods which had lain just behind the old German front lines, above Mametz and Montauban, would become the scene of fierce and terribly costly fighting.

### Trones Wood

One thousand yards east of Montauban lay Bernafay Wood. North east of Bernafay Wood lay Trones Wood, its northern tip pointing towards the higher ground of Delville Wood and Longueval village and its eastern border facing Waterlot Farm and the villages of Ginchy and Guillemont. Unfortunately, this proximity meant that Trones Wood was utterly commanded and overlooked from the north west through an arc of almost 180 degrees round to the east

*England's Heroes. Manchester Evening News 15 July , 1916*

# ENGLAND'S HEROES.

## Further Heavy Lancashire Losses.

### MANCHESTER'S PRIDE IN HER "PALS."

Further heavy casualties are reported to-day, the official lists of fallen officers alone containing four hundred and seventeen names.

The deadly nature of the fighting in which the Lancashire regiments have been engaged during the great offensive is again emphasised by the large number of casualties in these units.

In the records of the brave deeds that have cost so many of Manchester's sons their lives, it may have been noted that the use of the term "Pals," in connection with the city battalions of the Manchester Regiment, has again become popular.

When these men were recruited they were recruited as "pals." Later the name was dropped, largely because some of the men concerned preferred to be known simply as soldiers. Now, when they have won fame, the old name is being freely used again, alike by highly-placed military officials and by the men themselves—as well as their friends who are so proud of the "Pals."

Casualties reported to-day include the following:

### OFFICERS.
#### KILLED.

**A FORMER MINNEHAHA MINSTREL.**

Second-Lieutenant T. Stanley Greenwood, youngest son of the ...

---

#### ADVANCING UNDER FIRE.

Private Richard Hughes, formerly employed by the Manchester Corporation, in the lighting department, was killed on July 1. He was thirty-one, and leaves a widow and child, who live at 31, Garratt-street, Oldham Road, Manchester. Lieutenant Jackson writing to Mrs. Hughes says: "We were advancing in the open under fire when your husband was shot through the heart by a machine-gun on our left. It was a privilege to lead men like your husband."

Pte. Hughes.

Private William Langshaw, of 3, North-street, Hulme, was killed on July 1. He was employed by Rylands and Sons, Oxford-street. He was 23.

Previous to enlisting he was in the employment of Messrs. John T. Lewis and Sons, Ltd., manufacturers, 22, Fountain-street.

Private George Edge has died from wounds. He was employed by Messrs. S. and J. Watts and Co., Manchester. His home was at Heaton Mersey.

Signaller Emrys Edwards, for eight years employed by Messrs. J. Dilworth and Sons, Manchester, was killed on July 1. He was educated at the Warehousemen and Clerks' Schools, Cheadle Hulme, and his home was at Harpurhey.

#### A "PALS" WARRANT OFFICER.

Company Sergeant-major James Reddy, who died of wounds on July 6, served 21 years in the army and fought in the South African campaign. He was 44 years of age, and his home was at 11, Blanchard-st., Cambridge-st., C-on-M. Before the war he was employed at the Parcel Post Office, Morton-street, Strangeways. His son, Lance-Corporal James Reddy, is in Melton Mowbray Hospital wounded.

Co. Sgt.-major Reddy.

Lance-Corporal Maurice Roberts, 113, Waterloo-street, Lower Crumpsall, an employé at the Crumpsall Workhouse, has been killed. He was a married man 33 years of age.

Private Bousfield Nicholson was killed in action on July 1. He was the second son of M. B. Nicholson, 99, Coupland-street, C-on-M., and nephew of the late Chief Superintendent Philip Corden, of the City Police Force. His younger brother Arthur, who served through the Gallipoli campaign with the Royal Marines, is now fighting in France.

Lance-Corporal James Thomson, a former employé of Messrs. Hans Reynolds, Burnage, has been killed. He was 28, and leaves a widow, who lives at 32, Bradshaw-street, Moss Side. A brother of Thomson is fighting in France.

Private Charles Higgins, eldest son of Mr. and Mrs. Higgins, 7, Gleaves Road, Eccles, was killed on July 1. Formerly employed by the Co-operative Wholesale Society, Ltd., he was 21.

When about to send a birthday greeting to Private Tom Hampson, of the Manchester "Pals," in the trenches, his mother, who lives at New Mills, received a letter from another "Pal," stating that Private Hampson was killed on the morning of July 1. He would have been 24 years old to-morrow. His brother, Private Harry Hampson, is also at the front.

---

Private M. Corrigan (21), wounded by ... Now in hospital in Rouen. His home ... Hawkeshead Road, Queen's Road, Ma...

Lance-Corporal Arthur Howatson, ... stone Road, Irlams-o'th-Height, for... ployed by Messrs. Richard Hudson ... Ltd., 49, Newton-street, Manche...

Private Robert Kerr, 5, Denstone Roa... o'th-Height, are in the Lord Derby ... pital, Warrington. Kerr was in the e... Messrs. William C. Jones, Ltd., ... Road, Manchester, before enlisting.

Private Alf. Southern (19), wounde... shoulder and back. His brother, ... A. E. Southern, was wounded in Ga... June 4 last year.

Private T. Allen, whose home is at ... rill Grove, Levenshulme, has been s... through the right thigh. He is now... County of London Hospital, London... the war he was employed by Messrs. J... and Brown, Ardwick Green.

Private Joseph Maloney, of 13, Upper... street, Hulme, wounded July 1. He is... Beaufort Hospital, Fishponds, Bristol.

Private F. Edwards is in Rouen Hos... with gunshot wounds in his legs. Bef... war he was employed by Mr. H. Morris... Lane, Chorlton.

Corporal M'Kay is in the King's... Hospital, Liverpool. He was in the employ of Ty... and Holbrook, Deansgate, Manchester.

Lance-Corporal W. Owens (21), of 118,... Lane East, Moss Side, is in Rouen Hos... France. He was employed at Messrs. H... Pickles, Port-street, city.

Private James Alfred Peers, 37, Woo... street, Bury New Road, an employé of ... S. and J. Watts, was one of the first ov... "top" in the great advance, and afte... hours hard fighting was hit by two pie... shrapnel.

Lance-Corporal W. J. M'Nally, wounde... both thighs, is in hospital in France.... home is at 31, Lower Russell-street, Miles ... ting. He was employed by Messrs. John... wood, Ltd., Deansgate, Manchester.

Lance-corporal A. Hurst, of Longsig... member of one of the Manchester "P... battalions, wounded in the leg, is in ho... in Manchester. He was employed by S. ... Barlow and Sons, Manchester.

Wounded in three places, Private H. B... of Denton, also a member of the Manch... "Pals" Regiment, is in hospital in Birm... ham. He lived at Denton.

Signaller Joseph Forsyth, whose parents ... in Barmouth-street, Bradford, is anothe... in the Manchester "Pals" Regiment.... He was employed by Messrs. S. and J. W... of Portland-street.

Private Wm. McClure, of 36, Bluestone R... Moston, has been wounded in the left fore... is an inmate of Mill Road Infirmary, Li... pool. He was employed in the general of... of Messrs. Baxendales.

Dangerously wounded by shrapnel Priv... Sydney Bond, of the Manchester "Pals," is ... hospital at Rouen. He was employed ... Messrs. Latham and Wilson, Indian Hou... Whitworth-street, Withington. His parents live in H...

Private H. Green has been wounded in t... back, and is now in hospital in France. ... was a member of St. Stephen's, Salford, an... was employed by Messrs. Bower and Co., Ma... chester. He lives at 88, Hamilton Roa... Longsight.

Private Oswald Clough, who received a sha... nel wound in the leg, is now in hospital ... Newcastle-on-Tyne. His home is in Moreto... Avenue, Stretford. He was in the employ ... Messrs. Barlow and Jones Limited. His... brother, who is in the Navy, went through th... Jutland battle safely on one of the ship... mentioned in Admiral Jellicoe's despatch.

Private John Howarth, Manchester Pals ... wounded. He is the son of Mr. and Mrs. Harr... Howarth, of Walmsley Road, Bury, and this ... the second time he has been wounded.

Private Joseph Rodgers, Manchester Regi... ment, son of Mr. William Rodgers, 365, Wal... mersley Road, Bury, is in hospital at Sutton ... Coldfield, wounded in the left knee.

Signaller Eddie Jones is in Oldham Union ... Infirmary. Before enlisting he was employed ... by Messrs. G. and R. Dewhurst, Ltd., and his ... parents live in Greenheys.

Private W. McDonald Shearer, of the Man... chester Regiment, son of Mr. and Mrs. W. ... Shearer, of Southleigh, Heaton Mersey, received ... July 1, a dangerous gunshot wound in the thigh on ... July 1. He was educated at the South Man... chester Preparatory School and the Manchester ... Grammar School.

---

CSM Reddy of the 1st City Battalion, with his son, Lance Corporal J Reddy, photographed together at Heaton Park. CSM Reddy died of his wounds, received at Montauban, on 6 July. He had served twenty one years in the army and had fought in South Africa. His son had been wounded soon after the 1st City Battalions arrival in France.

*Bois des Trones*

*Bois Faviere*

*Waterloo Chimney*

*Longueval Church*

*Part of a panoramic photograph showing Longueval, Trones Wood and Faviere Wood. In the foreground can be seen the barbed wire which lay in front of the British trenches, just northeast of Maricourt Wood. This photograph clearly pre-dates the artillery bombardments which destroyed these woodlands during the summer of 1916, and also pre-dated the taking over of the trenches east of Maricourt by the French Army during the spring of 1916.*

and south. If it could be captured it could only be held with the compliance of the German artillery, or if the German positions in Longueval and Guillemont were overrun. The two woodlands were thus important stepping stones towards the piece by piece advance which Rawlinson was now forced to seek, Haig's hopes for a breakthrough on the 1 July having failed to materialize along the western arm of the battlefield. The two actions which resulted first in the taking of Bernafay Wood and secondly Trones Wood were each marked by tragically and sensationally different circumstances.

Since the Liverpool men who secured the Briqueterie had patrolled into an almost empty Bernafay Wood on 1 July, the pressure had been on XIII Corps Commander, Congreve, to take the woodland. He understood that once Maltz Horn Farm and Trones Wood were captured the task of the 30th Division would be to form a defensive flank, guarding the advance of Fourth Army through the German Second Line positions running west from Longueval. Already two days had been lost in the widespread preoccupation with consolidation. Further patrols on 3 July, by men of the 9th Division, confirmed that Bernafay was still empty save for a few demoralized men from the 51st Reserve Regiment. At 3.15 pm Lieutenant General Congreve issued orders for the 27th Brigade of 30th Division to take Bernafay Wood. Later that evening at 9.00 pm the Brigade's two assaulting battalions moved out over very exposed ground to advance. Expecting decimation at any moment, the men covered the open ground, entered the wood and occupied it up to the far side, creating an acute salient in the British lines here. Miraculously these attacking battalions, the 6th K.O.S.B. and the 12th Royal Scots had suffered just six casualties. Further patrols were then sent out towards Trones Wood but it was discovered to be held by a number of machine gun detachments. XIII Corps' command, therefore, postponed any immediate thoughts of capturing the wood. The eventual orders to undertake the capture of Trones Wood were to be considerably delayed.

Much debate surrounded the problems created by the conjunction between the British and French armies. Gaps in understanding, the difficulty of timing attacks to suit both and the lack of clearly understood strategic objectives meant that the preparation of attacks at those locations where the British and French armies joined was hesitant. When these difficulties had been addressed the initial assault on Trones Wood was made by 21st Brigade of 30th Division. During the wet afternoon of the 7 July these men, including the 19th Manchesters, were marched up from the Bois des Tailles to Talus Boise. From there D and B Companies of the 19th Manchesters moved to Glatz Redoubt whilst A and C remained in the old British front line north of Talus Boise. In preparation for the assault four parallel lanes had been cut by the pioneer 11th Battalion of the South Lancs through the confines of Bernafay Wood, to

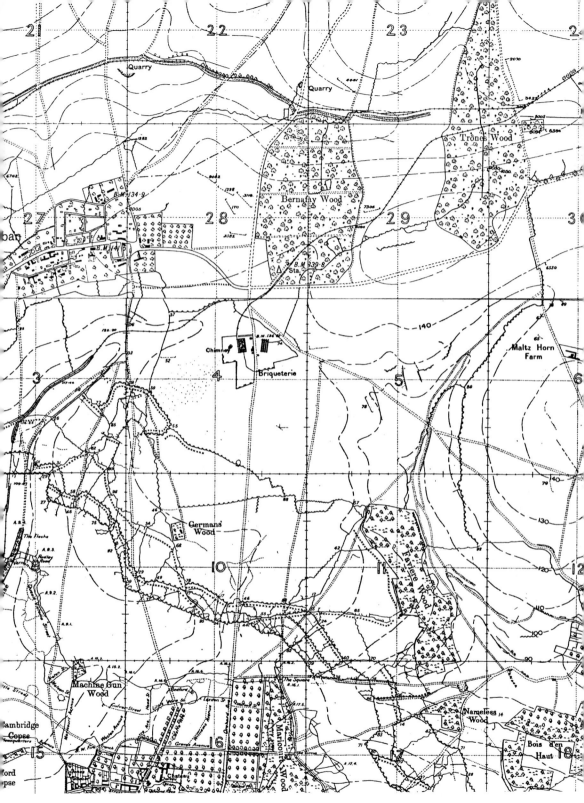

*The scene of the 30th Division's battles during the first two weeks of July 1916.*

allow access for the attacking troops. During the initial planning of these attacks the 18th Manchesters were taken from 90th Brigade and were attached to and placed under the command of the 21st Brigade. The 21st Brigade's first attack on Trones Wood was timed for 8.00 am on 8 July.[3] Under now clear skies, and in bright morning sunshine, the initial assault was undertaken by the 2nd Green Howards and met with disaster in the face of field artillery firing over open sights alongside overwhelmingly heavy concentrations of machine gun fire. Nevertheless, on their right an attack by the French, two hours later, took Maltz Horn Trench, but the Frenchmen's left flank was still exposed to machine gun fire from Trones Wood. At 12.20 pm Major General Shea was told to advance his troops from the Briqueterie and take Trones Wood, with the objective of covering the French left, even if he had to employ his whole division to achieve this. The scene was set for a future series of 'take it at all costs' attacks on Trones Wood by the 30th Division.

Soon after mid-day, one company of the 2nd Wiltshires under Captain Ward gained the head of Maltz Horn Valley and then worked down into Maltz Horn Trench.[4] About 3.45 pm the Wiltshires here were reinforced by B Company of the 19th Manchesters who brought up two very welcome machine guns into a position between the Wiltshires and the French on their right. Ammunition for these guns was carried by twenty men of D Company. Earlier, by 1.00 pm the remaining 2nd Wiltshires had attacked out of Bernafay Wood and were into the southern edge of Trones, and were entrenching along its south eastern edge and to the north in order to protect their left flank. As the afternoon progressed they were joined by one further company each from both the 18th and 19th Manchesters. At this point in time the wood still maintained the semblance of a canopy of green, which shaded and darkened the deadly scene being acted out below. This company of the 19th Battalion, D Company, remained in the wood under the command of 2nd Lieutenant Keefe alongside the men of the 18th Battalion, until mid-day on 9 July. Their initial task was the construction of a fire trench running east to west across the southern portion of the wood, the process being completed by 2.00 am the following morning. During these long hours the slightest movement above ground brought an instant response from German snipers. Throughout the afternoon and early evening the whole area of the southern end of the wood was also subjected to steady shelling. Nevertheless, after 6.30 pm, the remainder of the 18th Manchesters began to arrive to help secure this position in Trones Wood, whilst C and A Companies of the 19th Manchesters moved into positions in Maltz Horn Trench on the flanks of the Wiltshires and B Company of the 19th Manchesters, who were already there. Three times during the night the thin line of men from the 18th were forced to repel bombing attacks from the north.

Clearly the positions within Trones Wood were, at best, tenuous. It became clear that it would be essential to deploy another Brigade to grasp the position firmly. The assault would be by units of the 90th Brigade.

Therefore, at 1.00 am on the 9 July, under the cover of darkness, the 17th Manchesters were taken across country from the area of Talus Boise, by guides of the 2nd Yorkshires, to the Briqueterie. Two hours later, at 3.00 am, the British operations designed to secure the remaining portion of Trones Wood still in German hands were expected to restart with a vengeance. The two assault battalions were the 2nd Royal Scots[5] on the right and, on their left, the 17th Manchesters, who were due to advance out of Bernafay Wood, either side of the light railway which then passed north eastwards through Trones Wood. However, German gas shelling forced the Manchester's men to wear respirators which soon became misted in the cool drizzle and half light of early dawn. Inside the confines of the wood the guides became disorientated. It was only by 6.10 am that the Manchester's men were in position to attack the eastern fringe of Trones. The attack commenced at 6.40 am. As they moved across the exposed ground between the two woods, some men on the left were fired on by artillery directed from their north, but the speed of the advance and the sparcity of shelling meant that few casualties were suffered. Extraordinarily there was little resistance elsewhere and the whole of the 17th Manchesters pushed on into Trones Wood by 7.15 am, entering it at S.29.b.4.0, and there greeting men of the 18th Manchesters and briefly making contact with bombers of the 2nd Royal Scots. The exhausted ranks of the 18th had been ordered to support the 17th's new attack and parties duly followed northwards, picking up equipment and ammunition from the bodies which now carpeted the woodland floor. Central Trench and the dugouts within the northern portion of the wood were all carried without difficulty by bombing parties. The 17th Manchesters had then occupied the bulk of the woodland. By 8.00 am the 17th Manchesters HQ was established in Central Trench and the four companies were arranged along the eastern and northern perimeters of the woodland. Parties of the 18th Manchesters were in occupation of the south west aspect of the wood with the 2nd Wiltshires to the south east, although touch was lost with the 2nd Royal Scots in the face of progressively increasing shellfire. Apart from isolated nests of Germans, the whole of Trones Wood was now in British hands. At this time, before the increasing shellfire made movement impossible, the water bottles and rations of the dead were collected by men of the 17th and 18th Manchesters in anticipation of a prolonged wait before relief. It seemed quite unnatural and false that such a crucial position could have been taken with what, initially, seemed to be so little loss of life.

Unfortunately, this atmosphere of relative calm and optimism soon began to collapse as the intensity of enemy artillery fire further increased. German gunners began a systematic and cruel sweep through the jagged stumps and crumbled earth which now marked the wood. It proved impossible for the 17th Manchesters to make contact with South Africans believed to be north of the wood in Longueval Trench, although the reconnoitering party of the 17th Manchesters met and captured some Germans in their attempt to reach the Longueval Alley trench. Soon after midday the shelling further accelerated and began to fall on the wood in the sort of concentrations which made the place quite untenable. Almost every available German battery from Maurepas to Bazentin-le-Grand had observation over Trones Wood. It now became a lethal trap within whose shrieking and splintering confines the 17th Manchesters suffered terribly. In the smoking and dust-ridden centre disorientated clusters of men wandered in a dazed confusion among the crashing timbers and suffocatingly thick fumes of cordite, desperately in search of direction and shelter. In the face of such intolerably heavy shellfire it was impossible to man the very edges of the wood where shrapnel and splinters tore into anyone unfortunate enough to be exposed there. The German communication trenches running into the east of the wood therefore provided relatively safe and unobserved access for men massing to counter attack the wood. Since the 17th Manchester's left flank was in the air, and a counter attack seemed imminent, a withdrawal was ordered at 3.00 pm. The bulk of the battalion withdrew along the communication trench, Trones Alley, running towards the eastern edge of Bernafay Wood where they took shelter, with orders to be prepared to advance again later. The battered confines of Trones Alley were littered with the bodies of wounded and dead men. The overcrowding in the trenches at Bernafay Wood meant that some of the 17th's men were sent further back to the Glatz Redoubt, where the Advanced Dressing Station had been located. Unfortunately, one party of forty men was left stranded in Trones Wood after the messenger sent to recall them was killed. One of the officers whose body now lay dead inside the wood was 2nd Lieutenant Kenneth Callan-Macardle.

The 18th Manchesters[6] were then forced to retire on the Briqueterie, leaving D Company in the south eastern corner of the wood under the command of Captain Hobkirk. At 3.30 pm, German counter attacks began to mass and advance, along a line from Maltz Horn Farm to

*2nd Lieutenant Kenneth Callan-Macardle, 17th Manchesters. He was reported as missing during the battles for Trones Wood on 9th July 1916. He was one of the most graphic chroniclers of the life of Manchester's Pals battalions. Had he lived he would almost certainly have become one of the war's most significant observers and diarists.*

the northern tip of Trones Wood. Along with the 2nd Royal Scots, the isolated company of the 18th Manchesters repulsed these attacks, causing heavy casualties amongst the Germans advancing past Arrow Head Copse in front of Guillemont. North of the Guillemont Road, however, the withdrawal of the bulk of the 17th Manchesters meant that the northern part of the wood above the light railway line was overrun. The isolated party of forty men from the 17th Manchesters resisted to the end, being either killed or taken prisoner. Some other men had been rather more fortunate.

*Myself, and a Lance-Corporal who came from the USA to join up, were captured by a party of about thirty Germans. We could not keep any formation in the Wood – heavy fire, trees crashing down – it was pure hell. Towards dusk the party moved off – they had removed our equipment and searched us, taken our watches. We had been going about fifteen minutes when rifle and machine gun fire opened up in front of us. Some Jerries were hit near me and in the confusion I ran some distance and dropped in a shell-hole. I was lost in the wood which was full of dead and wounded men. Eventually I arrived on the edge of the wood and heard Scots voices [soldiers of the Brigade's Regular Battalion, the 2nd Royal Scots]. I made myself known and joined them after finding rifle and equipment to wear – there was plenty of equipment lying about. I picked up a petrol tin of water which I shared with the Jocks. It was very welcome for no water or rations had turned up since the battle started. We occupied a trench and were ordered to deepen it. I took my equipment off but the officer spotted me, he said, 'Put your equipment on, your not with the Manchesters here!' The Jocks were taking their time digging and the officer kept urging them on saying the Jerries would attack. Sure enough they did but they were beaten off. Heavy shelling then started – one burst near me, knocking me out for about an hour. The lads later told me that shell killed two and wounded four men.* Private Paddy Kennedy. 18th Manchesters.

Having observed its infantry re-occupy the bulk of Trones Wood up to its western edge the great swathe of German artillery positioned to the north and east of Trones Wood were then turned onto Bernafay Wood, causing many casualties amongst the 17th Manchesters and other 30th Division's troops assembled there. However, no German infantry attacks developed in this area east of Bernafay Wood out of Trones Wood.

By 5.30 the officer commanding the 17th Manchesters was injured by a shell burst. Although his battalion was now divided and in no shape to engage in offensive action, the CO received orders at 6.00 pm to re-occupy Trones Alley between Bernafay and Trones woods and return to Trones Wood. At this point Lieutenant Whittall took command of the 17th battalion.

His arrival at Brigade HQ seeking clarification resulted in those orders being cancelled and the 17th Manchesters then spent the entirety of the 10 July in the sunken lane east of the Briqueterie.

Lieutenant Alan Holt's letter home, written on 12 July, captures some of the anxiety and despair which this battalion was suffering during this Trones Wood episode.

> *We cleared the Germans out of the wood, taking some prisoners, and started to dig ourselves in on the far side, but the shelling was so bad that this became impossible, and after spending eight hours in the wood under an intense bombardment, we were forced to withdraw to a new position about a thousand yards back owing to our heavy casualties. Here we spent the night and next day waiting to give the Boche something if he tried to push through to the south of the wood Our new position was a road about ten feet below the level of the fields each side. We dug holes for ourselves in the bank so as to get a little protection from the almost ceaseless hail of shrapnel and pieces of flying shell.* Lieutenant Alan Holt, 17th Manchesters.[7]

It was now the turn of the 16th Manchesters to try their hand at Trones Wood. During the mid afternoon of 9 July the 16th Manchesters had left Glatz Redoubt under heavy shellfire and were assembled within the confines of the sunken road east of the Briqueterie. At 6.40 pm the men moved forward with the intention of covering the left flank of the 2nd Royal Scots Fusiliers who were still in occupation of Maltz Horn Trench. Moving swiftly, the 16th Manchester's men were able to avoid the worst of the hostile barrage. Initially they penetrated well into the wood, to a point along Trones Alley at S.29.b.8.4, leaving a standing guard just inside the western edge of the wood in front of three companies who occupied Trones Alley and a new trench which they had dug to the south west edge of Trones Wood about sixty yards from the shattered woodland, keeping in contact with the parties of men from the 18th Manchesters who were now in occupation of its southern tip, having relieved the 2nd Wiltshires here. That night, 9/10 July, the 16th Battalion received orders to clear the wood. The following morning, at 4.00 am, a standing barrage was placed by the Divisional artillery to the north of the wood and machine guns were being sent up to assist in the defence of the area. Alongside a South African Scottish company, platoon groups of the 16th Manchesters then pressed forward through the tangled undergrowth of the wood, meeting little opposition and reporting that the bulk of the wood seemed clear. To the west and north of Trones Wood, including parts of Longueval Trench running from Bernafay Wood past the tip of Trones towards German second line positions east of there, observation had been gained and it seemed as if the it would be possible to secure Trones. However, once again the men's hopes proved unfounded as German counter attacks from the direction of Guillemont swept through the wood at 5.00 am, capturing a number of the South African's and Manchester's patrols, under command of Lieutenant Oliver, and then forcing their way

*Private Paddy Kennedy. Paddy Kennedy of the 18th Manchesters had already been in action on the opening day of the Somme offensive. Seven days later his battalion had been temporarily placed under the command of the 21st Brigade for the purposes of that Brigade's attacks on Trones Wood. It was here that Private Kennedy was captured by, and later escaped from, his German opponents within the confusion and chaos which was Trones Wood. During these actions the 18th Manchesters suffered a further 270 casualties amongst the men and eleven amongst the officers to add to the already heavy toll incurred a week earlier on lst July. Pawson*

through to the western edge of the wood again. By 5.30 pm, the 16th Manchester's reserve company was sent up to drive the Germans back from the southern edge of the wood. This they achieved, along with the re-occupation of the new trench just outside the south western perimeter, but it proved impossible to occupy the actual edge of the wood in view of the many German snipers and bombers who knew the ground here intimately and used their advantage to deadly effect. Throughout the day many attempts were made to get back into the wood to make contact with the beleaguered parties belonging to the 16th Manchesters now cut off in its confines. These attempts were unsuccessful.

By 8.00 am some men of the 18th Manchesters had arrived and were placed under the orders of the officer commanding the 16th Manchesters, being sent forward to reinforce the new trench south west of Trones. Throughout the day patrols kept Brigade informed, and it was decided that one company of the 17th KLR would attack Trones Alley and the south west corner of the wood at 9.30 pm. The remnants of the 16th and 18th Manchesters and the South Africans would 'conform'. As the attack started a number of green rockets sent up from inside the wood summoned the German SOS barrage. By 10.30 pm, the British barrage forced all the units south west of the wood to withdraw towards the sunken lane near the Briqueterie, from whence the 16th and 18th Manchesters then advanced again to reoccupy the new trench south west of Trones. The following day the Signals Section of the 16th Manchesters recorded its own feelings about the severity of the Trones Wood actions this summer day, through the brevity of an entry in its sergeant's diary.

*10 July – Another attack at dawn, but lost most of our men. Then big bombing attack by enemy. Our line again this side. A Company reinforced Our 'phone at that end in a shell hole (manned by Kaye, Griffiths and Kershaw). Sniping murderous. Geo Hill hit mending wire. Awful strain. Another big 'strafe' 9.30-10.15. Relief and one big mix up. Every battalion in the Division knocking about. Another attack by Liverpools on Wood. Don't know position now. We made our way back to Maricourt. In our trenches during day. Feeling absolutely done up. Lost four more Sigs. and nearly all my Sergeant pals, as well as lots more. Absolute hell.* Sergeant Pennington. 16th Manchesters' Signals Section

Amongst the Signals Section, Freddy Davies and Jimmy Cochrane had been captured. Geoffrey Hill had been shot through the lung by a sniper, but had struggled back to safety and eventual recovery.

Before that relief by the 18th Division, the 16th and 18th Manchesters were 'strengthened' by the shattered vestige of the 17th Manchesters, now only one hundred strong in number, who went forward to support the new trench garrison. Amongst them Lieutenant Holt recorded the seemingly endless process by which thousands of troops were being ushered, relentlessly, into the maelstrom of these attacks on Trones Wood.

*About 12 o'clock that night I was ordered to take fifty men forward and occupy a trench forty yards to the south of the wood which was then occupied by the Germans. It was like going to certain death for every one of us, but we held the trench for three hours when I got a message to retire, which I did but not without being seen by the enemy who followed us with a hail of shells. On my way back I met lines of fresh attacking troops who passed through my line, and drove the Germans out again. I have just learned that they have been counter-attacked and that, having inflicted heavy losses on the Boche they were forced to retire to the line on the south of the wood. We came right back here yesterday and tomorrow we go further back. The dear old regiment is now a mere handful but it has made itself famous. To me now, everything seems like an impossible nightmare... How I wish I had a Blighty!* Lieutenant Alan Holt, 17th Manchesters.

*Trones Wood became, during the July fighting, an extraordinary chaos of splintered timbers, shattered earth and the terrible detritus of war.*

*Private Frank Nixon, an original 'Pal' serving with the 18th Manchesters, who was unfortunate enough to become another of the men taken prisoner of war in Trones Wood. Before the war Frank Nixon had become a school teacher in Northwich. His terms of imprisonment were made bearable through an exchange of prisoners in Holland during the summer of 1918. He was one of six brothers, four of whom joined the Cheshires, one the RAMC, and Frank the Manchesters as a consequence of his earlier schooling at a number of Manchester schools. In later life his health recovered sufficiently from the privations experienced inside prisoner of war camps to enable him to become a Headmaster during the 1930s.* Nixon

On the morning of the 11th, the men of the 16th, 17th and 18th Manchesters were relieved from these dreadful circumstances, marching back to the trenches at Maricourt.

During the coming two days other units of the 30th Division continued to attempt the capture of Trones Wood. Increasing urgency was given to this task, as the date for the general assault of the German's second line positions on the 14 July was fixed. During the five days in which it had been engaged at Trones Wood the 30th Division had lost over 2,300 of all ranks. Amongst the already depleted ranks of the 16th, 17th, 18th and 19th Manchesters the casualties totalled in excess of 750 men and officers.[8] The 30th Division were replaced at Trones Wood by the 18th Division before the dawn of 13 July. The wood was eventually taken on the 14 July. It had become a crazy tangle of shell holes, impenetrable brambles and splintered hardwood within which lay a multitude of reeking and torn bodies. In the summer heat the sound of buzzing, bloated flies filled the air, and for many hundreds of yards the air was loathsome with the sickly stench of death. Outside, opposite the eastern edge of Trones Wood, the soldiers of the 54th Brigade who had finally taken the wood could make out the buildings and trees which marked the next important position eastwards, Guillemont village.

### The 14 July: A soldier's view. Private Pat Burke, 20th Manchesters

*Private Pat Burke.*

Pat Burke was one of the most prolific of the Manchester Pals' letter writers. Even within the exhausting circumstances facing every ordinary soldier he often found time, usually every week of his active military service and sometimes more frequently, to write at length to his family at home. That family lived within the public house of which his father was landlord, barely two miles from Manchester City centre, just behind the Roman Catholic Cathedral of Salford. Pat Burke had been, during the events of 1 July, fortunate enough to survive the 20th Battalion's costly attacks south of Fricourt, about which he had written so excitedly. By the middle of that month he had become a battle-hardened veteran Lewis gunner. During this period, in the days and weeks after the opening of the 1916 Somme battles, Private Burke's letters begin to give a more measured and objective insight into the battle of attrition of which his battalion was now a part. That battalion, part of the 22nd Brigade of the 7th Division, was now engaged in the terrible struggle which was being waged for the observation and dominance offered by control of High Wood.

Written on 17 August from billets at Dernancourt, his letter describing the impact of the battalion's reconstruction after their losses on 1 July, and its part in the attacks on the Bazentin Wood area below High Wood, on 14 July and soon after, is very revealing. Pat Burke's clarity of written style and continued belief in his cause are remarkable, but the florid and excited writing of his earlier letters has now been spent.

> Well it was a very short rest we had after our first attack, just a matter of reorganizing the battalion, which has been filled up with drafts of all sorts of regiments. My word it's a very different battalion now, there are very few of the old lads left, in my own platoon there's not a one I know, there were only nine left after July 1st and those have clicked for various jobs. I was offered a Corporal's job, but would have meant me going back to the company, but I prefer to remain a Tommy in the gunners with the old Belle Vue lads.

In fact, during the days after 1 July one draft sent to Pat Burke's 20th Manchesters was 160 Irishmen! This was just at a time when it was proving difficult to find any recruits from Ireland for the Irish units in the British Army. The 7th Division knew that a further attack using these hastily reconstructed units, towards High Wood, was imminent. Once Mametz Wood had been cleared, by the evening of 11 July, orders were issued to prepare for an early morning assault on the German second line positions in front of Delville Wood, Longueval and the Bazentin area.[9]

> For the twelve days this said action lasted we went through an awful time, far more trying and severe than the last affair, and that indeed was Hell – but this time it was – well – terrible. We were only in reserve, it sounds cushy, but proved very far from it, you will have read in the papers no doubt the part we were active in. The attack took place [in the half darkness of early dawn] on 14 July – we followed up immediately and my word we were needed, as usual our objective was taken, but it was the holding of it and consolidating same where we caught socks. The night before the attack – such a bombardment, one cannot describe it, nor could one realize it until he has been actually in it.

The 7th Division's assault had been made at 3.25 am by the 20th Brigade, past the Snout and

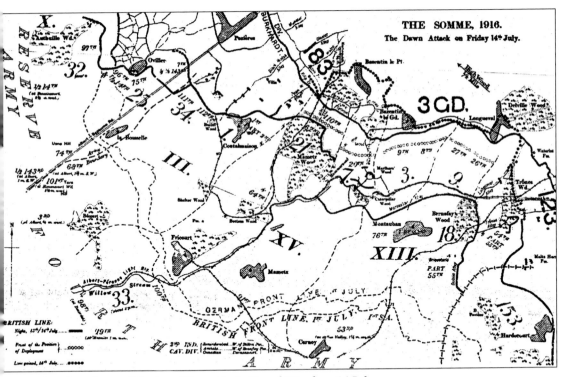

*Attack and consolidation of Bazentin le Grand Wood on 14 July.*

through Bazentin-le-Grand Wood. The assembly had been carried out at night without detection. The attack had been preceded by a short but devastating bombardment of incredible power which had lit the skyline with miles of awesome orange and steel blue explosions. The desperate German counter barrage fell behind the troops whose silent advance had carried them beyond No Man's Land, and few casualties were caused. Many of the German defenders were dead. Those who had survived were often caught in their dugouts before they had time to man their parapets. By 4.25 Bazentin-le-Grand Wood was in the 20th Brigade's hands and the 22nd Brigade passed through to begin its attack on Bazentin-le-Petit.

> *What a sight when we followed our front line up, under heavy shell fire of course all the time, by gad but the effect of our bombardment was wonderful. It was very woody country and the woods were absolutely thinned out, the lanes were covered with fallen trees and other things which you will understand are too gruesome to write about. Our first job was to dig ourselves in – there was no cover for us until this was done, and then it didn't provide much. Our next order was to take the gun into the woods which was not yet clear of the bounders, and hold same at all costs. Fortunately they did not break thro' our front line [facing High Wood], although we were there for forty-eight hours under very heavy stuff. After that we were withdrawn for a nights' so called rest but the next afternoon we went up with the company to hold the front line, just a roadway with bits of holes dug into the side for a little cover. This we stuck to until we were releaved [sic], suffering many experiences, and going through Hell on Earth...*

What Pat Burke was unable to see here was that on the 7th Division's front a vital opportunity was missed on the morning of 14 July. By 10.00 am all German opposition had faded in front of High Wood. British Brigade and Divisional officers were able to walk the slope above the Bazentin Woods without being fired upon.[10] Major General Watts, who

*Major General Sir Herbert Watts, KCB., KCMG.*

commanded the 7th Division, proposed to send the 21st and 22nd Manchesters as part of the 91st Brigade forward to capture High Wood.

The way was clear but Watts was prevented from sending his men on. This failure to allow Watts and the other divisional commanders to go ahead was disastrous.[11] Throughout the day delays occurred whilst the 2nd Indian Cavalry Division were brought forward from Morlancourt. They finally attacked at 7.00 pm, along with the 2nd Queen's and 1st South Staffs of the 91st Brigade, who got into High Wood without great loss. On their right flank were the 21st Manchesters who had moved forward towards Black Lane, at the southern tip of the wood. Unfortunately, it proved impossible to clear the wood in its entirety. The following day A, B and D Companies of the 21st Manchesters were sent up into High Wood with orders to clear it north of the Switch Line trench running across its northern tip. The machine guns sited there ensured that progress was impossible. That night the 21st Manchesters and the survivors of the Queen's and South Staffordshires were withdrawn from High Wood by Lieutenant General Horne, leaving the wood to be kept under fire by divisional artillery.

*One morning during these trying days a brigade went over just in front of us to take a certain wood [High Wood] just to our front, so you can guess how we went thro' it on this occasion. It was there [sic] turn to paste us and they managed it well, but we obtained our objective once more – but could not hold it, owing to very heavy fire. There were attacks and counterattacks which no doubt you read about, things are jolly*

*The Deccan Horse, photographed on 14 July near Carnoy, whilst waiting to move forward towards the Bazentin area and their expected attack against High Wood. Had less emphasis been placed on a cavalry breakthrough and more on developing the opportunity afforded by the infantry's successful attack on the Bazentin area the notorious High Wood could have been taken on 14 July by the men of 91st Brigade.*

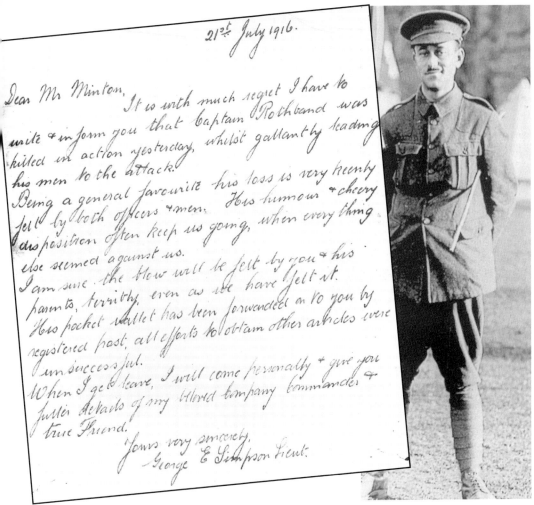

*21st July 1916.*

*Dear Mr Minton,*

*It is with much regret I have to write & inform you that Captain Rothband was killed in action yesterday, whilst gallantly leading his men to the attack.*

*Being a general favourite his loss is very keenly felt by both officers & men. His humour & cheery disposition often keep us going, when every thing else seemed against us.*

*I am sure the blow will be felt by you & his parents, terribly, even as we have felt it.*

*His pocket wallet has been forwarded on to you by registered post, all efforts to obtain other articles were unsuccessful.*

*When I get leave, I will come personally & give you fuller details of my beloved company commander & true Friend.*

*Yours very sincerely,*
*George E Simpson Lieut.*

*Captain Jacob Rothband, of the 23rd Manchesters. Captain Rothband was Killed in Action on 20 July whilst taking part in an attack with the 35th Division south of Trones Wood. Before the war he had been an officer with the Jewish Lads' Brigade in Manchester. Initially his body was buried where he fell, 500 yards south of the wood, but was later disinterred and re-buried at Flat Iron Copse Cemetery as a result of the clearance of many small battlefield burial sites in this area during the immediate post-war period. The letter informing Jacob's family of his death is from his subaltern, George Simpson, who would himself be killed in action on 22 October 1917 at Houthulst Forest north of Ypres. The letter to Jacob's brother Louis from another brother, Baron, serving nearby states that, "His Regiment was in Trones Wood and was ordered to make an attack at 11.30 on the morning of the 20 July. The men were very shaken after being heavily hammered for days, and just prior to the attack Jack walked right along the parapet to rally his men, without the slightest fear, and led them magnificently. He was shot through the head, almost immediately after he had shouted to his men 'Come on boys, dont be afraid of their guns', and death was instantaneous. From all accounts he was buried by a party of the 20th Lancs Fusiliers, but where I don't know. They say that he was the best officer in the battalion and I'm sure he was." Letter dated 28 July 1916.* Rothband

*rotten under these conditions, you can imagine what its like. One afternoon a Fritz plane came over followed by one of ours and such a scrap took place, ours got over him and drove him low. All we boys in the line opened fire on him with machine guns and rifles and set him on fire and down he came amongst us in flames – didn't we yell and cheer, we might have been in the Gods at the theatre. There were lots of other things happened Reg, could go on writing for ever, but must close with telling you how we finished up. As we were being releaved [sic] there was an acceptional [sic] heavy straf on and he was sending his gas, poison and tear shells over, it was jolly uncomfortable I assure you, and we got away in quick time. Our casualties once more reached between 200 and 300, but it was the most fearful time we have ever experienced living on biscuits and water (½ pint a day).*

*When we left the line we marched a devil of a way, absolutely done up, but we did it cheerfully to get away from that Hell Hole. After resting for a few hours we entrained for [Hangest] from which we have just returned after a short but peaceful and enjoyable rest.*

*Here we are again awaiting order once more for more duty work, not anxious – OH NO – but nevertheless ready and willing.*

*Smile dam you – smile.*

*Your loving brother Paddy."*

During the period covered by this letter of Pat Burke's the 20th Manchesters had been in the front line and immediate support for seven days, from the 14 July to the 21 July, when they were relieved by the 2nd Worcesters. It had certainly been an enormously harrowing week, and one in which the 21st and 22nd Manchester battalions also suffered heavily, to the tune of over 500 casualties between those two units. During these actions around Bazentin and High Wood the 7th Division as a whole lost 125 officers and 3,443 men. The casualties were very nearly as high as those suffered on 1 July. During the July of 1916 the 22nd Manchesters lost over 700 men. The 20th and 21st Manchesters lost over 500 from each battalion.

### The 19th Manchester's Attack at Guillemont. 23 July 1916

Orders were received on 21 July that the 19th Manchesters were to attack Guillemont on the morning of the 23 July. On their north the 2nd Yorkshires would attack the northern part of the village. The Manchesters' objectives included all of the village south of the road running east to west through the village, within T.19.c.d. In support were the 2nd Wiltshires, with the 18th KLR in reserve. The artillery support would be by the 35th (Bantam) Divisional artillery, wire cutting being undertaken by their 18 pounder batteries. Unfortunately, that relatively inexperienced artillery had not succeeded in knocking out many, if any, of the German machine-gun positions, nor had the wire been sufficiently cut to allow the attacking battalions a chance of clear progress. This attack by the 21st Brigade was, therefore, destined to be recorded as an utter disaster for the 19th Manchesters. From Corps through to Divisional and Brigade levels of command the staff were aware that the narrow frontage of attack ran the risk of failure. So it proved to be.

On the 22nd the men had moved up to Silesia Support trench, still very familiar to a number of the 'old hands' from 1 July. It was clear that the movement had been observed as the whole area was then subjected to a persistent and fairly heavy shelling. At 10.00 pm the Manchester's men were moved further forward to the ground west of Trones Wood where they dug in and sheltered until about 2.00 am on the

**Guillemont village and its church before the battles of late July 1916.**

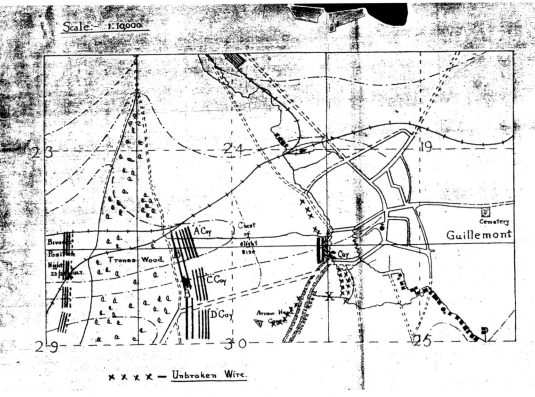

× × × × — Unbroken Wire.

*19th Battalion dispositions at Guillemont. 22/23 July 1916.*

morning of their attack. It was the last time that the bulk of the original members of the 4th Manchester Pals would be together. The men then passed through the unreal and still hideously reeking wood to take up their company positions facing east. That passage was however made somewhat easier by lanes which had been cut through the woodland by the pioneers of the 35th Division. The attack of the 19th Manchesters began at 3.40 am in the face of heavy rifle, machine-gun and shell fire.

The 2nd Yorkshire's attack was marred by a loss of direction, many of the Yorkshires veering north towards Waterlot Farm, others inexplicably turning south and becoming intermingled with the 19th Manchesters left and centre companies.[12] North of the Guillemont road A Company of the 19th Manchesters gained the German front line. Already heavy fire was being directed from half a dozen machine-guns on either side of the men. Although gallant, almost hopeless, charges were made by groups of men and officers, no further progress could be made, and the remnants fell back into the German front line trench. In the centre of the attack C Company attacked alongside the Guillemont road, passing straight through the German defences and entering the village in the direction of the church. However, this group of men were effectively on their own, neither company on each side making a penetration to similar depth. Within minutes they were facing large concentrations of men to both their right and left. D Company had found progress through the German wire south of the road almost impossible. Both the first and second lines of wire were uncut by the artillery preparation and, although the first line was cut by hand and negotiated, the second line proved impassable. Here, between the first and second lines of wire, the Company was forced to lie down and engage the enemy with rifle fire. Because of the proximity of the German's bombers the men were eventually forced to withdraw before men of B Company could provide the impetus to move forward. As time passed, the position within the village deteriorated and C Company was progressively surrounded and cut off. To their north the few survivors of A Company, who were left within the quarry at T.19.c.1.4, were also gradually cut down. By 6.00 am it was becoming clear to both men and officers that these unsupported attacks against the Guillemont positions were untenable and that a withdrawal would be necessary. Unfortunately that withdrawal would have to be made over exposed ground with very little hope of regaining the start positions outside Trones Wood. 30th Division knew nothing of this disaster until 11.30 am, when telephone communication with the 19th's HQ was established. Throughout the period of the attack the only effective means of communication had been carrier pigeons. No runners sent back from the front companies had made it into Battalion HQ.

By 9.30 pm that evening, having gained nothing, the 21st Brigade was ordered to withdraw to their assembly trenches back at Glatz Redoubt. From the 19th Manchester's A Company's positions only a handful of men returned. Of C Company's men there was no news at all. D and B suffered slightly less, but the outcome had clearly been disastrous. 30th Division's records later showed that amongst the 21st Brigade there were 984 casualties this day, 571 of whom were members of the 19th Manchesters. Of those 571 casualties, 496 were recorded as missing. The 21st Infantry Brigade then returned to Happy Valley with, as the 30th Division's records show, 'two of its battalions, 2nd Yorkshire Regiment and 19th Manchesters, unfit for a further offensive after the heavy casualties they had just suffered.'

*Hubert Knox, originally of the 2nd Battalion, and attached to the 16th Battalion on the return of Lieutenant Colonel Petrie to England after the Battles of Trones Wood.*

Within days of the earlier conclusion of events at Trones Wood the 16th Manchester's commanding officer, Lieutenant Colonel Petrie had returned to England. His replacement was Major Hubert Knox.

Nor was the replacement of a commanding officer unusual. The CO of the 18th had been killed at Trones Wood, his post being taken by Major H. Williams of the 3rd Dragoon Guards. Lieutenant Colonel Grisewood took over command of the 17th Manchesters on 15 July. Amongst the ranks, the new drafts sent to replace the recent casualties suffered by the 18th Battalion came from no less than twenty seven different regiments! The numbers of original NCOs and Officers had dwindled to a mere handful. During the last two weeks of July these new men barely had time to familiarize themselves with the routines of battalion life. The problem was known at 30th Division's Headquarters. 'The South Country reinforcements did not mix well with the men from the North, and many Officers and men were complete strangers to one-another.' In truth the men and officers only had the Army's powerful sense of discipline to fall back upon and yet, just a week after Trones Wood, on the afternoon of 22 July, orders were received which despatched the 16th, 17th and 18th Manchesters from Happy Valley to Mansel Copse. From there the men moved to their old assembly trenches in Cambridge Copse and the following day moved to a position behind Bernafay Wood. From here patrols were sent to reconnoitre the land in front of Guillemont. The initial intention was to deploy two brigades between Falfemont Farm and Guillemont in an attack in conjunction with the French on the right, to take place on 25th. Anticipation and concern was everywhere, yet this period of waiting became a farcical sequence of orders and counter orders. Every morning for the next five days the men expected to be told that this was the day set for the attack. After the disastrous attacks by the 21st Brigade on the 23rd, the 90th Brigade's men all knew what a terrible mauling their pals in the 19th Manchesters had experienced. On the 24 July the attack was postponed until 27 July. The following day a further one day postponement was effected. The same happened on the 26 July, whereupon the 90th Brigade were withdrawn to Mansel Copse to practice their assembly for the attack upon Guillemont. Just when the arrangements seemed set in hand, the scheme was further altered. Now the 90th Brigade was to attack Guillemont from the north west, whilst the 2nd Division would attack Ginchy from the same direction, an attack now made possible by their recent successes in Delville Wood. The 35th Division would also take part in the attack, assaulting Maltz Horn Trench simultaneously with 90th Brigade's attack on Guillemont. The 89th Brigade would attack with the French on 1 August.

On the 28 July, fifteen hours before the attack would commence, the whole plan was scrapped. The plan to be followed meant that the 30th Division would, after all, attack the line Falfemont Farm to Guillemont in conjunction with a French attack on the right against Maurepas and the 5th Brigade of the 2nd Division on the left, against the station north west of Guillemont. Zero hour was put back from the relative darkness of 4.00 am to 4.45 am, to conform with the French. By this time the dawn would have arrived. Orders to this effect were finally received by the Manchester battalions in 90th Brigade on 29 July.

The 16th, 17th and 18th Battalions of the Manchester Regiment were all to be disposed in the same attack. Many of the 17th's men were already exhausted by having been out throughout the night of 28/29 July digging and deepening trenches for assembly purposes, east of Bernafay Wood. Already in the 18th battalion it had become very clear that their new drafts were not in any way knitted into the unit's collective pride. There was an almost complete lack of esprit-de-corps, discipline in the route marches was poor and officers were not optimistic that unit discipline could be maintained during the anxiety and chaos of an attack. Now, late on the evening of 29 July as they marched up towards Guillemont, the 18th's men were put to the most severe test. Already a heavy mist was forming and as they passed the rubble of the Briqueterie the order to put on gas helmets was issued as lachrymatory and poison gas shells fell around the wood. As they entered Trones Wood the pronounced blackness and crazily undulating ground meant that the men were unable to progress except by a tortuously slow single file, holding the equipment of the man in front. Some men risked all by removing their gas helmets, only to be assailed by the putrid stench of many hundreds of still unburied corpses. The 18th Manchesters emerged from the horror of Trones Wood at 4.30 am, into the assembly trenches facing Guillemont. Zero was timed for 4.45 am. Visibility at this stage was little more than twenty yards. Even the four battalion's headquarters, located in the eastern perimeter of Trones Wood, would have an impossible task in keeping contact with their men. Whether the 18th's unit discipline could hold would now be put to the test in the dullness and mist which shrouded Guillemont and its exposed approaches. Air observation had been obscured throughout much of the previous week because of the persistent mists, and little was known about the state of the German wire in front of Guillemont, it being hidden by a fold in the land along the Guillemont Road.

### The attacks on Guillemont by the 90th Brigade. 30th July 1916[13]

As the attack by the 90th Brigade got underway it seemed to the men and their company officers that the barrage was not all that it should have been. This was probably due to the marked contrast with the massive and effective barrage which had preceded them on 1 July's successful assault. Certainly Guillemont itself only received five minutes of intensive bombardment prior to the assault, the intention being to avoid German retaliation on the assembly positions in front of and within Trones Wood. Even within fifty yards of the

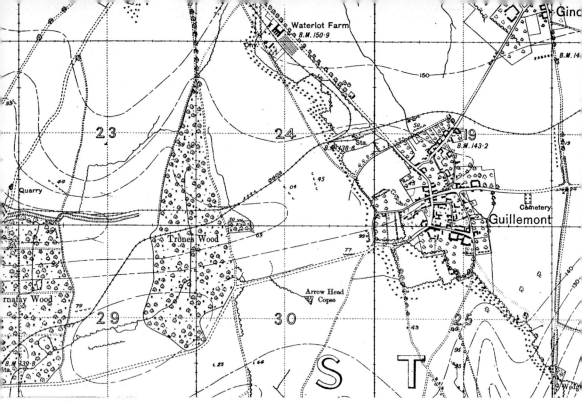

*The infamous Guillemont Road, between Trones Wood and Guillemont village, scene of further attacks involving the first four of Manchester's Pals Battalions during the last eight days of July 1916.*

*Captain Megson, the 16th Battalion's Signals Officer who, alongside his men, was forced to spend the whole of the 30 July under the most intense sweeping machine gun fire in hastily dug slit trenches between Trones Wood and Guillemont.* Nash

concussion and cacophany of the artillery's barrage it still seemed that there was a noticeable lack of weight to the shelling and only the 18-pounder field guns gave support to the men going forward into action. On the right of the attack the 89th Brigade, consisting of the 19th, 17th and 20th KLR, together with the 2nd Bedfordshires, attacked at 4.45 am between Arrow Head Copse and Maltz Horn Farm.[14]

The mist throughout the early morning was exceptionally dense, making it all but impossible to keep direction and maintain contact with units on either flank nor close contact with the barrage as it moved forward. The initial objective of the 16th Manchesters was the railway north west of Guillemont, in S.24.d. This was the left flank of the 90th Brigade's attack. Their assembly trenches were west of Trones Wood, in S24a, but en-route the battalion's guides had become casualties and the assembly was chaotic. The 16th's attack was led by B and C Companies, A and D Companies remaining in support east of Trones Wood. Because of the delay to a 4.45 am start the onset of daylight meant that the men were not able to push forward to a previously laid taped line, out in the open but nearer to their initial objective. Nevertheless, the 16th's men advanced steadily towards the railway. Here

*The shoulder title of the 8th City Pals, the 23rd bantam Manchesters.*

*A view of what was once the railway station at Guillemont.*

they wheeled part right and formed up again, pushing on towards the quarry and Guillemont village itself. However, as they came to the intermittent German wire along the north and west of the village's defences, in S.24.d, the weight of machine-gun fire from both the station and the quarry, at T.19.c.1.3, became intense. Without having made contact with the 18th Manchesters, the 16th were driven back to a position just a few yards in front of Trones Wood on the Guillemont road, at S.30.a.6.5. A few of the 16th's signallers under command of Captain Megson had dug in some fifty yards south west of the level crossing but it was impossible to get telephone lines out from their positions to connect with either HQs or the front line units in Guillemont. From now on the whole of the approach to Guillemont was continuously swept by intense machine-gun fire directed from the station and the quarry. This enfilade fire from north to south would make any attempted advance by the supports north of Arrow Head Copse almost suicidal.

Meanwhile the two leading battalions, the 2nd Royal Scots on the right and the 18th Manchesters, had gained the village but were now unsupported on their left. At 5.00 am one small party of Manchester's bantam Pals under 2nd Lieutenant Moore carried twenty boxes of SAA and fifty-six boxes of bombs into Guillemont for the men of the 18th Battalion. However, in the depth of the initial fog, D Company of the 18th had veered left in front of the 16th Manchesters and ended up attacking the station to the north of the village, where the attack by the 2nd Division was already floundering. Further south the rest of the 18th Manchesters under Captains Blythe (C Company) and Routley (A Company) were quickly into the western houses of the village, with the 2nd Royal Scots on their right. Initially their advance had been rapid, maintaining contact with the barrage until the line of the church had been reached from where the 2nd Royal Scots pushed on to the eastern face of the village, where consolidation was begun about 5.45 am. A and C Companies of the 18th Manchesters, however, could make no further progress. C Company had by this time amassed over one hundred prisoners of the 22nd Bavarian Regiment, but was now under heavy machine-gun fire from the quarry. Unfortunately, the German defensive barrage west of Guillemont now combined with the machine guns in the quarry to ensure that very few reinforcements and almost no further ammunition could reach the 18th's men. Under intense fire some men of the 17th Manchesters belonging to A and C Companies, under the command of Captain Fearenside, had, by 7.45 am, managed to get up to support the 18th's men in the west of the village. As these men moved forward astride the Montauban to Guillemont road they had been forced to search for a gap in the wire in front of Guillemont. One was found where the sunken lane in front of Guillemont cuts the road from Montauban. Here they met with other small parties of the 17th Manchesters who had been forced to follow the same course.

*149*

Captain Fearenside's men then made an attempt to compensate for the failure of the 16th's attack by bombing towards the quarry. However, because of the total lack of information, the British barrage was forced to concentrate on the far side of Guillemont and the German bombers, machine-gunners and riflemen hidden amongst the orchard on the western fringes of the village were, therefore, unchallenged and found themselves able to pick off many of the 17th Manchester's men crowded in the vicinity of this gap. B and D Companies of the 17th Manchesters, in support and under the command of the officer commanding the 2nd Royal Scots, had earlier deployed out of the eastern edge of Trones Wood, but it was deemed sensible to retain these men rather than order them forwards in an attempt to break through the curtain of German shelling to support the 2nd Royal Scots. These two companies then remained in assembly trenches, east of Trones Wood, throughout the remainder of the day.

During the morning two further groups of the Manchester Bantams did, however, manage to get through to the 2nd Royal Scots, taking up water and bombs at 8.00 am, and Very Lights and rockets at 10.00 am. This proved to be the last contact with the 2nd Royal Scots. Meanwhile the 17th's men in front of Guillemont found no-one on either flank with whom they could co-operate, and they, therefore, withdrew towards the trenches running intermittently north and south of Arrow Head Copse and parallel to the east of Trones Wood. They were now joined by 2nd Lieutenant Moore's bantams, whose men continued to hold the lines here throughout the remainder of the 30 July.

Their depth of good fortune in getting back was amply evident in the description of Lieutenant Alan Holt, who had been in the village with his men from the 17th Manchesters.

*I got up to the village in the mist with my men without any casualties, but after spending three hours there and losing a lot of men we were ordered to retire. It was then daylight and the mist had lifted; we had to walk back over 800 yards of open ground and how I got back I don't know; very few of my men did, as we were swept by two machine guns. I got a machine gun bullet through the sole of my boot, another through the holster of my revolver, also a piece of shell which went through the holster and smashed the handle of my revolver on the way. Just as we were leaving the village I was hit in the back with a small piece of shrapnel, but it is nothing serious and I was able to carry on 'till the Brigade was relieved on Monday morning The doctor took the piece out yesterday and I am on duty as usual – none the worse. Some luck, what!* Lieutenant Alan Holt, 17th Manchesters, writing on 1 August 1916.

Almost all of the runners now attempting to report the situation from within Guillemont were shot down. Patrols sent forward to find out the position either did not return or could not get near enough to find out what was happening. It was not until midday that Lieutenant Colonel Grisewood commanding the 17th Manchesters had any idea at all as to the whereabouts of his men. Inside the village of Guillemont the fighting was hand to hand and desperate. German counter attacks from the direction of the cemetery east of the village and also from the south east were successful in penetrating the positions of the 2nd Royal Scots and 18th Manchesters. Eventually the 2nd Royal Scots were surrounded and obliterated. One Forward Observation Officer reported seeing a party of soldiers surrender in the south west portion of Guillemont as late as 2.30 pm, when completely cut off and fired on from all sides. These were the remnants of the 18th Manchesters, amongst whom was Company Sergeant Major George Evans for whom, apart from enduring his life as a prisoner of war, the war was now over. The casualties amongst his battalion this day were 470 men killed, wounded or missing, together with all bar one of the battalion's company officers. Almost all the 18th Manchester's men had fallen in No Man's Land during the assault or been killed or taken prisoner in the village.

By 2.00 pm the Corps Commander had arrived at 30th Division's HQ to be told that the

*The Victoria Cross.
During the Great War two
soldiers serving within the
Manchester Pals would win
Britain's highest award for
military valour. The first
was won by CSM George
Evans on 30 July 1916.*

89th and 90th Brigades were incapable of further attacks, and that any assault by the 21st Brigade could only prolong the disaster. The station, the quarry and Guillemont itself were still in German hands, the approaches were swept by machine gun fire and heavily barraged by defensive artillery. The 30th Division was exhausted and arrangements were already in hand to pull them out. As those arrangements were undertaken it became clear from the large numbers of dead and wounded who were crowded in almost every shell hole what a catastrophe the attack had been. A small number of men from the 17th Manchesters and the City's Bantams were scattered around any shelter and trenches along the eastern perimeter of Trones Wood, the whole area being intensely shelled as dusk fell.

*About 10.00 pm an officer reported that he had been shelled out of the front trench*

*Company Sergeant Major George Evans. 10947. 18th Manchesters. George Evans was an old Scots Guardsman who had served during the Boer War in South Africa. In 1914 he had joined the Manchester Pals, travelled to France and become the recipient of the Victoria Cross, won during the attack on Guillemont Village, 30 July, 1916. The citation recording George Evans' outstanding and conspicuous bravery says: 'For most conspicuous bravery and devotion to duty during the attack at Guillemont on the 30 July 1916, when under heavy rifle and machine-gun fire he volunteered to take back an important message after five runners had been killed in attempting to do so. He had to cover about 700 yards, the whole of which was under observation from the enemy. Company Sergeant-Major Evans, however, succeeded in delivering the message and although wounded rejoined his Company, although advised to go to the dressing-station. The return journey to the Company again meant a journey of 700 yards under severe rifle and machine-gun fire, but by dodging from shell-hole to shell-hole he was able to do so, and was taken prisoner some hours later. On previous occasions at Montauban and Trones Wood this gallant warrant officer displayed great bravery and devotion to duty and has always been a splendid example to his men.'*

*During the attack on Guillemont on 30 July, the 2nd Royal Scots were virtually wiped out after they were surrounded in the depths of the village.*
Taylor

*The sunken lane in front of Guillemont, showing the utter devastation wrought by weeks of shelling and the numerous assaults which ground to a halt on these infamous acres of land. Although 1st July produced the most stupefying losses, the fighting throughout late July, August and on into October tested the resolve and personal courage of every participant to the very limits of endurance.*

*E[ast] of TRONES WOOD and forced to retire with some 70-80 men. Only twelve arrived with him, the remainder having disappeared on the way.*

*No touch had been established with any troops on our left and thus it seemed likely that a very considerable gap existed in our lines. I collected all the available men remaining at HQ and all the men I could find at the T.M. Battery – about 80 in all. They went forward in two parties with three officers & held the line pending the arrival of reinforcements.* Lieutenant Colonel Grisewood. 17th Manchesters.[15]

Five heavy Vickers guns were then brought up to deal with any possibility of German attacks breaking through the thinly held lines east of Trones Wood and along the Guillemont Road. Periodically small groups and individual survivors, bloodied and filthied from the attack, would writhe back over the bags and return to their start lines. Amongst them was Paddy Kennedy, rapidly becoming one of the 18th battalion's oldest hands. That night all the forward troops of the 30th and 35th Divisions in the area were relieved by the men of the newly arrived 55th Division. For some that relief could not come too quickly. Exhaustion and weariness meant that, for many, the night had been spent in utter oblivion to the spasmodic shelling which continued to wrack the area.

*Towards morning we were awakened by men of the King's Liverpool Regiment. They told us that very few of our men had returned. We made our way back to the transport lines and had a good meal of double rations, dead men's.* Private Paddy Kennedy. 18th Manchesters.

The casualties amongst the 30th Divisions two attacking Brigades had been extensive, approaching 3,000 men and officers in total. In the 89th Brigade the figures amounted to 1,314. Losses were even heavier amongst the 90th Brigade's men and officers. Including the

Manchester bantam's losses, the first three of Manchester's Pals Battalions suffered just over 1,000 casualties in front of Guillemont during this last day of July 1916.[16] The 18th Manchesters, who had lost so many men here, had now suffered the incredible total of one thousand three hundred casualties amongst its men during July, added to the 32 officers who had become casualties.

*This photograph shows men resting in a crater at Waterlot Farm, after it was seized on 15 July.*

Nevertheless the remnants of the battalion marched back to the Citadel to listen to the Divisional General, Major General Shea, speak of the attack as a success and of being of the greatest importance in breaking up an anticipated counter attack by large numbers of German troops in the Guillemont area. Those German troops defending the village of Guillemont then resisted a number of further and costly attacks until the 3 September when it was taken by men of the 20th Division. By this time the area was a mere sea of craters. The village buildings had been utterly obliterated by the effects of over sixty days shelling. Underneath the village, however, a network of tunnels connected the wells and many deep dugouts which had withstood the bombardment.

### Ginchy, 3 September 1916

One mile east of Waterlot Farm and a similar distance north east of Guillemont lay the village of Ginchy. On the day that Guillemont was finally captured by the 20th Division and men of the 47th Brigade of the 16th Division, Ginchy was the focus of an attack by the 7th Division. The British lines in front of Ginchy ran east of Delville Wood along the Longueval – Ginchy road for four hundred yards before turning south along Porter Trench in the direction of Guillemont. On the night of 2/3rd September the men of 22nd Brigade relieved the 91st Brigade within these trenches prior to the attack timed for mid-day on the 3 September.

The plan involved bombers belonging to units in the 91st Brigade, bombing out the Germans from the eastern tip of Delville Wood and thence along Hop and Ale Alleys, whose

*Delville Wood had, by early September, been reduced to a pulp in which it was almost impossible to dig adequate trenches.*

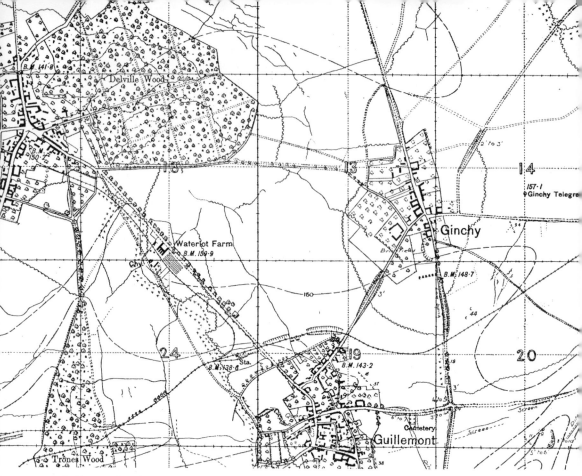

*Delville Wood and Ginchy village, scene of the attacks by the 20th and 21st Manchesters during 3 and 4 September. At the end of these events the 20th Manchesters had fewer than 130 original members of the battalion left.*

trenches dominated the ground across which the men of 22nd Brigade were to attack. This bombing attack was due five minutes before the main infantry assault. The artillery bombardment became heavier from 10.25 am, and intense just forty minutes before zero. At mid-day the main infantry attack got underway, the men's objective being the Ginchy Telegraph, 600 yards east of the village. Unfortunately, the preceding bombing attack on Hop and Ale Alleys produced no gains, and the 1st Royal Welsh on the left of 22nd Brigade's attack found progress against heavy frontal and enfilade fire almost impossible. The 20th Manchesters on the right, however, were far more fortunate. The German's defensive barrage did not open until 12.17 pm. The 20th's men were, therefore, able to keep up with their own barrage lifts and advanced into the southern portion of the village without difficulty, overcoming the defenders from the 1st Battalion of the 35th Fusilier Regiment and other men of the 88th Regiment. On the Manchester's left some small parties of the 1st Royal Welsh got into the northern part of the village, but were never heard from again. On the north western fringe of Ginchy some men from the 2nd Royal Warwickshires in support also gained the edge of the orchards. By 2.00 pm reports coming in from wounded soldiers and officers confirmed that the Manchesters had taken Ginchy. By 3.50 pm the 20th Manchesters were digging in along the eastern and south eastern fringes of Ginchy under severe and close range fire. Meanwhile the Germans in the northern part of the village were able to work their way into positions both north and east of the Manchesters, from which counter attacks drove some of the 20th Manchesters out of their positions in Ginchy. From here the men were forced westwards back towards Porter Trench, along with the majority of the 2nd Warwickshires.

However, at least one organized but small party of the 20th Manchesters held out in the sunken part of the Guillemont Road, just south west of Ginchy. Here they faced determined counter attacks in the mid afternoon by men of the 1st/88th and 1st/35th Regiments. These were driven off by Lewis Gun fire. Elsewhere the remaining isolated parties of the 20th Manchesters left within the confines of Ginchy were driven in by attacks made by men of the Ist and IIIrd Bns/88th Regiment and also by the IIIrd Bn/35th Regiment, as late as 6.00 pm. This hand to hand fighting saw men using spades, pick axes and entrenching tools as the likeliest weapons, but by 8.30 pm patrols sent forward by 22nd Brigade HQ had realized and reported that the village of Ginchy had been reoccupied by the Germans.

Amongst the battalion's officers this day there had been eleven casualties, amongst the men 275, of whom 108 were missing.[17] During the period of July, and up to 4 September, the 20th Manchesters had now lost more than 30 officers and 850 men. There were now only 130 men of the original Pals left within the ranks. Soon after these events the battalion required a draft of over 500 men, chiefly from the Cheshire Yeomanry, to make good their numbers.

The loss of so many of the 20th Manchesters at Ginchy did not, however, mark the end of the Manchester Regiment's involvement here. For the purposes of the assault on Ginchy, the 21st Manchesters had also been attached to the 22nd Brigade and the following day, at 2.00 pm, two companies of the 21st Manchesters were used in an easterly attack out of Delville Wood against Ale Alley. The attack was led by the battalion's bombers, supported by A and C Companies. However, it proved impossible to make progress against the fire of massed Germans who had gathered in strength between Hop and Ale Alleys. Another company attacked northwards out of Pilsen Lane against Hop Alley, but this attack also proved futile

*RAMC men search the packs of the dead and missing for any effects, letters and valuables which could be sent to the relatives of these men. This photograph was taken during the period 3-5 September, after the battles for the villages of Guillemont and Ginchy, in which a great many men of the Manchester Regiment became casualties.*

against well directed and intense machine-gun fire in enfilade from the north of Ginchy. Throughout the day the survivors were forced to lay out in shell holes until the cover of nightfall allowed their withdrawal.[18] During their operations here in front of Ginchy the 21st Manchesters suffered 227 casualties, almost all during the events of 4 September. Such casualties had now become the currency of success or failure in the war of attrition to which the 1916 Battle of the Somme had now, all too clearly, become resigned.

### The Transloy Ridges

During the August of 1916 the Manchesters in the 30th Division temporarily left the area of the Somme, moving northwards to the Bethune area. During September the 16th, 17th and 18th Battalions found themselves in the Festubert area, their first experience of Flanders and its notoriously wet conditions. So close was the water table to ground level around Festubert that many of the trenches were merely superficial ditches, surrounded by walls of sandbags for cover. The 19th Battalion were at Givenchy. However, these two months passed relatively quietly with few casualties, and by October the first four of Manchester's Pals battalions were on the move back to the Somme area. By early October the fighting had moved forward towards Bapaume, the British now close to the village of le Sars, having taken Flers and the remains of Gueudecourt village. On the 7 October the Battle of the Transloy Ridges was opened, in the hope that the Somme campaign could be ended by a victory leaving the British troops overlooking Bapaume's vital transport and railhead facilities. The village of le Sars fell that day. That night heavy rain began to fall and persisted throughout the next day as arrangements were made for the 30th Division to replace the 41st. Even after two months of rest, reorganization and recuperation in a quiet area, the Manchester's rifle strength was woefully inadequate, each battalion mustering less than 500 men as they marched in to replace the exhausted 41st Division.

On the 10 October the 16th's men were bivouacked on ground just west of Delville Wood, ready to go into action. The 30th Division was being made ready to take part in the assault of the Ligny-Thilloy ridge positions in advance of Flers. Unfortunately their knowledge of the ground was non-existent. Aerial photography was limited by the persistently wet and dull weather. The following day the 16th Battalion's men were marched forward to Flers Support, in M.23 & 24, and Grove Alley, where they stayed throughout the 12 October, forming the reserve for the 90th Brigade's tragically unsuccessful attacks towards Bayonet Trench, Le Barque and Le Transloy. The 17th battalion's part in that attack was to lead the assault, with the 2nd Royal Scots Fusiliers on their right and the 2nd Bedfordshires on their left. In support of the 17th Battalion were the 18th Manchesters. As the battalions gathered in the morning the weather was overcast and numerous heavy showers drenched the men waiting in their increasingly muddy trenches in front of Factory Corner on the Flers to Ligny-Thilloy Road. The attack took place at 2.05 pm, after just five minutes of intense artillery bombardment. As soon as the British artillery opened, a simultaneous barrage from the German artillery began to fall on the Manchester's front and support lines, as well as Battalion HQ in Gird Trench, located at N.19.a.1.2. Extraordinarily, it was possible to see the German marines lying in the open, some fifty to one hundred yards behind their own front lines, running east to west through M.18.c/d and N.13.c/d south of Le Barque and Ligny-Thilloy. As soon as the British barrage lifted these men rushed back to their forward positions from which they overlooked the attack of the 90th and 89th Brigades. From a number of German positions in these front lines, and more numerous ones to the rear around Ligny-Thilloy, an intense machine-gun barrage made progress impossible. As the first waves belonging to the 17th Manchester's right hand companies went over they were immediately cut down, nobody from A and C companies getting more than twenty or thirty yards beyond their own assault

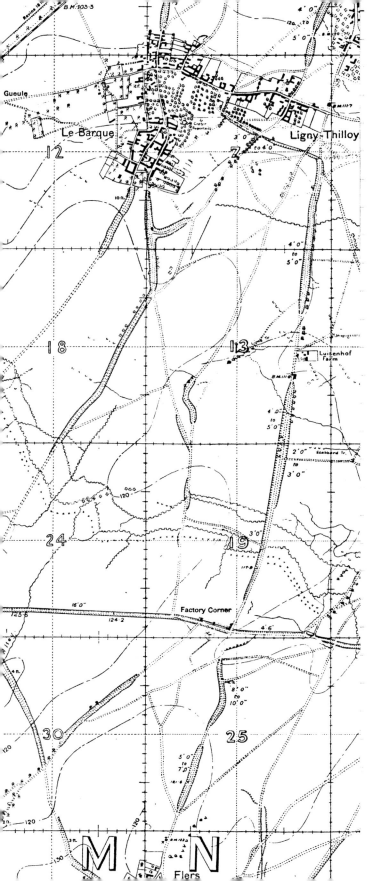

Lieutenant Aubrey Harris, 21st Manchesters, who was killed in action on 4 September 1916 at Ginchy. Before the war he was a schoolteacher, being gazetted to the 21st Manchesters in December 1914 and being promoted to Lieutenant in the April of 1915. Harris was one of the most experienced of officers within the 21st Battalion, and had long held the command of the battalion's bombers. He was buried within Delville Wood, but after the war his grave could not be found. His name is therefore commemorated on the Thiepval Memorial.
Guest

trenches. C.S.M. Ham, who went over with the third wave returned and, on his own initiative, ordered the fourth wave to remain in the front line trenches and stand to in case of counter attack. On their left the men of B and D made better progress and a few reached their objectives in Bayonet Trench, running across the south of M.18.d and N.13.c, where B Company's commander, Captain Sidebotham, was shot through the head as he looked over the parados towards Le Barque. By now

157

*Lieutenant Eric Goodwin. Killed in action on 12 October 1916 during the 17th Manchesters actions on the Transloy Ridges in front of Le Barque. Before the Great War Eric Goodwin had been a member of the Manchester University O.T.C. He was gazetted into the 2nd Pals in 1914, becoming a Lieutenant in 1915. Soon after his arrival in France he was wounded and forced to return to England. He rejoined the battalion in May 1916 after a period of recuperation.* Guest

five of the twelve officers who had gone over with the 17th's attack were dead, the remaining seven were all wounded and out of action. The 18th Battalion's men, coming up in support, also suffered terribly from the devastating machine gun fire. A small group of the 18th's men, together with number 7 and 8 platoons of B Company of the 17th Battalion, managed to get as far as a clump of trees south east of Le Barque, at N.13.c. central, near to Luisenhof Farm. The survivors were pinned down in the watery shell holes throughout the remainder of daylight. These heavy losses amongst the officers and men of both battalions meant that the surviving small parties were forced to withdraw, along with the remnants of the RSFs. The 17th Battalion's losses in this action were all twelve officers and 213 men. Of the three hundred and fifty from the 18th Battalion who went over in support, a further two hundred and fifty were killed, wounded or missing.

That evening the 16th Battalion's men moved forward to the front lines and Gird Support Trench where they reinforced the devastated companies of the 17th and 18th Manchesters. The following morning the area of Gird Support, where the 16th's HQ had been located, was heavily shelled. Whilst this shelling went on two hundred men of the 19th Manchesters were brought up to carry the wounded from the 90th Brigade's attack back to the dressing station from the wreckage of their front line positions. Lieutenant Colonel Knox was killed by a shell burst here whilst attempting to move his staff into a less perilous location. His loss was a tragic one for the 16th Manchesters, but it brought to the command of the battalion Major Wilfrith Elstob.

Wilfrith Elstob was a charismatic figure whose bravery and devotion to duty and his men was already legendary amongst the 16th Battalion. He was a strikingly tall, strongly set man and had then acquired the nickname 'Big Ben'. Of his own great physical strength he was almost unaware. He had been born in 1888, in Chichester, his father's third son. Within weeks his family moved to

*Soldiers wait patiently amongst the chaos of transport and artillery timbers, as they prepare to move forward to take part in the attacks on the Transloy ridges in mid October.*

*Men of the 16th Manchesters watch sadly as their dead are loaded onto narrow gauge railway trucks during the autumn fighting in the area of Flers and Ligny-Thilloy.* MRA

*Amidst the desolation of the battlefield a lone officer from the 16th Manchesters manages to find the time and motivation to write home, from 'somewhere in France'.* MRA

*Private Charles Titus Barnett, 43530, 21st Manchesters. Charles Barnett was training to be a teacher when he decided to join the 21st Manchesters in January, 1916. In August he was sent to France as part of the draft to replace the Somme casualties. On 25 November his battalion was moved into the indescribably horrible conditions in front of the 'Waggon Road', outside Beaumont Hamel on the Somme. Private Barnett was killed the following day by a sniper.* Guest

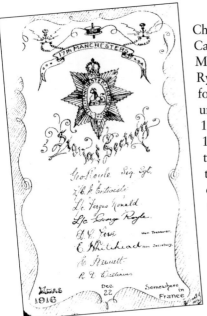

*The 17th Manchester's Signallers Section Christmas celebration menu, dated 22 December 1916. Of the section members mentioned, Fergus Ronald would be killed four months later at Arras.* Bradshaw

Cheshire, following his father's appointment as Vicar of Capesthorne and All Saints Church in Siddington, near Macclesfield. From his home nearby Wilfrith attended the Ryleys Preparatory School, in Alderley Edge, before leaving for Christ's Hospital school. Wilfrith Elstob then became an undergraduate of Manchester University, gaining his BA in 1909 and his teaching diploma the following year. During 1911 and 1912 he studied at the Lycee in Beauvais and then the Sorbonne in Paris, after which he embarked on a teaching career at Merchison Castle School, Edinburgh. He quickly became the senior French master. On the outbreak of war Wilfrith Elstob returned to Manchester, en route for London where he intended to enlist into one of the many units being raised in the capital. The day before he was due to leave Manchester Elstob accepted a commission into the Manchesters, as second-in-command to his lifelong friend, Hubert Worthington, company commander of A Company of the 1st City Battalion. By the time he took command of the 16th Manchesters, to whom he was devoted, Wilfrith Elstob was just twenty eight years old. His powers of leadership and motivation were immediately to be tested in conditions of the utmost severity.

During the week that followed, the 16th and 19th Battalions experienced all that was worst in the nightmare conditions of the Somme. By this third week in October the autumn rains had turned the chalk and clay into a sucking quagmire of filth. In the darkness of the early morning on the 14th, the 19th Manchesters were subjected to a heavy shower of gas shells and sleep in gas helmets proved to be impossible. The following day these same men were at work on the High Wood to Longueval road, in desperate attempts to improve the supply of ammunition and food to the front line positions. On the morning of the 16th both the 16th and 17th Battalions were digging new assembly trenches. The men watched as an enormous bombardment again pulverized the German lines in front of them, part of Rawlinson's methodical bombardment which churned the chalk and heavy clay soil into an almost impassable marshland slough. Many of the shells were falling short, because of wear on the gun's recoil mechanisms and barrels, and parts of the newly dug trenches were blown in, much to the men's disgust! On the 17 October A and D companies of the 16th Manchesters moved up into reserve for the attack which was to be made by the 21st Brigade across an area now utterly weighted against the chances of a successful attack. The approaches were a morass of water-filled shell holes; the location of the German trenches and gun pits unknown; the ground in front a quagmire; the assembly trenches, if they still existed at all, waterlogged. Zero was 3.40 am, two hours before sunrise.

Predictably the assault was a most terrible ordeal. The direction of attack was a compass bearing, the objectives unclear. Rifles and Lewis Guns were immediately jammed as officers and men slipped and stumbled in the darkness and ooze. On the right of 30th Division's attack, the 89th Brigade made no attack due to the failure of the lachrymatory barrage in their sector. The 21st Brigade's attack was supported by the 19th Manchesters but, as these men reached their own front lines, it was already apparent that the attack had suffered disastrous casualties. By 8.00 am a lone tank crossed the lines held by the 19th Manchesters and moved forward to Gird Trench, scattering the terrified Germans and killing many who fled north eastwards. Realizing that it was now possible to get the infantry forward, the tank's commander got out and waved the 19th's men forward. Unfortunately this opportunity was not followed up. The tank then went forward alone, along Gird Trench and up to its junction with the Le Barque road before retiring back through the Manchesters. Having missed this opportunity, the 19th Manchesters were then ordered to prepare to support another tank sortie at 4.30 pm. Perhaps fortunately, since no artillery support was promised, the tank broke down on its way forward and the operation was cancelled.

On the 18 October the 16th and 19th Battalions were in occupation of front line trenches. Two days later an inspection of the 19th's trenches revealed the dreadfulness of their circumstances. The men had been up to their thighs in mud for four days, and the dead were still unburied from the attacks of 18th. Many of the half trained drafts were exhausted and in a state of complete collapse. On this day, the 20 October, the 16th Battalion marched back to Montauban, having suffered just short of one hundred casualties during these trying experiences which presaged the awful conditions of Flanders in late 1917. The 19th were relieved on the evening of the 21 October, having completed the burying of the dead within the shell holes and shallow assembly trenches which sufficed for the job.

The months of November and December slipped away calmly. The men of 90th Brigade were now in the Bellecourt area, five miles south of Arras and opposite the German held village of Blairville.

It was a quiet sector, one in which reliefs could be undertaken in daylight, although sometimes attracting the sporadic attention of the German artillery. Soldiers were amazed to find that a number of villages just a mile behind the lines were still intact, with civilians conducting a normal daily routine. However, by the end of the year the communication trenches here were also reduced to an impassable, mire and the 90th Brigade were happy when, at the end of the first week in January 1917, they moved to Dainville and Bavincourt near Arras. Here the battalions providing working parties for the Canadians engaged in improving and extending the railway. The railway's purpose was clear. The spring of 1917 would see another initiative by the British and Empire troops around Arras and the Vimy Ridge area.

## Epilogue

For very many of Manchester's Pals the Somme offensive spelled the end of their active military service. One group for whom the war was over were the Prisoners of War, including a number of men who had been with Lieutenant Oliver at Trones Wood, when many of their patrol had been captured. Along with a number of Scots and South Africans these men had arrived at Duisberg Meiderich in Westphalia. Here the men had been put to work in the nearby coal mine. It was a moment of great tension.

> We were given clogs and tins as used by miners and marched to the pit 300 yards away. There we refused to take the lamps. We explained that prisoners of war in England were not ordered to work in the pits and that we should not do it. Lipman, the only one of us to speak German, was our interpreter. We were marched back to the prison, lined up, and told we were to be shot, the armed soldiers marching at the back of us. Lipman was pulled by the ears every time he was wanted to interpret some order.
>
> We stuck it out from just six in the morning until late in the afternoon, when only three of the original fifteen were left standing They were taken to their cells, and next day the same thing happened. We were again lined up and prodded and assaulted until several men fainted. We realized this could not go on, and we gave in. In the pit we were knocked about, but I gave one Gerry a good hiding, and the word was passed round that the English men were not to be struck. After that we had a comparatively good time. Food came regularly from England and we had our own jokes on the Germans.[19]

*Christmas 1916 in one of the many hospitals housing casualties from the Somme fighting. Many of these men belonged to the 20/22nd Manchesters.* Burrows

For others, the most severely wounded men, this would mark the start of many years anguish as they struggled to cope with the desperation of maimings, blindness and disfiguration. For a larger number, however, their more superficial physical wounds could be healed and these soldiers restored to active military service. In this race to heal and return the men, the role played by the nursing and medical services was a crucial one in the battle to ensure ascendancy of numbers in the war of attrition now being waged on the Western Front. Many of Manchester's Pals found their way back to hospitals in the north of England. A favoured location was the nearby holiday town of Blackpool, where men could complete their hospitalization in attractive and familiar surroundings.

Quite naturally the entertainment facilities of Blackpool were much sought after by men looking to recover their health and self confidence. The process of strengthening the men was undertaken at the nearby racecourse, where a facsimile of a complex trench system gave the soldiers a chance to flex their muscles again in the digging and construction of ever expanding lengths of trenches. Guided 'tours' of these trenches provided the men with the chance to recover their self esteem and meet with the many mill-girls from nearby Lancashire towns, who flocked into Blackpool that summer to unite with and pamper their soldier heroes.

*After my operation I had the time of my life for about three months. I went from Huddersfield and they sent me to Blackpool where we were billeted on the racecourse.*

*As young fellers we used to have a fresh girl every week you know, because we'd no money and these girls were making plenty, they used to come and play host to us at*

Taylor Chapman, originally of the 19th Manchesters but returned to active service with a different unit, initially with the 2nd Manchesters, then as a counter artillery spotter and range-finder and eventually as a wireless operator with 52 Squadron, RFC. For hundreds of original Pals, who after the Somme offensive found themselves serving away from their friends, the contrast often proved dispiriting. When he returned to France in the Spring of 1917 with the 2nd Manchesters, Taylor Chapman recalled that, 'I was with a different class of fellows than those that I had been with. These were the 2nd Manchesters and they were a line battalion and Regular soldiers. You couldn't leave your stuff in a billet otherwise it was stolen. After being with friends in the Manchester Pals it was a different life altogether, so much so that I applied for a commission to get away from them and was sent down the line to Etaps (Etaples).' Chapman

*Harry Westerman convalescing in Blackpool amongst nurses and other casualties from a multiplicity of different units. He is seated, second row, next to the end on the right. Private Westerman had been wounded whilst acting as the CO's runner during the attack by the 20th Manchesters at Bois Francais near Fricourt on 1st July. Now almost restored to health he would first meet his future wife here in Blackpool, before being returned to active service as part of the 7th Army Training School, as a machine gun instructor. This was a considerable surprise to a young scout with no experience as a machine-gunner whatsoever, the probable explanation being his prowess on the football pitch, which counted for much in inter-unit competitions!* Westerman

*Blackpool. So, we did not object, we might have Blackburn one week, we might have Bolton next week, it might be Preston the following week, but they were all the same, they were all very tied to us.*

*I remember one job I got there. I was detailed one day to go on a facsimile of the Loos trenches which they'd built and we was sent as guides. Oh it was money for a Burton for me, because you used to take these people round the trenches and tell them about it and so on and when you'd finished you put your hat down. I was making twenty pounds a week, which was enormous in those days.* Taylor Chapman. 19th Manchesters.

A number of Manchester Regiment units served the purpose of rehabilitating, retraining and returning the men to active service. These included the 3rd and 4th (Reserve) Battalions who were placed on coastal defence at Cleethorpes and the Humber estuary. However, the Manchester Pals units initially gave rise to their own reserve battalions. The 25th Reserve was formed out of depot companies from the 16th, 17th and 18th Battalions. The 26th Reserve from men of the 19th, 20th and 21st, whilst the 27th Reserve Battalion was formed as a local reserve from men of the 22nd, 23rd and 24th (Oldham) Battalions. On 1 September 1916 these units were designated the 69th, 70th and 71st Training Reserve Battalions, located at Ripon in Yorkshire and Altcar near to Liverpool. During the late summer of 1916 these units were filling with the newly recovered Pals who had been wounded during the early weeks of the Somme battles, many of whom were still keen to rejoin the war. Writing to his old company commander, Lance Corporal Aukland described his wounding on 1 July, the weeks in hospital recovering from the shrapnel wound to his left arm and then time spent in the 69th Training Reserve Battalion. Lance Corporal Aukland clearly regretted the days being wasted before he could join an Officer Cadet unit to pursue a commission.

*It was certainly not a serious wound, nevertheless my left arm was rendered quite*

*useless at the time and taking discretion for the better part of valour, made my way to the rear. Though I went up to Montauban in pretty quick time, it is up to me to say I came back a jolly sight faster. Eventually I thoroughly enjoyed thirteen weeks of hospital life at Manchester and seven at Eastbourne. To be made a fuss of by Sisters and Nurses suited me admirably, and my behaviour was such that one Sister actually told me I was a lady's man; of her dreadful mistake she remains in utter ignorance... It is now quite six weeks since I was accepted by the War... and am feeling a little annoyed and impatient at having to wait so long for instructions to proceed to Cadet Unit, especially as I have once more reached the keen on getting out stage. I must be passed being impatient and can arrive at the only natural conclusion that waste paper baskets are being used to accommodate surplus commission forms. Unless it be that the supply of would be officers is far and away in excess of demand. This is a very different unit to the old 16th and I am eagerly hoping to get away at an early date in anticipation of the time when I shall be showing a platoon the way to find the Boche.* Lance Corporal W. Aukland writing from 69th TRB at Ripon, 9/4/1917.

*Albert Hurst had fought his last battle. His foot wound meant that he would never be able to march and carry loads again. As a consequence was discharged and quickly returned to his pre-war employment as an engineer with the National Gas and Oil Company where, as in every other engineering and manufacturing plant in Manchester skilled and educated men were in desperately short supply.* Hurst

By contrast few, if any, events which occurred during the years 1914 to 1918 have given rise to more intense feelings and anguish than the use of military discipline to justify the execution of volunteers and conscripts accused of serious offences against the Army's codes and practices. The great majority of more than 300 men who were executed whilst serving in the British and Empire Forces were shot whilst serving on the Western Front. The largest number of these, by far, were accused of desertion. Without doubt the majority of these poor men were terrified and shocked by the circumstances which they endured so long. Four men serving within the Manchester service battalions were shot at dawn during the Great War. Three of the four men executed in the Manchester's Pals battalions came from the 18th Battalion, a unit whose casualties during the year of 1916 had been unremittingly severe. All four executed men had been charged with desertion. The circumstances within which their death's occurred were squalid and regrettable. One member of a firing squad remembered the events many years later with a terrible and vivid clarity.

The man due to be shot had only recently come to the unit as part of a draft sent to replace the July and August casualties.

> *... they wanted to make an example of him because the objective had failed – they used to do that. Early in the morning they brought him down a hill, sat him in a chair and bound his arms and legs – he wouldn't be blindfolded. One of the lads in the firing squad pleaded, 'I want nothing to do with this, he's a good lad, I knew him in the 1st Manchesters, he's done well.' His plea was ignored. One of us had a blank cartridge, so we could think 'maybe I had a blank', a conscience easer. The officer pinned a white handkerchief over the lad's heart and ordered us to aim there. Our hands were shaking We fired, but the shots richocheted, going under his arm-pits somehow. His head was lolling but he wasn't dead. 'My God' the officer said, 'I've got to finish him off.' He placed his pistol upwards to the lad's ear and blew his brains out. We were then ordered to place the body on a stretcher. He was swilling in blood and later we had to hose the stretcher to swill away the blood. The lad was buried in a corner of a cemetery at Bailleulmont. On a cross was his name and killed, not killed in action...* Private Paddy Kennedy. 18th Manchesters.

164

*The headstones of all four members of Manchester's service battalions who were shot at dawn. Albert Ingham and Alfred Longshaw are buried together. The magnificent inscription on Albert Ingham's headstone reads, 'Shot at dawn. One of the first to enlist. A worthy son of his father.'*

Private William Hunt. 1957. 18th Manchesters.
*Shot at dawn on 14 November 1916.*

Private Albert Ingham. 10495. 18th Manchesters.
*Shot at dawn on 1 December 1916.*

Private Alfred Longshaw. 10502. 18th Manchesters.
*Shot at dawn on 1 December 1916.*

All three men are buried at Bailleulmont Communal Cemetery. Albert Ingham and Alfred Longshaw were friends from their pre-war days as employees of the Lancashire and Yorkshire Railway Company at the Salford goods yard. Both were original members of the 3rd Manchester Pals. They had enlisted together and were executed together. The fourth man to be executed was from the 19th battalion was:

Private Ellis Holt. 26685. 19th Manchesters.
*Shot at dawn on 4 March 1917.*

His body is buried at Berneville Communal Cemetery[20] in a corner, along with just two other men.

## Notes

1 Lieutenant Alan Holt, 17th Manchesters.

2 In fact 2nd Lieutenant Callan-Macardle had attributed to General Shea a message actually sent by General Sir Henry Rawlinson who had wired on 2nd July, 'Please convey to all ranks 30th Division my congratulations on their capture and defence of Montauban. They have done excellent work and will be attacking again before long.'

3 Initially by the 2nd Green Howards, followed later by the 2nd Wiltshires, in a move designed to coincide with French attacks on Maltz Horn Farm to the right. The 19th Manchesters were in Brigade support with the very much weakened 18th KLR in reserve.

4 The other three companies of the Wiltshires made an attempt to take Trones Wood at 1.00 pm, suffering heavy casualties in a replica of the earlier Green Howards attack, but this time succeeding in entering the wood and digging in along its south eastern edge. During this, the second attack on the wood the 2nd Wilts CO was wounded and their adjutant killed.

5 Moving forward along the sunken road leading south east out of the Briqueterie, the attack by the 2nd Royal Scots succeeded in taking Maltz Horn Farm and were then able to bomb northwards towards Trones Wood along Maltz Horn Trench, up to its junction with the Guillemont Road. The Divisional Diary records this as 'a brilliant little action', 67 Germans surrendering at the farm, two machine guns and 110 prisoners belonging to the 38th Reserve Regiment being captured in Maltz Horn Trench together with the killing of some forty to fifty more of the enemy.

6 The 18th Battalion's CO, Lieutenant Colonel William Smith, was fatally wounded about 4.00 pm this afternoon

by shellfire at his HQ. Major Godlee took over command of the battalion at 2.00 am the following morning.

7 Imperial War Museum, Department of Documents. Reference 82/16/1.

8          16th Battalion:    182 men and  8 officers.
                  17th Battalion:    200 men and 10 officers.
                  18th Battalion:    270 men and 11 officers.*
                  19th Battalion:     69 men and  4 officers.**
                  Total:          721 men      33 officers
                  * See 90th Brigade War Diary. PRO ref: W095/2337.
                  ** See W095/2327.

9 The attack was to be carried out by four divisions, the 9th, 3rd, 7th and 21st. In the 7th Division the 20th Brigade was to lead the attack through Flatiron Trench south of Bazentin le Grand, to be followed through by the 22nd Brigade, including the 20th Manchesters in Brigade reserve, who were to attack Bazentin le Petit village. The 91st Brigade, including the 21st and 22nd Manchesters, were in Divisional Reserve.

10 Brigadier General Potter of the 9th Brigade, 3rd Division, was able to say later that, after seeing the processes of consolidation begun that morning, 'I walked out alone to examine the ground in front. It was a lovely day; the ground was very open and sloped gently up to a high ridge in front, so I wandered on until I found myself approaching a large wood which continued over the crest of the ridge. There was no sign whatever of the enemy, so I walked into the edge of the wood but saw no sign of a German, nor any defensive works. As I had advanced about a mile, and was quite alone, I considered it time to return...' Quoted in Terry Norman, *The Hell They Called High Wood*. [William Kimber, 1984]

11 Even the normally anodyne Official History concludes that it was, 'in the highest degree unfortunate that, at a moment when fresh troops were at hand to maintain the impetus of the advance, such a delay should have been imposed by higher authority. Resposibility might well have been delegated to the divisional commanders, both experienced and capable leaders, who were in the best position to know what could, and what could not, be done... High Wood was not to pass completely into British hands until after two whole months of bitter and costly fighting.' [*Military Operations. France and Belgium 1916. Vol 11.*] See also *The Dawn Assault – Friday 14 July 1916* by T R Moreman, an article which contains a very great deal of detail and a complete Order of Battle for these actions. [*Journal of the Society for Army Historical Research, Autumn 1993*]

12 To the north of the 2nd Yorkshires an attack by the 3rd Division was also going badly, the 30th Division's diary records that 'The troops of the 3rd Division appeared to have no idea of their whereabouts as several small parties of Shropshire L.l. were discovered firing S.W. into TRONES WOOD.'

13 The carrying parties detailed to move ammunition and other supplies forward this day came from the 23rd Manchesters, the Manchester Bantam Pals. The Bantam's route was from the Briqueterie to the advanced dump of S.A.A., grenades and rockets held at S30c.4.6. The report on these operations from 90th Brigade HQ says that: 'These men did their work excellently, generally under heavy shell fire and at least two parties got on to the outskirts of Guillemont and dumped their loads there, in the earlier stages of the operations.' The Bantam's casualties during the Guillemont actions were 51 men, of whom 5 were killed, 29 wounded, 4 gassed and 13 missing. [P.R.0 ref: WO95/2310]

14 See *Liverpool Pals*, pp 114/124 for a full and graphic description of the 89th Brigade's costly attack.

15 PRO ref W095/2339.

16          16th Manchester Battalion casualties on 30 July =  8 Officers and   211 Other Ranks
                  17th Manchester Battalion casualties on 30 July =  5 Officers and   274 Other Ranks
                  18th Manchester Battalion casualties on 30 July = 14 Officers and   470 Other Ranks.
                  23rd Manchester Battalion casualties on 30 July =                  51 Other Ranks.
                                    Total: = 27 0fficers     1006 Other Ranks.

17 Source WO95/1631.

18 Ginchy finally fell on 9/l0 September to men of the 56th Division.

19 This story was told by Rowland Heathcote, 16th Manchesters, in an article which descibed a reunion of the POWs in April 1929. The other prisoners who shared his ordeal were Tommy Atkinson, G E Charlesworth, Harry Maylett, Wally Howarth, Harld Helsby, Leslie Scotter, James Scrimgeour, Arthur Peers and Pte. Wood of the 16th Manchesters, together with Lipman and two other South African soldiers and two Scots. See *Daily Dispatch*, 9 April, 1929.

20 See Julian Putkowski and Julian Sykes, *Shot at Dawn*, Leo Cooper/Pen and Sword Books Limited, for details relating to these unfortunate cases. Although the authors wrongly identify Albert Ingham and Alfred Longshaw as having arrived in Egypt in November 1915 rather than France as should be recorded, their sensitive and careful documentation of the cases, along with the other soldiers shot by authority of the *Army Act* is very informative of the callousness and inhumanity which surrounded all too many of the executions.

## Chapter Seven

# 1917, Arras and Passchendaele

*"Daddy thinks it is a disgrace and a shame that such distinction is shown."*[1]

If 1916 was to be remembered in the future one reason would certainly be the terrible attrition suffered by the largest volunteer army ever raised in the United Kingdom. Nevertheless, no thoughts about their place in history were entertained by the survivors of the Somme and the many new faces within Manchester's service battalions. Their duty would remain to see the conflict through to its bitter end. As the coldest of the war's winter months unfolded, the drafts of Derby men, recruits who no longer bore the stamp of the enthusiastic volunteer, began to reach the battalions. By the end of 1917 the conscripted soldiers, for whom enlistment had been a matter of either reluctance or simply the arrival of an eighteenth birthday, began to fill the gaps in the ranks. As the months of 1917 and their terrible events unfurled, each draft bringing the newest members of the battalions often possessed only a tenuous knowledge of Manchester and its regimental pride. But the life of their units had to go on. Indeed, these new men's part was just as significant as that of the Pals, and came to be marked by the same standards of valour and determination once they were faced with the realities of war on the Western Front.

However, the enormous sacrifice given by Kitchener's Army had not been without effect. German casualties upon the Somme had also been enormous. Many of her best units were drained of their original and most competent soldiers. France's position at Verdun had been relieved. Strategically the Allies could now harbour great hopes of victory in 1917. The central question for Germany was how to cope with the overstretching of her military

*Private Bill Mathers, 47972, 21st Manchesters. Bill Mathers was a Derby Scheme recruit, initially placed in the 5th Manchesters at Wigan as Pte 5916. Throughout his military service he compiled a diary, as if written by his small daughter, in which he recorded his own thoughts on the iniquity and sorrow of war. Before embarkation he received just three months military training. He was sent to France, during January 1917, passing through the notorious Etaples transit camp where he undertook three weeks of final preparation and hardening, between January 12th and February 3rd, before being posted to a front line unit. In March he found himself with the 21st Battalion at Beauquesne. One of his first tasks was to be engaged in the clearance of bodies from the battlefields in front of Bapaume. His 'diary' entry for March 18th, 1917, reads as follows: "Daddy is sent along with a small party to search the Battlefield of Bapaume, to find Dead Comrades who fell in the Battle of Nov and Dec 1916. They find several Privates, 2 Sergts and an officer of their Regt. They carried the officer to a grave about three and a half miles back. The Privates were buried where they lay. Daddy thinks it is a disgrace and a shame that such distinction is shewn."* Andrews

*Private Bill Mathers*

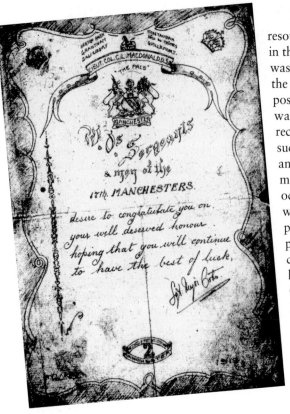

*From the Warrant Officers and men of the 2nd City Battalion to Major (Temporary Lt. Col.), Charles Leslie MacDonald on his receipt of the D.S.O. Lt. Col. MacDonald's D.S.O. was gazetted on 1 January 1917 whilst he was seconded to the 30th Divisional School. He would also win a bar to his D.S.O. whilst attached to the 19th Manchesters, later in 1917.*
Bradshaw

resources across the dual fronts in the west and in the east. One tactical move within her power was the essential shortening of her positions on the Western Front, the withdrawal to the positions of the Hindenburg lines. The purpose was to release men for longer rest, recuperation and training. The retirement was successfully undertaken during late February and throughout the March of 1917. This move resulted in the German Army occupying a superior defensive position, whose defences in depth were extravagantly protected by massive wire fortifications and purpose built concrete strong-points. By contrast, the Allies were soon handicapped by the appointment of Robert Nivelle as Chief of the French Army's General Staff. His ill advised great offensive was planned for the spring, a hoped for 'surprise attack' which would end the war. As a preliminary to Nivelle's offensive, the British First and Third Armies commanded by Generals H S Horne and Sir Edmund Allenby would attack the German Sixth Army at the proposed Battle of Arras. Before that huge initiative could begin a number of German occupied villages south of Neuville-Vitasse and in front of the Hindenburg Lines proper had to be reduced. One of these was Croisilles, south east of where the Manchesters serving within the 7th Division had arrived.

## The 21st and 22nd Manchesters at Croisilles, 2 April 1917

The 21st and 22nd Manchesters' pursuit of the retreating German Army had begun on the 24 February when, under the cover of a misty morning, their patrols discovered that Serre village lay empty. The following day an advance, undertaken slowly and methodically, had started. The 7th Division pushed on through Puisieux towards Bucquoy across a land initially devastated by shellfire and later, as their advance progressed, by the destruction wrought to buildings and roads by the retreating German Army. Bucquoy itself proved to be an unpleasant and wasteful experience for the 22nd Manchesters. The order to attack, received from Fifth Corps just hours before, gave little time for artillery preparation and wire cutting. The initial attack, due to be made at 10.00 pm on the 13 March, was postponed. The pre-arranged barrage was, however, fired, but only served to put the German's on their mettle. At 1.00 am on the morning of 14 March, surrounded by utter darkness and pelting rain, a welter of muddy conditions and belts of unbroken wire, the 22nd Manchesters advanced to take Bucquoy and Arnim Trenches, from L.10.a.5.6. to the railway at L.9.a.8.8, and then on through the east side of the village. On their left, to the west, were the 2nd Queen's. No-one could see where they were going. Within minutes every man's rifle was jammed with mud and

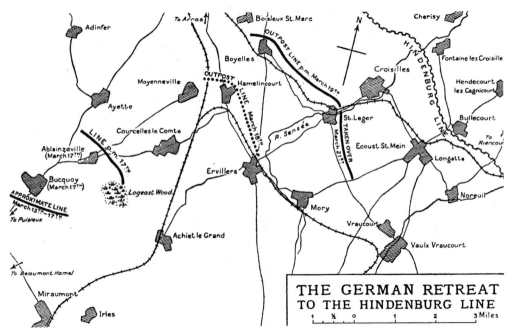

*The German retreat to the Hindenburg Line, on the 7th Division's front.*

grit. The left hand company was unable to get through dense masses of barbed wire which protected the village. A few of the right hand company of the Manchesters managed to get into Bucquoy and Arnim trenches, taking eight prisoners. However, they were unable to hold on in the face of counter attacks by superior numbers and, after the Manchesters' grenades ran out, the men were forced back before 6.00 am. One small party of an officer and 35 men did manage to hold on just outside Bucquoy, at L.9.b.5.5, but they were withdrawn at nightfall. The battalion's losses were an officer and 70 men missing amongst a total casualty list of almost 150 men. Casualties amongst the Queen's men were similar. A parallel attack

*Part of sheet 51B.SW4, corrected to 2 February 1917, showing the Croisilles area.*

*Mopping up amongst the concrete fortifications which abounded in the village of Croisilles.*

on Bucquoy from the west by men belonging to the 46th Division also met with the same outcome. It was a particularly pointless loss of men, especially when viewed with the benefit of hindsight since, on the 17 March, following their withdrawal from Bapaume and Achiet-le-Petit, Bucquoy was also evacuated by the Germans opposite the 7th Division.

The way forwards was now free again and the 7th Division's men advanced past Ablainzeville, through a further area of destruction and booby-traps left for the careless or unwise. By the 18th the Division was up to Hamelincourt and Ervillers, the following day to St. Leger, in front of Croisilles. The village of Croisilles was known to be stoutly defended by

*Part of sheet 51B.SW1, corrected to 4 March 1917, showing the area of St Martin-sur-Cojeul.*

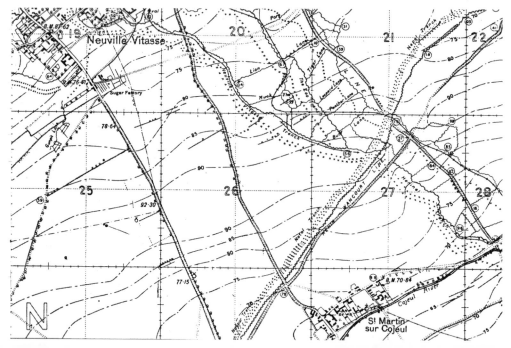

barbed wire, in some places more than twenty yards deep, as was Ecoust St. Mein a mile and a half to the south. These villages now held the key to a successful attack on the German positions at Bullecourt, in the Hindenburg Line.

The attack on Croisilles was made by the 22nd Manchesters, with the 1st South Staffordshires on their left. At 5.15 am on 28 March the troops advanced out of St. Leger to get close up to the barrage, timed for 5.45 am. As soon as the 22nd Manchesters approached Croisilles they came under heavy direct machine-gun fire. One small party, commanded by Captain Duguid, managed to get into the village, but the rest of the men were forced to dig in, outside the wire. An attempt to outflank the defences by the reserve company was defeated by concentrated machine-gun and artillery fire. The South Staffordshires' attack was similarly inconclusive. All that could happen was that the men would hold on to their gains until darkness. At this point the 21st Manchesters relieved the Staffordshires, and the Queen's went into the line established by the 22nd Manchesters. Little had been gained.

A further attempt was then arranged for 2 April. This was to be a massive attack, along a frontage almost ten miles in length, the 4th Australian Division on the right, to their left the 20th Brigade, to its left the 91st Brigade attacking Croisilles again. On the extreme left the 21st Division would attack against the higher ground between the two rivers, the Sensee and Cojeul. In the meantime a persistent bombardment was fired with the intention of clearing the wire, which had proved so formidable during the relatively small attack made on the 28 March. The objective of the new attack by the 91st Brigade was the railway line south and east of Croisilles, after which patrols would push out behind the village and link up with men of the 21st Division, cutting off the retreat of the Croisilles defenders. The 21st Manchesters would attack towards Croisilles railway station and then on past the Croisilles to Bullecourt road towards the east bank of the Sensee. On their left were the 2nd Queen's. On the Manchester's right were the 1st South Staffordshires. Zero was at 5.15 am.[2] The 22nd Manchesters were placed in Brigade reserve at St Leger, with orders to clear the village or support the main attack.

In front of the Manchester men the railway embankment south east of Croisilles was forty feet high and covered with brambles, wire and hidden machine gun emplacements. The men's assembly was carried out in exceptionally clear moonlight, which ensured that some of the 2nd Queen's men were seen, resulting in a barrage being fired across the shallow valley in front of the railway embankment. Fortunately the barrage was so clearly defined in its extent that succeeding companies were able to avoid the limits of the shellfire and continue their assembly unmolested. As the attack started the Queen's, on the left, were straddled by the British barrage, fired short, all their lead company officers being hit. Nevertheless, the battalion was reorganized and continued, successfully although behind schedule, to the attack. On the right the 1st South Staffordshires gained their objectives easily, and began to cause heavy casualties amongst fleeing Germans. The advance of the 21st Manchesters in the centre was also quickly thrown into confusion as the British barrage opened fifty yards behind their left company's start lines and then swept through these men. Nevertheless, the battalion moved forward without hesitation and reached the embankment with men of B and D Companies. In the face of their advance two machine guns, one on top of the embankment and one located in a culvert beneath, fired incessantly. All along the top of the embankment sniper posts had been dug deeply into the stone ballast of the rail track. These snipers, the two machine guns located at the top and base of the embankment and now some guns firing from Croisilles where the 2nd Queen's were held up, all caused casualties and the fighting was desperate, without any quarter being given. All four of D Company's officers were killed or wounded and the command was exercised by CSM Lucy.[3] After a heroic struggle the embankment was carried by 6.30 am. D Company on the right then got a Lewis gun team over the embankment and engaged a machine gun firing from the sunken road to the north. By 10.00 am after small parties had successively rushed over the embankment and, quite incredibly, through the culvert, the Manchesters established themselves in the sunken road. C Company were then leapfrogged through towards the final objectives on the east bank of the Sensee. The 21st Manchester's casualties were two officers killed, three officers wounded, together with twenty men killed and sixty eight wounded. The subsequent clearing and mopping up within Croisilles cost the 22nd Manchesters a further five officers and thirty nine men who fell victim to snipers, shellfire and booby-traps. This battalion had advanced from a position two hundred yards north east of St Leger Wood at 11.30 am on a line either side of the Sensee River. Their objective was the sunken road north east of the village. In the confines of the village, which still contained a large number of Germans who had been unable to make good their escape, there was sharp fighting from mid-day onwards. Eventually the support company was ordered up at 1.45 pm and the remainder of the battalion a few minutes later. During the ensuing action Lieutenant Robinson's men found a number of dugouts still occupied. These were engaged by Lewis Guns and then rushed. Robinson himself killed an officer and three men before taking twenty two prisoners. Apart from Croisilles village which

*Private Bill Mathers, 21st Manchesters. Before the actions at Croisilles Bill Mathers was severely wounded and taken prisoner of war during a raid on an outpost in front of St Leger His 'diary', written as if by the hand of his daughter, explains how this came about. '23 March 1917, it is evening. Orders arrive by runner from Headquarters that Daddy's platoon must attack the enemy outpost, at the point of the Bayonet. A Soldier (and Daddy's Comrade) named J J Dawson and Daddy are selected by the Lieutenant in Charge to proceed with Bayonets fixed, with instructions not to fire unless absolutely neccessary... 24 March 1917, It is early morning – Very Dark – Daddy overcomes the first German sentinel – leaving him Dead and is challenged by another – no sooner had the challenge come than a shot was fired – (a revolver shot) an explosive bullet entered Daddy's right ankle. It blew Daddy's Boot and puttees into the air... 24 March 1917, it is evening – Daddy awakens in a shell hole – having got there by crawling after being wounded in the morning. Daddy did not know where he was, so decided to try to crawl to the British lines for safety... 25 March 1917, it is just breaking dawn – Daddy thinks it is a good chance to crawl back to British lines and commences. After crawling about ³/₄ mile, a shot from a sniper's rifle pierces Daddy's left arm. Daddy could not move then as the bullet fractured his arm, between elbow and shoulder. Two German soldiers crawl to look at Daddy. It must be about 10.00 am. The German soldiers come back and decide to carry Daddy to their dugout...'. Just over two weeks later, on 9 April, Bill Mather's foot was amputated in a German hospital at Douai. Five days later he was sent to Germany. From being posted to the 21st Manchesters until his capture Bill Mathers experienced forty-nine days at war. Amongst those forty-nine days Bill Mather's diary records that twelve had been spent in assisting the RE's in railway construction at Bertrancourt, ten days in rest at Beauquesne, one day spent during a battalion attack on Serre, three days in Battlefield clearance near Bapaume, twenty days 'in the line' or close support trenches and three days in the attack during which he was taken prisoner in front of St Leger.* Andrews fell to the men of the 91st Brigade this attack had also seen the village of Ecoust St. Mein fall. The way was now open for the battles for Bullecourt, on the far side of the Hindenburg Lines, to begin.

Meanwhile, the Battle of Arras proper began on the 9 April, on a front running from Henin-sur-Cojeul, just south east of Arras, to Givenchy-en-Gohelle across the Vimy Ridge. It was initially marked by an extraordinary success at Vimy Ridge for the Canadians. That afternoon the 16th Manchesters were moved up into support positions just south of Mercatel. The following day the battalion were ordered to move forwards, with the intention of crossing positions in the Hindenburg lines, opposite the village of Heninel, which the Germans were believed to have vacated. At 2.00 pm the men were met with heavy machine gun fire at the cross roads west of St Martin-sur-Cojeul. Thus began a period of three weeks almost constant engagement with the German Army, which eventually reduced the 16th, 17th and 18th Manchesters to less than one hundred effectives in each battalion by 27 April.

It soon became clear on the afternoon of the 10th April that the Germans occupied the portion of the Hindenburg lines from Nepal Trench running to the south east. The 16th Manchesters were positioned in Nagpur Trench, with D Company along the Neuville-Vitasse and St. Martin road. Positions were set up between Neuville-Vitasse and the St. Martin road. Later that night it was decided to attack the Hindenburg positions here in the flank, by bombing down from the north west, where Natal Trench cut the Hindenburg lines, in order to take 'The Cot', on the south east side of Natal Trench, roughly 1000 yards west of Heninel, at N.28.c. This operation was carried out by A Company, in conjunction with men of the 1/9th London and 7th Middlesex Regiments. Further to the south attacks towards Bullecourt, yet to be undertaken by the 62nd Division, were planned. In the darkness of 4.30 am on the 11 April, the position of the Cot was attacked and carried by 2.00 pm. That same day the 18th Battalion were also engaged in fighting along the Hindenburg lines from an area known as 'The Egg', at N.20.d, past Panther Lane towards Nepal Trench, a mile north west of Heninel. The following day the 16th Battalion were relieved, and returned to Souastre where they were given more training and made ready for the second phase of the Battle of Arras, due to begin on the 23rd. But the 12 April was memorable for an extraordinary achievement by the 18th Battalion, who continued their minor operations of the previous day into a full scale attack along the fire trenches and support lines of the Hindenburg positions, into Heninel village. Thus 1700 yards of massively fortified positions were overrun in a flank attack by the bombers of A, C and D Companies of the 18th Manchesters, which thus allowed the 21st Division to pass, relatively untroubled, into this location. It was by any standards an attack to have been proud of and, for once, had resulted in relatively light casualties, just six men killed and twenty seven wounded. Their haul included relatively few prisoners but vast quantities of ammunition, grenade launchers, rifles and other weapons. German dead were strewn thickly around the whole area, but the complexity of the trench system and a number of connected tunnels had allowed the majority of the garrison to escape. The exhausted troops were now under the greatest of strain, the weather was intensely cold, with snow falling much of the time which made the trenches greasy and inhospitable. A period of consolidation and preparation was essential before a further advance could be considered.

### 23 April, the 30th Division's attack at Cherisy

This day the 30th Division were due to attack in a south easterly direction from positions just east of Heninel towards the village of Cherisy. Cherisy lay three miles north east of Croisilles, but this time the attack would be made behind the Hindenburg positions. The assaulting Brigade was to be the 90th, commanded by Brigadier-General J H Lloyd. His orders meant an advance of roughly one mile in an assault which would see the 50th Division attack

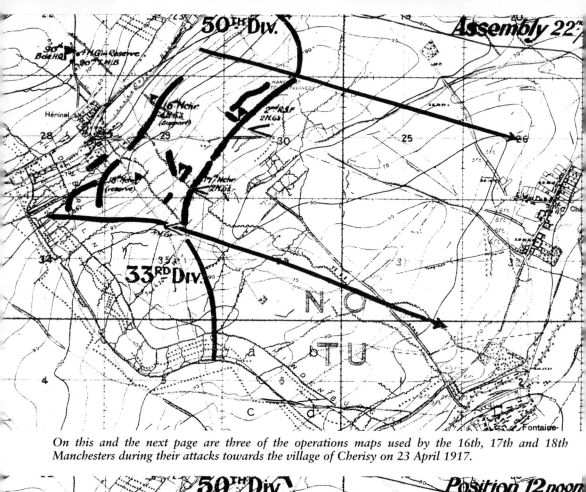

On this and the next page are three of the operations maps used by the 16th, 17th and 18th Manchesters during their attacks towards the village of Cherisy on 23 April 1917.

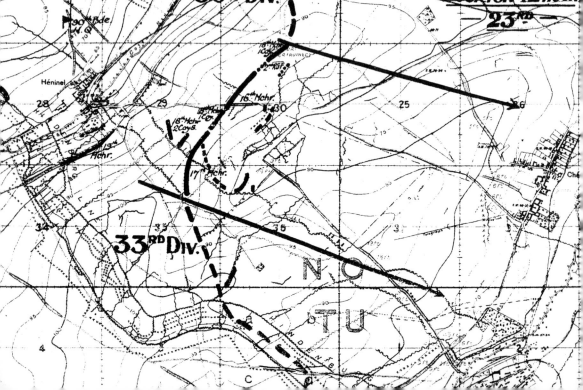

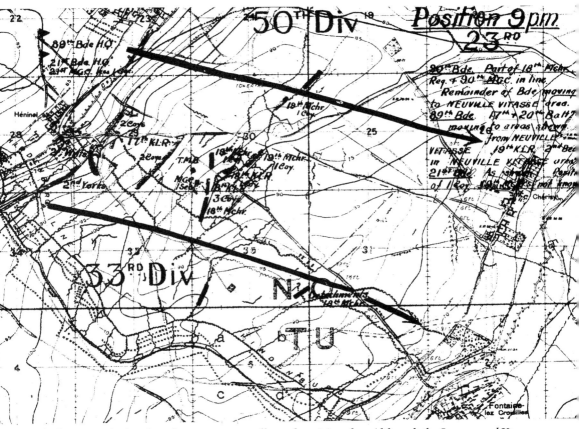

*The locations depicted on these maps are well worth a visit today. Although the Somme and Ypres sectors are frequently seen by visitors to the battlefields, the villages around Arras are quiet, often revealing many features which are unchanged since the events of 1917.*

towards the north of Cherisy and the 33rd Division attack to the south, towards Fontaine-lez-Croisilles. On the left of the 90th Brigade's assault were the 2nd RSF, on the right, the 17th Manchesters. In immediate support were the 16th Manchesters, with the 18th Manchesters in reserve. If all went according to plan the 16th Manchesters would provide mopping up parties to both assault battalions, as well as furnishing parties of men to consolidate a line of strong-points from the Quarry, in N.30.b, to the Sunken Road, at N.36.b.1.8. The ground over which the attack was to be made was difficult terrain. South East of the Cojeul River the German positions were on high ground, behind which a valley was commanded by a further spur running across the line of expected advance, from 0.31.a. to 0.26.c. Everywhere behind the German front positions numerous sunken lanes provided cover for abundant reserves and for the machine gunners who dominated the bare countryside. However, 30th Division was optimistic about the chances of success, the two opposing lines were close to each other, there was believed to be a lack of German wire, the preparatory bombardment had been heavy and two tanks had been allocated to support the assault. Most importantly, the earlier events of April meant that the Hindenburg defences were now breached. The 90th Brigade's attack would now be going in across land which had, until two weeks earlier, been behind the Hindenburg Lines' support positions. On the right of the 90th Brigade's attack the 33rd Division would actually be fighting south eastwards, along and parallel to the Hindenburg Lines, towards the Sensee River running between Fontaine-lez-Croisilles and Croisilles village.

Events however ensured that the 30th Division's report would later be forced to make clear that such optimism had been unwarranted.

*Captain Robert H Megson (without helmet) and another officer of the 16th Manchesters. Megson had been with the battalion as Signals Section commander and a Company Commander since Heaton Park. He was killed in action in front of the village of Cherisy on 23 April 1917.* Nash

> *In actual fact the German front system [south of Wancourt Tower in N.30] proved to be a highly organized and thoroughly prepared Trench system, holding a large garrison whose morale had not been destroyed by our barrage and previous bombardments, and who fought with exceptional bravery and tenacity and handled their machine guns and snipers with great skill. The difficulty of the task was certainly underestimated by us.*[4]

Opposing the 30th Division were the 35th German Division, with the 141st I.R on the right, the 61st I.R in the centre and the 176th I.R on the right. Initially everything had gone well for the Manchesters and the 2nd RSF. Before their attack, the process of digging assembly trenches had gone smoothly in the area out of German observation between the British front line and the Cojeul River. The assembly and the location of the 19th Manchesters in close support of the 90th Brigade attack also went well. The weather was fine, although early morning mist and clouds of smoke did hamper observation throughout the early part of the actions until its dispersal by 8.00 am.

Zero was at 4.45 am. Casualties were immediately seen to be heavy amongst the 2nd RSFs. As soon as A and B Companies of the 16th Manchesters, in support of the 2nd RSFs, left their assembly positions more casualties from machine gun fire were experienced. By 6.20 requests were being made by the 17th Battalion's Adjutant, to the 16th Manchesters, to provide two platoons to reinforce the 17th Manchesters. Accordingly two platoons of D Company were sent forward. Lieutenant-Colonel Elstob was not one to shirk the opportunity to find out what was happening, and he decided upon a personal reconnaissance to clarify the position. His report graphically describes the confusion and complexity of the circumstances facing the remnants of the assault battalions in their outposts.

> *I went along the left of our old front line and down the trench going east from about N.30.a. 7.2. Some 150 yards down this trench I found another trench leading off to the left and a few yards along that trench I found Lieutenant Wright of the 2nd RSF with their*

HQ Coy – He informed me that Colonel McConaghy and the Adjutant had gone forward and had not been seen since, though he had heard that both of them were wounded.

A number of men of RSF, 16th and 17th Manchester Rgt scattered about in isolated parties in shell holes. Enemy very active with snipers and MGs which it appeared had held attack up.

Bde signals got a line up to this point (N.30.a.9.1 approx) and I communicated with the Brigade Major mentioning that situation was very obscure but that I was endeavouring to clear it up and that a flank attack up the valley from the right would probably clear the enemy out.

Received instructions to take charge and organise this attack.

Instructed Lt Wright to take charge of the 2nd RSF and any of their parties of men near lines and to organise a defensive position along the trench he was in, also to thin out the men and form them into groups under a N.C.O. or a senior private.

Then went forward to try and discover where our front line actually had got to – on the way met Capt Hendrie of Stokes Mortar Battery and explained my intention of organising an attack up the valley, arranging for him to bring fire to bear on the left to occupy the attention of the enemy as soon as he saw party approaching up the valley. Capt Hendrie then went to reconnoitre the position for his guns.

I then went on towards the QUARRY and, leaving the trench, formed up some more isolated parties of men in shell holes – It was necessary to crawl the whole time as ground was covered with M.G and rifle fire – I could not find any officers, so instructed each party that I came across to continue consolidating the shell holes that they were in and to hold on to them.

In the most forward shell hole that I reached I found one of our Sgts and 3 men. This Sgt informed me that the enemy were only about 25 yds away - He pointed out where he thought our left flank was (about N.30.b.4.4) and told me that at about 8.00 am 60 Boche had attacked from a trench but had been driven off by Lewis Gun and Rifle fire. He said it was impossible to move from the shell holes without being shot.

I asked this Sgt whether he thought he was strong enough to hold the Bosche on his immediate front and he replied, 'Certainly sir, we've done it once and we can do it again.'

I told him that I was going to organise a flank attack up the valley from the copse on the right and that he was to be ready to give covering fire with the men around him – He thoroughly understood the position and the tactics to be employed.

At this time, (about 9.00 am) enemy apparently did not know where his own line was as he was shelling positions held by his troops.

I then returned to my Bn HQ at N.29.d.8.9 and carried on as per report already sent...[5]

The 30th Division's narrative of these events confirmed just how severe this fighting had proven to be.

At 8.00 am the situation of the 90th Inf. Bde. appeared to be as follows:

On the night the right company of the Right Assaulting Battalion (17th Manchester Regiment) had reached neighbourhood of N.36.a.6.8. The left Company of this battalion had been practically wiped out. Practically all the officers in these two companies had either been killed or wounded.

The enemy held in strength N.36.a.6.8. and N.36.c. 7.1. also the sunken road in N.36. b...

On the left the assaulting battalion, 2nd Royal Scots Fusiliers, had been practically wiped out and their Commanding Officer (Lieutenant Colonel McConaghoy) had been killed, and all their other officers either killed or wounded.[6]

The two tanks, of whom much had been expected, failed. The right hand tank caught fire and stuck fast in a position just in front of the junction between the start lines of the two assaulting battalions (N.30.c). The left hand tank in front of the 2nd RSFs initially did well, but overheated after an advance of 500 yards and was returned to its initial rendezvous point. In neither case were the tanks of any real assistance to the infantry. By 9 o'clock more men, this time of the 19th Manchesters, were crossing the Cojeul River to the slope south east of Heninel. The Battalion's role here would in fact be marked by all the chaos which the circumstances of battle so often produced. Success, if any this day, would be bought by weight of numbers rather than the decisive and skillful manipulation of arms and troops.

It was realized at Divisional HQ that, south east of Wancourt Tower, the 2nd RSF had made just a few yards progress in the face of murderous machine gun fire. A few men had pushed on heroically towards Cherisy, where they had all been killed. Both of the machine gun teams of the 90th's Machine Gun Company, advancing with this battalion, had been wiped out immediately. The experience of the personnel of the gun teams with the 17th Manchesters was more fortunate. Although they experienced heavy casualties, the guns were brought forward and gave support to the Manchesters throughout the day. Nevertheless, almost all the German defences in front of the 2nd RSFs and to the left of the 17th Manchesters (in N.30.b.,c. and d) were still intact. Indeed, much damage had been inflicted on the advancing troops by German soldiers who left their trenches, fighting in the open using flexibility and mobility to disrupt their enemy's advance.[7] As a direct consequence of Wilfrith Elstob's personal reconnaissance and report the 16th Manchesters, along with two Companies of the 18th Battalion, were ordered to undertake his suggested flank attack against the German positions in front of the RSF's attack. This would take the form of a move north eastwards from positions gained by the 17th Manchesters (up the valley through N.36.a to an area known as the Picture Ground, in N.30.c.&d, and on towards the Quarry, at N.30.b. Unfortunately, within the heat of battle, little was realized about what events were unfolding on the 50th Division's front to the north. In fact their attack, initially successful, had been subjected to two counter attacks in strength during the half hour after 11.00 am. The 50th Division was in fact being driven back to their starting positions north west of Wancourt Tower. With their left flank in the air the 90th Brigade was in trouble, and the composite 16/18th Manchesters were immediately diverted from Elstob's planned flank attack to form a defensive line south of Wancourt Tower. By noon it also seemed that the 33rd Division were being counter attacked with sufficient severity to force them back upon their own start lines. Only the two right companies of the 17th Manchesters had made progress, in places more than 600 yards towards Cherisy, but it was now clear that their own left flank was dangerously exposed and the 30th Division's attack as a whole in danger of collapsing. At this time the 19th Manchesters were located in the sunken road just south of Heninel, in N.28.d and N.34.b, from where they were ordered to move forward to occupy the left hand of the Division's start lines near Wancourt Tower. Their move, however, was observed and, in the face of artillery and machine gun fire, their companies and platoons became intermingled, the majority of A Company ending up on the left instead of the right as expected. As the afternoon progressed some attempt was made to reorganize the men.

In the midst of this situation an order from Lieutenant-General Snow, commanding VII Corps, was received by 30th Division to the effect that, at 6 pm that evening, the assault towards Cherisy was to be resumed, 'and that all resources were to be employed'. This attack was to be undertaken by the 21st Brigade, reinforced by a battalion of the 90th Brigade. For once this meant that the 18th and 19th Manchesters, the 3rd and 4th City Pals, although in different Brigades, would attack side by side, the 18th on the left and the 19th on the right. However, those orders were only revealed to the CO of the 19th Battalion, Temporary

Lieutenant-Colonel Whitehead, when he was sent for at Brigade HQ to be given the news that his men were to go over the top in the approaching twilight. Their objectives were those originally stated for the failed attack in the early hours of that morning.

On returning to his HQ and with just minutes to go Lieutenant-Colonel Whitehead, his adjutant Captain Duncan, and the company commanders were in conference. A hasty plan suggested the men would attack in three companies, each with a depth of two waves, C Company on the right, B in the centre and A on the left. D Company, which only had three platoons, would provide support of one platoon for each company's assault. A compass bearing giving direction was issued. Unfortunately, as he was returning to his men, Second-Lieutenant H W Purdy commanding D Company was killed by shellfire. The remaining company commanders had, at best, six minutes to organise their platoon commanders. At 6.00 pm the assault got underway, but the men knew nothing other than a direction and an estimate of the distance over which they were expected to advance. It was a recipe for failure. Side by side the 18th and 19th Manchesters moved south eastwards. D Company of the 19th Manchesters, of course, knew nothing of the attack and remained in their assembly positions. In the face of sustained machine gun fire the attack's progress was patchy. The 18th King's Liverpools, who had been expected to provide further support platoons and parties of 'Moppers Up', did not arrive behind the 19th Manchesters in the confusion and hurry. Nevertheless, some small groups of the 18th Manchesters pushed ahead towards Fontaine, although by this time having only two officers of the original complement left. By 8.00 pm as small parties less than one hundred strong in total got into the trenches in front of Fontaine, sharp hand to hand fighting took place during which both sides lost casualties. Within twenty minutes a counter attack drove these men out of their gains, and the remnants were forced back to their starting positions, fifty three men making it back to their positions between 9.30 pm and midnight. The 18th Battalion's casualties were fifteen officers and 346 other ranks, killed, wounded or missing. The 19th Manchesters had also made only limited progress, except for some men of the left companies who had advanced 400 yards towards Cherisy, south east of Wancourt Tower. Lieutenant-Colonel Whitehead, of the 19th Battalion, revealed his distaste for what had happened in his subsequent report.

> At 6.00 pm the attack was launched and the result was very much as I had expected. The frontage was too wide for the Coys. to keep in touch and an entry into the enemy trench was effected at isolated points. During the advance a good many casualties were suffered from our own barrage. When the men came under machine gun fire, they doubled forward and the officers and sergeants were unable, in the noise and excitement, to hold them back. A and B Coys. were able to join up in the German front line. The trench on the left of A and on the night of B was still full of the enemy, and there were no signs of the battalion who, I had been told, were to do the mopping up. Heavy machine gun fire was coming from the enemy second line trench. As A Coy was by this time reduced to about nineteen men and B Coy. to about sixteen men, it was impossible to advance further without leaving behind them an unmopped trench full of the enemy. All the officers of both Coys. had become casualties and the NCOs in charge decided to hang on to what they had won. A similar state of affairs existed on the right where a sergeant of C Coy. with thirteen men had assaulted, and was holding on to, a portion of the German front line trench, the only difference being, that whereas A and B Coys. held on all night, the C Coy. party was ordered by an officer of another regiment to withdraw after dark. All these parties made their flanks secure with bombing posts and eked out their supply of bombs and ammunition by using those of the enemy.[8]

*John Guest, with pipe, together with some of the other youthful subalterns who joined the 16th Manchesters early in 1917.* M. Guest

In the face of German counter attacks at about 8.30 pm, the 2nd Yorks were dispatched to support the sparse and scattered men of the 19th Manchesters in their attempts to hold on to their forward positions. This they managed to achieve throughout the hours of darkness.

The following day, the 24th, it became apparent that the Germans were pulling back towards Cherisy, and the 2nd Yorks were able to advance to take the objectives which had eluded all attempts by the Manchesters the previous day. Subsequently the positions in front of Cherisy were held by 89th Brigade, including men belonging to three of the Liverpool Pals Battalions, the 17th, 18th and 20th King's Liverpool Regiment, until their departure some days later. One of the new subalterns with the 16th Manchesters wrote home to announce that he had survived the first hurdle. He had been fortunate. All four of the 16th Battalion's company commanders had been killed this day.[9]

*Here I am in the same old dugout, safe and sound. I have been into my first battle and I hope I do not go into many more. It was the worst day I have ever experienced and I hope I never experience another anything half so bad... I shall have a long tale to tell when I get in front of a fire in the dining room. I shall be glad when that day comes. I am a home bird after this war is over.* Second Lieutenant John Guest. 24 April 1917

The 30th Division's casualty roll for the period 19-29 April reveals just how severe were the losses amongst 90 Brigade's units. The Division's total Infantry casualty list amounted to more than 1,700. Of these 1,307 had been incurred by 90 Brigade. Total casualties amongst the Manchester's four battalions present at these events were close to 1,000 men, the 16th Manchesters now being reduced to less than one hundred effectives.[10]

In fact the Manchesters and Liverpools were not the only long standing members of the 30th Division to depart the area in late April. Major-General Sir John Shea, was removed from the command of the Division which he had served and commanded so conscientiously throughout his men's active service. He was sorely missed by his officer colleagues and the rankers who he had commanded. His replacement was Major-General W de L Williams who continued in command of the 30th Division until the end of the war. Shea himself later resumed his successful career, serving with Allenby during the Palestine campaign.

Writing two weeks later of the battle, Wilfrith Elstob was philosophical about the losses, dangers and humanity experienced within war.

*I hardly dare mention the losses, for my heart is full and I know how you will feel. On the battlefield as one moved amongst shells and bullets – Death seemed a very small thing and at times enviable. Here we are – English and German – we or rather those damned Journalists talk about Hate – it seems to me to disappear on the battlefield, people who have not been there talk a lot of damned nonsense. We are 'blind', as a private soldier on the night after the battle said to me – 'We know it is not their quarrel sir' – this spontaneously.*

*Our fellows, it is always cigarettes or hot tea or something like that when they take prisoners, and the Germans fed and kept alive our fellows in the midst of the bitterest Trones Wood fighting last year. Thank God. Humanity and unselfishness are higher than a damned lot of talked nonsense by certain petty minded people.*

*Hubert we have lost Meggy, Willy and Hookie whom you knew – Sergeants Ashton and Dawson and poor little Jimmy Mayors, Lance Corporal Gibson with you at Montauban and Private Ogden of A Coy. Sergt Ashton is missing and Clegg (both believed killed). I haven't written to their next of kin yet in the case of these last two for there is a shadow of uncertainty. Hubert, Knowles (Transport Officer) and myself are the last of the two very originals out here. I should be miserable if I were taken away from the Battalion. I want to be with them in the battles, and if I were taken on the battlefield I feel that I could die happily.* Lieutenant Colonel Wilfrith Elstob. 6 May 1917

## Bullecourt

After an abortive attack in front of Bullecourt by the 62nd (2nd West Riding) Division, undertaken on 11 April, the 21st Manchesters were sent forward on the 14 April to relieve one of the 62nd Division's battalions opposite Bullecourt. The 62nd Division's attacks on the 11 April had corresponded with the assault by the 30th Division at Heninel. Now that the 7th Division was back in the line, opposite Bullecourt, all of the first seven of Manchester's Pals battalions came to be within just a few miles of each other during the Battle of Arras. There now began a period of steady attrition which proved just as trying a time for the Manchester battalions within the 7th Division as it did for those units serving with the 30th. Patrol activity on the 7th Division's front was heavy, and advanced posts suffered casualties from the increased frequency of German raids here during the weeks of late April in front of Bullecourt.

In the middle of that month, on 16 April, Nivelle's vast 'surprise attack' had been launched on the Aisne between Soissons and Rheims. Before the end of April it would be checked, having achieved none of the surprise, and little of the expected gains. In places the French Army were reduced to a sullen indifference, occasionally mutinous, in units which had suffered heavily during the much vaunted Nivelle offensive. It was Haig's belief that the British Arras offensive would have to be extended in order to relieve the pressure on the French Army. In this respect the constant involvement of the Manchesters, within the 7th Division, in attacks on Bullecourt village during April and May of 1917 were of an almost sacrificial nature. These attacks were often carried out with little chance of tactical success but being deemed necessary for the greater strategic good.

On 3 May a further action was undertaken by the men of 22 Brigade. This was part of 7th Division's support for an attack on Bullecourt again being made by the 62nd Division. The 62nd Division's attack employed men belonging to 185 Brigade on the right and 187th on the left, supported by men of the 7th Division, including the 20th

*The Hindenburg defences were marked by carefully prepared concrete fortifications as well as the use of extravagant belts of barbed wire in front of fortified villages such as Bullecourt.* Taylor

*2nd Lieutenant H S Grimshaw, 21st Manchesters. Harold Grimshaw had left his job as a schoolteacher in 1916 to join the Honourable Artillery Company [H.A.C.] and later the Artists Rifles. He was gazetted into the 21st Manchesters during January 1917 and was severely wounded whilst on outpost duty in front of Bullecourt on 30 April. He died as a result of those wounds on 24 May 1917 and is buried at Achiet le Grand Communal Cemetery Extension.* Guest

Manchesters. It was an extraordinarily clear example of how the futility of the continuing Arras offensive resulted in the loss of so many more lives than should ever have been the case. The narrowness of the frontage meant that many German artillery pieces were turned onto the attackers. As the 62nd Division's attack faltered in the face of the defensive barrage and strength of the village's garrison, the 20th Manchesters were sent up to positions below the railway embankment south of Bullecourt. To the east of Bullecourt a significant number of Australians were just holding onto a stretch of the Hindenburg Lines, but that hold was precarious and impossible if Bullecourt was not secured.

As a consequence, 22 Brigade of the 7th Division was ordered, that evening, to attack Bullecourt. At 10.30 pm the 2nd Honorable Artillery Company (which had replaced the 2nd Royal Irish in this Brigade) and the 1st Royal Welch Fusiliers attacked. These men suffered heavy casualties from machine guns north west of Bullecourt, at U.20.b and U.21.a, which enfiladed their advance. That attack failed in the darkness and by 2.00 am the Brigade was arranging for a renewed bombardment, 'with view to two fresh battalions going in'. Still in the darkness, and unfamiliar with their objectives, the 20th Manchesters and 2nd Warwickshires were ordered to repeat the process at 3.00 am on the 4 May. As the men were forming up on the line of the railway embankment they were hit by an accurate German barrage. The 20th Manchesters battalion suffered eighty casualties but their attack was not made until 4.00 am, by which time the men had been reorganized. Small parties of the Manchester's men got into the south east of Bullecourt but were unable to hold these positions. Throughout the day attempts were made by Brigade HQ to find out what had happened, but most patrols were badly shot up by Germans who were clearly still in Bullecourt in strength. On the 5 May, 22 Brigade was pulled out. It had suffered almost 800 casualties for no gain. The 20th Manchesters had got off lightly, two officers wounded, fourteen men killed, 88 wounded and four missing. They were soon to be back. Over the next three days 20 Brigade of the 7th Division were engaged in further attacks, which did gain a few yards in the south east of the village, but also suffered extensive casualties of the same magnitude as those already experienced by the 22nd Brigade. By the 10 May it was 91 Brigade's turn, including the 21st and 22nd Manchesters this time round. On the late morning of 12 May some of the 22nd Battalion were sent forward towards the 'Red Patch', located in U.27.b central, after an attack by the 2nd Queen's and 1st South Staffordshires was held up. Each of these two battalions had been supported by a

*Major-General T H Shoubridge, CB, CMG, DSO, who came from the command of a brigade in the 18th Division to command the 7th Division from April 1917 to the end of the war.*

Part of Sheet 51B.SW4, corrected to 2 February 1917, showing Bullecourt village.

Inset: Bullecourt village, photographed from the air on the 6 April and again one month later on 9 May, 1917. The incredible destruction wrought by five weeks of shelling fired by both sides to the conflict for supremacy in this few hundred yards of land can clearly be seen.

*Right: Private Albert Morris, of the 22nd Manchesters' A Company, No. 3 platoon. Wounded in action at Bullecourt, 11 May 1917. 'Gunshot wounds, head multiple, l.arm, l.hand, l.thigh l.side, and abdomen, severe…' Evacuated to England where he recovered, later being returned to something like fitness with the 3rd Manchesters at Cleethorpes and then returning to the Western Front, with the 17th Manchesters, in the spring of 1918. At Bullecourt he had been saved from further severe wounds by the fortunate intervention of his pay book and mirror which, between them deflected the grenade splinter from his chest into his left arm.*

*Left: Private Herbert Austin Thomas, 32669, Manchester Regiment. Before the war Herbert Thomas had been a commercial traveller for J & N Philips. He was captured during the battles for Bullecourt and for six months was 'missing, believed killed.' Not until November of 1917 did a series of post cards from Herbert, now whiling his time in Gustrow Kriegsgef-Lager, Mecklenburg, reveal that he was alive and well.* Lamb

183

company of the 21st Manchesters and had gained some little ground in the south east portion of Bullecourt. However, the arrival of three companies of the 22nd Manchesters only succeeded in overcrowding the communication trenches in which they were forced to take shelter until nightfall. By mid-day things were at a standstill and, utterly worn out, Brigadier-General Cumming was temporarily replaced as GOC 91st Brigade by Lieutenant Colonel Norman of the 21st Manchesters.[11]

The following day, the 13 May, saw another attack by the 22nd Manchesters in the hope of making further progress through the village by securing the G1 trench which protected the south west of the village, running from U.27.b.7.2 to U.27.b.1.9. This trench, although isolated, stubbornly refused to be captured, and still controlled the western portions of Bullecourt. The 22nd Manchesters were due to move from north east to south west and they would attack in conjunction with the 2nd Royal Warwickshires, who would attack the same trench from the south west, using the bayonet only. Two companies of the 22nd Manchesters, A and D, were lined up fifty yards north of the road running north west, from U.27.b.7.5, through the village towards the crucifix. A Company was on the right, nearest to the crucifix, which was thought to be held by men of the 62nd Division. Their attack was another disaster. At 3.40 am the barrage on G1 trench in fact fell north of the road amongst the 22nd's men causing many casualties and demoralization. As the remaining men went forward through the shattered brickwork and devastation towards the G1 trench they were met by heavy machine gun fire, both from that trench and also from positions around the crucifix on their right. The attack was 'held up'. Some parties of the 2nd Royal Warwickshires came along the road running into Bullecourt past the G1 trench and apparently ran into some men of D Company and took these men along northwards, such was the disorientation of the men and their officers. Both A and D Company commanders were wounded. Wounded men straggling back described the attack as having failed. The survivors were scattered across ground still swept by machine gun and aimed rifle fire. Casualties were relatively light, two officers killed, two wounded, one missing believed killed, 106 other ranks killed, wounded and missing.

On 14 May the 20th Manchesters were back in Bullecourt again, although the village had, by this time, been reduced to mere rubble and dust. The 20th Manchesters' left lay on the site of the almost imperceptible village church. To their left were the Honourable Artillery Company, holding a lodgement to the north of the Red Patch. Scattered along the eastern and southern perimeter of the village were groups of the 21st Manchesters. At dawn on the 15th a German attack by two fresh battalions of their Guard Fusiliers was made under cover of another barrage. Its intention was the recapture of the village of Bullecourt. The centre left of the 20th Manchesters line initially gave way, along with the Honourable Artillery Company on their left. At once the headquarters staff, servants, cooks and signallers were turned out to defend these positions, followed by a successful counter attack by the 20th Manchesters' reserve-company. The position was restored. The following day, the 16 May, the 20th and 21st Manchesters were relieved from duty at Bullecourt, able to say that the village was still safely in British hands. They left this area of utter desolation with the rest of the 7th Division's tired and exhausted units. Bullecourt cost the 7th Division 128 officer casualties and a further 2,554 amongst its men, 879 being recorded as killed or missing.

## Ypres

By 1917 one name had became virtually synonymous with the futility and catastrophe of the Great War: Ypres. At some point in almost every unit's history there was an occasion when they passed through the terrible Salient. It caused only heartache to the men unfortunate enough to be there. And within the many battles, small and large, which were fought out around the city of Ypres, in four years of stalemate, none grew to have a more oppressive and sinister ring to

*A group of NCOs, drawn from many regiments, at a Sergeant's weapons instruction course held at Strensall Camp in the July of 1917. In the centre of the back row is Tom Andrews, 6946 of the 16th Battalion, who had by this time recovered from the serious back wound which he received during the fighting at Trones Wood in July 1916.* Capper

the British public's ear than that of Passchendaele. It was the late summer and autumn of 1917.

By the middle of June the Manchester Service Battalions, raised as Pals but now with just a handful of original members, arrived in the Ypres area. On 14 June the 16th, 17th and 18th Manchesters were at Hooge, near the Menin road, later moving to Zillebeke Bund by the end of the month. Behind them, but soon to share a tour in the lines, were the 19th Manchesters. The period in the Hooge trenches was a difficult one with many casualties from rifle grenades, sniping and gas poisoning. Later, throughout July, the men were trained and equipped for the opening phase of the Third Battle of Ypres. This was due to start on the 31 July and, it was hoped, would exploit the successes gained on the Messines Ridge on 7 June[12] by pushing eastwards across the Passchendaele Ridge, through the Germans supply positions and on towards the north Belgian coastline.

The attack was to be undertaken by five Corps, each of four divisions, with two in the assault and two in reserve. From north to south the Corps were the XIV, XVIII, XIX and the II as part of Gough's Fifth Army, with X Corps as part of Plumer's Second Army to their south. The 30th Division were part of II Corps, commanded by Lieutenant-General Sir Claude Jacob. The other divisions under Jacob's command were the 8th, 18th and 25th. The

*The shock of seeing the once prosperous city, reduced to mere rubble, would always stay in the minds of men who survived the terrors of 'the Salient'*

attack of II Corps was towards Polygon Wood, the 30th Division aiming to fight their way through Sanctuary Wood across the Ypres-Menin road and on past second objectives in Glencorse Wood, Inverness Copse and Dumbarton Wood to their final objective in Polygon Wood. These devastated woodlands, full of shattered tree stumps, debris and broken ground, on the approaches to the Gheluvelt plateau were immensely well sited for defence, and the 30th Division was known to have a hard task to carry out. All four of the Manchester Service Battalions raised as part of the city's First Brigade would attack together this day. On a line running north-south through Sanctuary Wood, 90 Brigade were to the north with the 21st Brigade to the south. South of the 30th Division's men was the 24th Division, whilst to the north of the 30th Division the attack would be made by men of the 8th Division.

### The 30th Division's attack on 31 July, 1917

During the few days prior to his battalion's attack Wilfrith Elstob had organized a reconnaissance in strength behind the German outposts. On the night of 27/28 July, Elstob personally took charge of that reconnaissance and penetrated as far as the German support positions. On the party's return to Stanley Trench, without having suffered any casualties during their penetration into the German trenches opposite, the officers and men were lucky to survive a heavy German shelling. However, their fore knowledge of the likely fall of shot of the German SOS barrage gained by this experience meant that the 16th Manchester's assembly positions on the morning of the attack were designated as only fifty yards from the German front lines in Sanctuary Wood. On the right of the 16th Manchesters would be one of their sister battalions, the 18th, whilst on the left of the 16th in the attack were to be the 1st Worcesters. The 18th Battalion had been just as thoroughly prepared as the 16th, and their reconnaissance had been undertaken during daylight on the 26 July when they had raided the German lines known as Jam Trench, from J.24.b.9.8 to J.19.a.2.4, south west of Stirling Castle. Although this raid cost the battalion thirteen casualties, including three men killed, they obtained useful information about the German positions and an identification of the units opposing them.

Late on the night of 30 July the assault battalions were moved into position. Unfortunately, as the men assembled, no contact with the Worcesters, who were code named as ARTFUL for the purposes of this attack, was able to be made. As the silent gathering was completed the weather was chill and misty, perhaps fortunately so in that the men's advanced position was

Private Norman Bamford, 203018, 18th Manchesters. One of the many hundreds of men drafted into the Manchester Pals units to replace casualties incurred on the Somme and at Arras. Like his predecessors in the Pals battalions, Norman Bamford had received an elementary training at Heaton Park. After serving with the 18th Manchesters he was later transferred to the 4th Loyal North Lancs, with whom he was awarded the M.M. Bamford

*Right: The area between Sanctuary Wood and Polygone de Zonnebeke which was to be the location of the Manchesters' attacks on the first day of the Passchendaele offensive on 31 July 1917.*

*One of the Manchester's battalions after a tour in the Ypres Salient. The farmland west of Ypres was a depressing and flat plain on which the men's billets were never beyond the constant rumble of shellfire and the noise of preparation for the forthcoming offensive.* Taylor

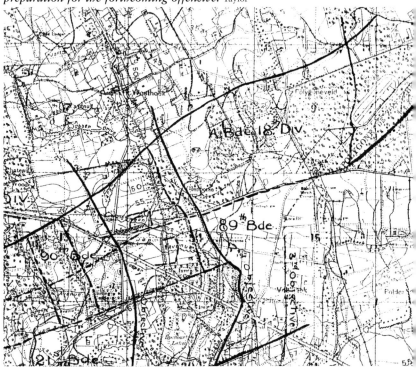

not discovered by the German observers in Sanctuary Wood. Later, as the hours progressed through the coming day, the overhanging clouds gave vent to rain which, by the evening, turned into a persistent and heavy deluge which lasted for three full days. This combination of unseasonably wet weather, saturated ground, broken drainage and incessant shellfire would soon give the already featureless landscape an air of terrible unreality.

At 3.50 am, when their attack was made, the men of the 90th Brigade moved forward confidently, behind an immensely powerful barrage. The pace had been set at twenty-five yards each minute. No hostile barrage was opened, and the first half dozen of the 16th Manchesters' casualties were incurred as their initial wave advanced too quickly into its own protective barrage. The 18th Manchester's first objective was Stirling Castle[13] at J.13.d.5.3,

*2nd Lieutenant Benson Waldron, 19th Manchesters, Killed in Action on 31 July, 1917. Benson Waldron had enlisted as a private soldier into the 1st City Battalion in 1914 and had been wounded at Montauban on lst July 1916. After convalescence he trained as an officer and was commissioned into the l9th Manchesters. He was shot dead by a sniper whilst leading men forward on the opening day of Third Ypres. The letter to his father from Lieutenant Colonel Macdonald, written on 6 August 1917, was both sincere and typical of the many which were sent during the coming months from the Ypres trenches. '...He was preparing to advance further and was climbing out of the trench to give his men a lead when he was hit by a bullet through the heart and killed instantaneously. I was beside him at the time and saw him fall. He was so good a soldier that I know this is just how he would have chosen to die, but he will be a great loss to the regiment. Your son was one of the best officers I had. His men were devoted to him and would have followed him anywhere. If you were proud of your son before you may be ten times prouder of him now. His death must be a terrible blow to you but there is consolation in the thought that if he had lived to old age he could have done nothing finer than he did on 31 July.'* Westerman

now reduced by artillery fire to a mere mound, whose wire and machine gun posts rose bleakly amid a sea of shattered earth and already sodden shellholes. The trenches of Jackdaw Support were quickly overrun, the 16th and 18th Battalions each taking about fifteen prisoners. The 16th's immediate objectives were just between Clapham Junction at J.13.d.9.9, and a position just north of Surbiton Villas at J.13.b.4.5, and involved crossing the Ypres-Menin road in the direction of Glencorse Wood. However, because almost no-one had a reliable idea of direction, or where they were, the fighting degenerated into small individual actions, many of the German troops in their outposts being cut off from their unit's support positions. A Company of the 16th Manchesters got into their initial objectives in Jackdaw Support trench, at J.13.c.5.5, within twenty five minutes, encountering practically no opposition. A number of B Company's men, disorientated in the confusion and smoke, fought their way forward and south into the ruined stables of Stirling Castle. C Company arrived at Clapham Junction on the heels of the barrage which had badly damaged the whole area. Over forty prisoners were taken here, together with large numbers of machine guns and trench mortars found amongst the dugouts which abounded. However, the whole scene at Clapham Junction was quickly becoming one of great confusion and inertia. Within ninety minutes of the attack starting men of eight different battalions were engaged in crossing the Ypres-Menin road at this point,[14] and many casualties were being incurred from machine guns located on the higher ground towards Glencorse Wood. After clearing the dugouts just north of the bend, in the ruins of Surbiton Villas, the 16th Manchesters established a strong point there, at J.13.b.2.4, to command the ground lying around Surbiton Villas and up towards Clapham Junction. In this context some of the men detailed to mop up the German lines had extraordinary success, the most remarkable being Private 37552 Pigott, a veteran of the Boer War and Mons but now serving with the 18th Manchesters. Single handedly he was responsible for capturing and bringing in nineteen Germans, including two NCOs, a feat of arms for which he was awarded the DCM. This attack by the 16th and 18th Manchesters was quickly supported by the 17th Battalion, whose men were leapfrogged through the positions gained by the 16th Manchesters in an attempt to continue the attack's momentum. However, it proved impossible to gain or make any real progress towards the second objectives because of very heavy machine gun fire and the men were forced to dig in, in front of the German positions known as Jargon Trench which protected the perimeter of Glencorse Wood.

From 5.00 am onwards an intense German barrage began to fall over the whole of the Sanctuary Wood area, making communication by telephone lines in front of Brigade headquarters impossible. In addition a number of low flying German aircraft were firing at artillery positions and any concentrations of troops seen moving above ground. The position of the Manchesters here in front of Glencorse Wood and Inverness Copse was indeed desperate, but no knowledge of their circumstances was known at Divisional or Corps Headquarters until much later in the day as runners began to get through.

The start to the 19th Manchester's attack, in support of 21 Brigade's assault, was marred by the severity of the German SOS barrage which delayed the men's exit from their assembly dug-outs, A and B Companies being located in Crab Crawl Tunnel and C and D Companies in Maple Copse, at I.23.b.d. The chaos as the wounded thronged the tunnel entrances meant that A and B Companies' attack was decimated by lack of cohesion and heavy casualties. Troops exiting this tunnel were only able to leave in ones and twos, making a coherent assembly almost impossible in view of the heavy barrage on the British front line positions. Half the company officers from A and B were lost even before the front line positions were reached. C and D Companies fared little better, being badly shot up by an accurate bombardment as they moved along the Observatory Ridge Road, at I.24.c. C Company was the only remaining organized body of men. By the time these remaining men of the 19th Manchesters were in a position to support the assault battalions of 21 Brigade's attack, the western approaches to Dumbarton Wood were swept by German machine gun fire and the momentum of the assault was lost, even though a number of tanks arrived at the scene between 6.30 am and 7.30 am. Consolidation was immediately embarked upon. The men began to adapt any cover amongst the shell holes and ditches surrounding the wreckage of the Jam Lane communication trenches, located at J.19. central, alongside another group who had penetrated to a strong-point on Jasper Drive, just south of Stirling Castle.

Although these attacks had been honestly and honourably pursued in the face of a determined defence by the German Fourth Army, the abiding memory retained by the Manchester men who were there was created by the weather. By mid-day on the 31 July the latticework of shellholes had begun to fill with mud and rainwater. Drowning was now a serious threat to those badly wounded who could not move themselves to safer positions. Progress by units in support of the original assault became virtually impossible and the attack predictably ran out of steam before it was able to establish itself on the higher ground of the Gheluvelt plateau. Now, throughout almost thirty six of the most insufferable hours, the battalions' stretcher bearers laboured to clear the battlefield before the 16th, 17th and 18th Battalions were relieved on the morning of 1st August. The 16th Manchesters casualties were in excess of 260. The 17th's casualties exceeded 180. The 18th Manchesters casualties were in excess of 230. The 19th Manchesters, now literally up to their waists in water and sludge, had to wait until the night of 2/3 August before they were able to march back to Chateau Segard. They had suffered fifteen officer casualties, three of whom were killed, and 283 casualties amongst the battalion's other ranks. Almost 1,000 officers and men from the first four of Manchester's Pals battalions had been lost. In the 30th Division as a whole there were over 3,500 casualties between 31 July and the Division's withdrawal from the Hooge area on 3 August. The combined casualties of the British Second and Fifth Armies for these four days were over 33,000 men and offficers[15]. The German Fourth Army, who were opposed, suffered casualties in the region of 40,000 men during this period. It was no wonder that the Third battle of Ypres would be so indelibly imprinted upon the minds of so many families, both in the Manchester area and elsewhere. And this was just the opening hours. The fight which was destined to culminate on the slopes in front of Passchendaele village would go on for more than three months.[16]

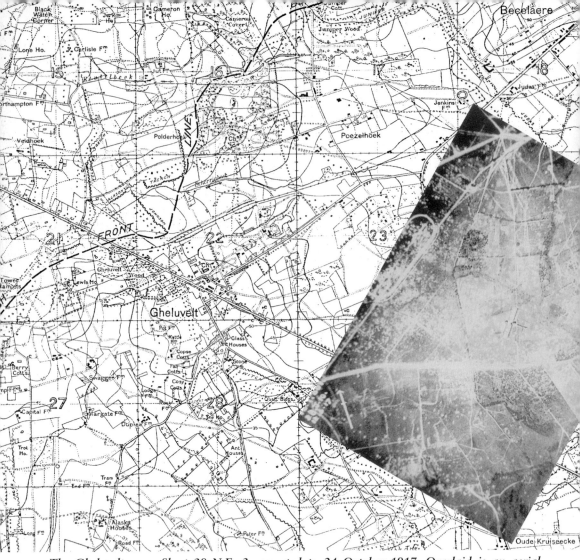

*The Gheluvelt area, Sheet 28 N.E. 3 corrected to 24 October 1917. Overlaid is an aerial photograph, dated 12 June 1917, showing the same location before the majority of the destruction wrought by artillery fire was effected.* Taylor

### The 7th Division at Gheluvelt

For the Manchesters in the 30th Division, the first hours of August marked the end of their active involvement in the Third Battle of Ypres. But for the 7th Division, the continuing fighting would involve them in a protracted and costly engagement. They arrived at the end of September to take over positions in Polygon Wood, in the region of which two months of fighting had advanced the line roughly two miles from the starting positions of 31 July. For a few members of the 7th Division this location might have brought back memories of their actions here during First Ypres. For the majority, though, it simply brought to life the rumours of horror within the Ypres Salient. In many places the land surface was devoid of vegetation and the earth had subsided into an almost impenetrable, featureless wasteland of saturated filth and debris, above which a few cracked and withered splines of timber marked where woodlands had once stood. Since July the shelling and counter shelling had reduced the whole

*Somewhere to the East of Ypres the forlorn view from a watery bunker is punctured by the explosion of yet another artillery round. Already the destruction of the drainage system has raised the water table to just below the surface within days of the offensive's start to the battlefield was reduced to a quagmire. This picture dates from late September during the battle of Polygon Wood.* MRA

*Even before the onset of winter conditions inside any trench or sap had become impossible.* MRA

area to one only passable by duckboard tracks. However, each pathway was known and registered by German aircraft and was capable of being straddled by artillery at any time. Movement in the daylight hours was to invite disaster. To fall at night was to risk drowning in the stagnant pools of mud and filth. The stink of putrid flesh was everywhere.

On the 1 October 1917 the 20th Manchesters were given their baptism of fire in the Salient. They were holding lines at the eastern end of Polygon Wood in Jubilee Trench, alongside the 1st RWFs to their south in Jetty Trench. The positions were roughly 1,000 yards west of Noordemdhoek. At 5.00 am an enormously heavy German barrage was rained onto these locations, the precursor to a series of attacks by the Germans still seeking to regain

*This photograph of the Butt in Polygon Wood was taken on 11 October 1917. It was a position well known to Manchester's battalions in the 7th Division, a number of battalion HQ's being dug into the reverse slopes. Today, the bodies of two Manchester battalion commanders are buried in the magnificent cemetery which was constructed below the Butt. (Lt. Col. D R Turnbull. Kia 1 October 1917 and Major C Kemp DOW 9 October 1917).*

ground lost here during the Battle of Polygon Wood on 26 September when a magnificent attack by the 5th Australian Division had pushed the Germans back eastwards through the wood. The German bombardment ran along a 1,500 yard frontage from the Reutelbeek to Polygon Wood and covered a thousand yard depth back to the British reserve positions. At 5.30 large numbers of German soldiers belonging to 45th Reserve Division and the 210th R.I.R. appeared, their greatest strength concentrated against the RWFs and 20th Manchesters in Polygon Wood. The successful defence mounted by these two battalions was the result of a typically solid and well rehearsed pattern of skills, with just a touch of good fortune. There was effective defensive artillery, which responded on four further occasions throughout the day to the rockets launched from the front lines, signalling the need for aid, disciplined rifle fire from soldiers on the very limits of personal endurance and, fortuitously, the foul mud which so slowed the assembly of every wave of attackers and softened the impact of every incoming shell's explosion. At 7.15 am the 20th Manchesters lost their commanding officer, Lieutenant-Colonel D R Turnbull, who was shot dead by a sniper whilst in the front line trenches encouraging his men. His immediate temporary replacement in command was Captain J S Gemmell. Throughout the day more casualties were incurred by the men of the 2nd Royal Warwickshires as they attempted to bring replacement small arms ammunition up through the persistent German barrage falling behind the Manchesters. By the day's end the line had been successfully held but at a cost of more than 100 casualties in both the 20th Manchesters and the RWFs.

Within four days the 7th Division were due to take part in a massive attack along the higher ground running from just south of Polygon Wood, north past Zonnebeke and Poelcappelle to the Ypres-Staden railway. This would be the Battle of Broodseinde and, in the 7th Division's sector, it forestalled a planned German attack which was already massing soldiers in readiness for an assault on the morning of 4 October. The expectation of the British attack was that it would press the Germans back from their positions overlooking the east of Ypres. The 7th Division were fortunate to have the 1st Australian Division on their left, whilst the 21st Division were expected to attack on their right. In all, twelve divisions would attack this morning. The artillery preparations were meticulous and ponderous. A huge bombardment would be launched as the attack got underway. The advance would be screened by a creeping barrage moving slowly forward to a red line just short of the Broodseinde-Becelaere road. A halt and further bombardment before the final push forward to the blue line 600 yards beyond, which would give control over the dominant observation positions around Reutel and In der Ster Cabaret. The artillery plan had recognized the need for a slow moving barrage to protect the infantry's move across the shattered land, but on top of an already brutalized landscape more shelling would create even greater desolation and difficulties underfoot. In preparation for this attack the men of the 21st and 22nd Manchesters sheltered in the filthy dug-outs on the railway embankments west of Zillebeke, during the evening of 2 October. Late on the evening of the following day the men were taken up in darkness to assemble within Polygon Wood astride the Polygonebeek, just east of the Racecourse. They were in position by 2.30 am.

As the attack got underway at 6.00 am the initial advance of 91 Brigade towards Red Line first objectives was undertaken successfully by the 1st South Staffordshires, and the 22nd Manchesters advanced to a position 400 yards in advance of the South Staffordshires' forming up tapes. The rain which had begun to fall did nothing to slow their advance and large numbers of Germans were taken prisoner, others streaming away in retreat to the east. Meanwhile the men of the 22nd Manchesters awaited their orders to advance behind the shelter of a further ninety minutes of barrage, which searched the area beyond the red line. At 8.10 their advance towards the blue line re-started, but it was immediately clear that things were now going to prove much harder. Although German dead, belonging to the three divisions who had been massing here, were thickly strewn around the whole area, the defence now stood firm[17] and it was clear that the attack by the 21st Division on the Manchester's right had not developed as expected. Advancing towards In der Ster Cabaret, the 22nd Manchesters were caught in enfilade by machine gun fire from Joiner's Rest. At 9.30 am D Company of the 21st Manchesters were sent forward to support the attack. During the early afternoon, about 2.00 pm, C Company of the 21st Manchesters was also sent up to help make these positions secure. A defensive flank to the right was thrown back to link with the men of the 21st Division, whose progress had been less rapid and the process of consolidation was begun.[18] It was cold and only a bare minimum of shelter could be scraped before meeting the welling water which oozed upwards within the saturated and broken soil. The only consolation was that the land gained was held, and the wounded this time had the chance to be pulled out and taken back to hospital before the onset of gangrene. The men of 20th Manchesters who were now brought up to effect the consolidation had a hard time. A week earlier they had lost the commanding officer, killed. Now, on the way up towards Noordewdhoek past Hooge, Lieutenant-Colonel Turnbull's replacement was himself struck by a shell splinter and forced to leave his new charges. The following day Major Charles Kemp DSO of the 21st Manchesters arrived to take command, but, tragically, the following day Kemp himself was mortally wounded. Within hours Major Healing, who had been Lieutenant-Colonel Turnbull's first permanent replacement, was drafted back in to take command. In the space of just ten days the 20th Manchesters had experienced four changes of

*Acting Captain Brian Conway, 22nd Manchesters. Killed in action on 4 October 1917 during the attacks towards In der Ster Cabaret. His service during the Great war encompassed a number of different units. He had enlisted into the RAMC as a private soldier, previously having received two years training as a medical student. He went to France in 1915 as a Sergeant Major. Later that year he was commissioned into the Durham Light Infantry and was later transferred into the 22nd Manchesters.*

*This photograph shows lightly wounded men at a dressing station in a ruined farm near to Wieltje on the Broodseinde Road. The photograph was taken 5 October 1917 whilst the 20th, 21st and 22nd Manchesters were engaged at Polygon Wood.*

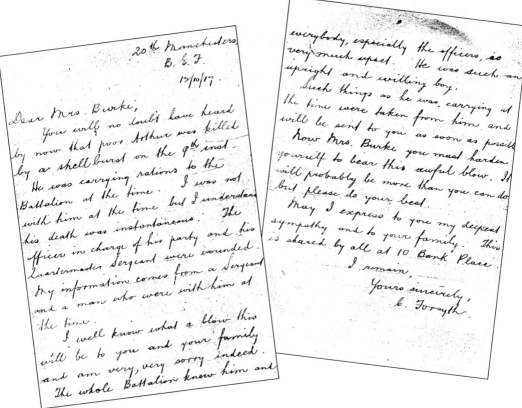

The letter of condolence written to Private Pat Burke's mother by one of her son's Pals and comrades, C. Forsyth. Pat Burke had been an original Pal and had survived unscathed since the days when his battalion had first appeared on the Somme almost two years before his death. His Company Commander wrote of him, 'In the line he showed that spirit which made him popular amongst the men – of cheerfulness which is so helpful when things look bleak. He was a real worker and as brave as any man I had known. He was always to be relied on for his thoroughness and in all his duties, so conscientious. His loss was a real one to me and the whole company regretted it. He died in the front line and is buried with his comrades.' Letter from Captain Frank Nicholl, dated 16 November 1917. I.W.M.

command and the deaths of two of their commanding officers. During this period the battalion suffered eight officer casualties and, among the other ranks, 55 killed, 185 wounded and 30 missing. One of those killed was Pat Burke, who had been one of the most prolific of letter writers within the ranks of the 20th Battalion. The casualties amongst the 21st Manchesters had been four officers killed and ten wounded; amongst the other ranks 35 men were killed, 148 wounded and 19 missing. In the 22nd Battalion the figures were worse still, two officers killed and seven wounded together with 279 other ranks killed, wounded or missing. The 22nd Battalion was relieved from these positions on 7 October.

On a more positive note, the positions won here enabled the British Army to overlook the Flemish lowlands in the direction of Dadizeele. This secure position was not, however, matched further north where the Battle for Passchendaele would continue for some time into November. These attacks towards Noordemdhoek and Reutel therefore did not mark the end of the Manchesters involvement in the fighting on the Gheluvelt plateau. However, the 7th Division were now given a period of rest and recuperation west of Ypres where they received drafts and were reorganized and issued with fresh clothing and equipment. However, the replacements were insufficient in number to close the gaps in the ranks or amongst the

*The problems of supplying the troops with food and munitions were immense. By October, and the 7th Division's attacks at Gheluvelt, the Menin Road had become a cratered wasteland over which it was difficult to move horsedrawn vehicles. As the front lines were approached everything had to be carried by hand across the duckboards which skirted the water filled shellholes. The reality was that no continuous line of trenches existed, the men simply scraping a shallow ditch between any suitable line of craters. The photograph above shows the village of Gheluvelt some days after the fighting had passed through to positions further east.*

officers. A number of the new men were now ex-labour corps, reclassified following the reduction in the stringency of medical rules governing the fitness of combat soldiers.

Having been out of the line for some ten days, the men's return to the Gheluvelt area shocked all but the most battle hardened. Morale was at a low point. The mud of autumn was now indescribably thick and cloying on the approach tracks. The front line trenches were merely shell holes, at best connected by shallow ditches, which offered no protection from the elements at all, and little from enemy shelling. Only the glutinous mud cushioned and limited the impact of each incoming shell's explosion. On October 26th the smear on the mudscape which had once been the village of Gheluvelt would become the focus of attacks by the 7th Division in what were planned as diversionary attacks on the right flank of the Second Army's front. As soon as the plans and orders were issued to him Major General Shoubridge had felt that the event was suicidal and stood little or no chance of success. His private concern was of course of no importance, and this late October day would therefore see the third attempt by 7th Division men on Gheluvelt. The attack by 90 Brigade would employ the 21st Manchesters in the centre of its attack towards Berry Cottage, at J.27.a., and Swagger Farrn, at J.27.b. In support were the 22nd Manchesters with the 20th Manchesters placed as further support behind them. Again the artillery had, somehow, been dragged forward to provide a barrage. The weight of shell would be impressive. 144 18-pounders, 48 4.5″ howitzers, 32

*Everywhere east of Ypres on the slopes below Passchendaele the signs of intense fighting abounded. Between 31 July and 12 November the British and Empire troops suffered over 244,000 casualties, the German Army lost 'about 400,000'. The Highlanders whose bodies are pictured here did not belong to the units referred to within the text, they were in fact killed during the storming of Zonnebeke on 20 September.*

medium and 20 heavy howitzers. The barrage would be established 150 yards in advance of the forming up lines, the division's front line of shell holes being just in advance of the forming up positions. After the first four minutes of barrage the artillery would lift forwards 100 yards, then a further 100 yards after six more minutes, followed by two more lifts of 100 yards now at eight minute intervals and finally, twelve minutes later, another lift of 100 yards. Thus forty-five minutes after zero the troops were expected to be in Gheluvelt and ready for the second phase advance past the village! The actuality of this attack was incredibly different.

The whole event was a grotesque tragedy which spoke eloquently about the futility of war.

Even before the attack started, casualties were being incurred through shelling and snipers as the 21st Manchesters assembled between Ambrose Farm, at J.21.c.0.1., and Tower Hamlets, at J.21.c.0.6. Many of the men's feelings were now cynical towards the whole idea of further attacks in conditions which were almost certain to cause failure. Rifles and Lewis Guns were so caked with mud that they were already incapable of being fired, even before the advance began! Just southwest of Gheluvelt the valley of the Kroomebeek was awash with a huge depth of slime. The only dry ground which was available, next to the Menin Road, was swept by machine guns located in pillboxes just in front of the village, within Gheluvelt Wood. At the first glimpse of light at 5.40 am the attack started. On the right of the Manchesters some progress was made by the 1st South Staffordshire's men. Elsewhere the Kroomebeek's mud and the open field of fire afforded to the German machine gunners meant that the attacking troops quickly lost the protection of their barrage. A Company on the left of the 21st Manchesters' attack had barely managed to make their own front line positions before machine gun fire from the pill boxes at Lewis House, in front of Gheluvelt Wood, caused the attack to falter at 6.02 am. Three minutes later B Company on the right came under exceedingly heavy machine gun fire from Berry Cottages, and were amazed to see a group of seventy or eighty Gordon Highlanders passing across their front utterly lost in the confusion of battle. The 21st Battalions Diary reported that,

> There is every reason to believe that officers and men of A and B Companies were able by chance to continue the advance after zero plus 22 and zero plus 30 although the barrage was lost — nothing is known of their fate and no trace could subsequently be found of them although they are reported to have gone on.[19]

C Company's advance continued for thirty five minutes until the force was reduced to just four men who together scraped shelter just south of Lewis House. For a period of time small bands of soldiers north of the Menin road fought their way into the village, but the cloying mud meant their weapons were choked and useless and they also were forced to fall back as supplies of grenades dwindled. Before long all the positions in front of the initial attack, including some actually taken by the South Staffs, were being shelled by 7th Division's own artillery in an attempt to prevent any German counter attacks from building. What had been a gallant attempt to achieve the impossible was abandoned. Two and a half hours after the attack had started all the available men of the 21st Manchesters, the 2nd Queen's, 1st South Staffordshires, 2nd Gordon Highlanders and the 2nd Borders were organized under Lieutenant Buckley and Company Sergeant Major Lucy in the original line of posts from which the attack had begun.

*Private William Williamson, 38069, of the 22nd Manchesters, killed in action at Gheluvelt on 26 October 1917.* Stainton

The chances of pulling casualties from the quagmire were nil. Many men who were wounded and presumed missing simply sank. The whole diversionary assault by 7th Division had made no progress whatsoever, although it had served a purpose in holding a number of German reserves in the area, preventing their moving north to reinforce the defences where the main attack was being driven home. The 7th Division's total casualties this day were 110 officers and 2,614 men. In the 21st Manchesters the figures were seven officers killed, five wounded and one missing. Amongst the men twenty seven were killed, 173 wounded and 92 missing (almost all of whom were in fact killed or died later in No Man's Land).[20]

### The 23rd Battalion's attack at Houthulst Forest, 22 October 1917

The 23rd Battalion of the Manchester Regiment, the 8th City Battalion, had been established in 1914 as a bantam unit. It had been placed within 104 Brigade of the 35th Division. All the other three units within this brigade had also been established as bantam battalions, when raised in late 1914 and early 1915. The other battalions were all Lancashire Fusiliers; the 17th and 18th who were raised in the Bury area and the 20th Battalion, the 4th Salford Pals. Prior to the 35th Division's move up to the Flanders front, the battalions had been

*The operations map used by the 23rd Manchesters during the battalion's attacks south of Houthulst Forest on 22 October 1917.*

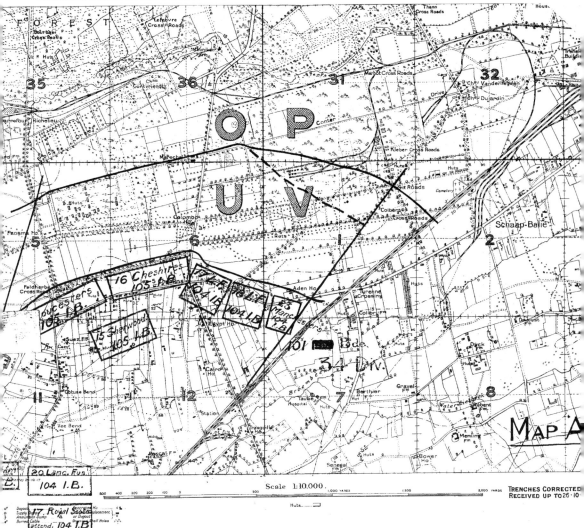

*The approaches to Houthulst Forest were almost impassable to the bantams of the 35th Division. The attack proved to be a disaster and marked the end of almost all the units originally established as bantams, in 1914-15.*

numerically strengthened by the arrival of many drafts of men, who had been combed out of other units with little infantry training. Their destination was Houthulst Forest. Before the war the surrounding countryside had been a maze of tidy hedgerows, tracks and small holdings. The area was dotted with hamlets and farm buildings whose owners had been preoccupied with the agricultural and commercial prospects of their small plots of fertile and heavy soil. As an area of slightly elevated land the whole position had now taken on a significance far in excess of its pre-war anonymity.

Here in front of Houthulst Forest, north of the Ypres Salient, the 35th Division was under the command of the Fifth Army's XIV Corps. The plan which Fifth Army had settled upon involved an attack whose tactical purpose was to strengthen the left flank of the main battle front's attacks on Passchendaele. On the right of XIV Corps would be XVIII Corps, whilst on the left would be the First French Corps. The preliminary attack of the 35th Division, timed for 5.45 am, would take place across a fan shaped front northwards into Houthulst Forest. This would be followed by a subsequent attack in a north easterly direction towards Schaap-Balie. The first part of this would be undertaken by 104 Brigade on the right, with 105 Brigade on its left. Within 104 Brigade, the 23rd Manchester's objectives were the Six Roads junction, one thousand yards west of Schaap-Balie, at V.1.b.7.7, to a position some two hundred yards west. These two Brigades moved into their battle positions on the night of 20/21st October, relieving 106 Brigade. The frontage for 104 Brigade ran from Aden House, where the 23rd Manchesters were in the forward positions, to the Columbo House – Marechal Farm road.

Opposing them were men of the German 26th Reserve, 58th and the 40th Divisions. There were no organized trench systems. Instead a random pattern of watery shell holes provided the minimum of cover to men in the most forward positions, around which the wreckage of scattered farm buildings attracted the desperate or unwary. The backdrop was an almost indistinguishable pattern of tracks, ditches and coppices which had once formed a tranquil rural scene but which was now constantly riven by machine gun fire and terrible bursts of high explosive. Some hundreds of yards to the rear a series of pockmarked pillboxes, shell-proof blockhouses and signalling stations provided some cover to battalion headquarters, signallers and forward dressing station staff. They were utterly stripped of any pretence at camouflage and stood starkly above the expanse of dark and watery waste.

One man's moving account of his experience here with the 23rd Manchesters is particularly graphic. He was Private G Barker, a Derby Scheme recruit who had only joined the battalion in early 1917.[21] Still forty-eight hours before the attack was due and having lain out all the previous night in support, terrified, in the sulpherous stink of a water filled shell hole he was ordered up to a more forward position.

*An officer emerges from a pill-box, and with a whisper tells us to make for the distant ruins of a farm. Panting with nervous fear we each make for it, and our steps are shaky as we proceed. I try to run but my limbs are like lead. Plonk-za! – a near shave that time. Some of us manage it, others get hit and join their unfortunate companions in death. Wounded men must make for safety as best they can until stretcher bearers can get to them.* Private G Barker, 23rd Manchesters

Throughout that night the men sheltered in the farm's crumpled brickwork. The following morning Private Barker's rations were gone, eaten by the rats which infested the whole place.

*All at once I hear and see a German aeroplane coming, and one of the lads foolishly goes and exposes himself by standing near the open door. Suddenly the machine turns tail, proving to me that our hiding place has been discovered. We haven't long to wait before Jerry tries to annihilate us with a terrific bombardment. Shells are bursting all around us every few seconds. One comes near me and a fragment hits me like a kick from a horse at the top of my thigh. I am paralysed for the moment and feel I am burning, and in looking down I find my trousers cut and a terrible gash in my flesh. I can see my leg hanging by a sinew with layers of fat and lean showing like the remains of a bullock that has just been killed; then blood flows profusely.* Private G Barker, 23rd Manchesters

Fortunately he is with friends who bandage and staunch the flow. For twenty four hours Private Barker struggled back amongst the mud, the corpses and the sounds of shelling, sometimes being carried on the backs of stretcher bearers who found handling their stretchers an impossibility in the depth of mud and cratered ground. Before his arrival at a Casualty Clearing Station he had been twice dumped into the foul ground and oily water as his bearers slipped and struggled for many hours to save him.

During this fraught build up

*Right: Drummer James Adams, photographed with the bugle which he carried throughout the war in his capacity as a bandsman. In this role his duties also included that of stretcher bearer during any engagement with the enemy. He served throughout the war and was present in the terrible circumstances of the actions at Houthulst Forest.* Horsfield

to the attack any communication from the front to rear had been exceptionally difficult, being confined to just two duckboard tracks which ended on the line between Vee Bend and Louvois Farm, at U.11.a to U.11.d. For the most part each unit's preliminary reconnaissances had been carried out by battalion commanders, since daylight movement by large bodies of troops was impossible. Forming up was done on a taped line laid by the engineers. Although the officers had a good idea of direction the men were ill informed. The columns assembled soon after dark on the night of 21/22 October with virtually no casualties and waited throughout a terribly cold night, during which heavy rain began to fall in the early hours. The men could not have been filthier or more saturated. As zero approached the 23rd Manchesters pushed out patrols with the intention of making contact with the 16th Royal Scots of 101 Brigade, 34th Division, who were supposed to be there on the Manchester's right flank. Unfortunately no such contact was made until after the attack began, when it proved all but impossible to stay in touch. On the left of the 23rd Manchesters were the 17th Lancashire Fusiliers, and both units here were in close contact with each other and the 18th Lancashire Fusiliers who were in immediate close support.

When the attack started at 5.45 am the 35th Division's artillery barrage moved forward at a rate of 100 yards every eight minutes. German aeroplanes were again immediately active, and harassed the troops with low flying swoops to machine gun the lines of men struggling forward. A gap formed almost immediately on the right flank of the 23rd Manchester's advance. Nevertheless, the first 400 yards were covered with few casualties. Soon after cresting a small rise, just north of V.1. central, the 23rd's men were engaged in hard fighting on the right of their progress, roughly 600 yards from their start lines, at V.1.b.2.2. Some small groups of men then battled forward to their final objectives, where they unfortunately became separated and were either killed or taken prisoner. The 18th Lancashire Fusiliers' attack was made as close support for the 17th Lancashire Fusiliers and 23rd Manchesters; it immediately lost direction and moved rather too far to their left. This left the huts, at V.1.a.3.2, on the road in front of the 18th Lancashire Fusiliers and on the left of the 23rd Manchester's attack almost unmolested. Allied to the failure of the 16th Royal Scots on their right, the situation left the 23rd Manchesters very isolated with parties of Germans to their rear who had been missed in the initial mopping up operations. Very soon machine gun fire from the railway and the huts, at V.1.d. where the 16th Royal Scot's attack had failed, took the 23rd Manchesters in their right flank and the rear. Fire from the huts missed by the 18th Lancashire Fusiliers also took the 23rd Manchesters in the left flank and rear and there was also heavy machine gun fire from the direction of Six Roads and Colbert cross roads in front of the 23rd Manchester's attack. Casualties were very heavy amongst the men. All the company officers who were allocated to the attack became casualties, one missing, eight killed and five wounded.

*Officers of the 16th Manchesters, probably photographed during the course of late 1917.* M. Guest

Meanwhile the 17th Lancashire Fusiliers had reached their objectives near Marechal Farm by 6.50 am, but the lines of the 18th Lancashire Fusiliers and surviving elements of the 23rd Manchesters were then swung back to their starting positions towards the right of 104 Brigade's attack. At this point, 8.10 am, the situation was critical and two companies of the 4th Salford Pals were ordered up to stabilize the flank between the 18th Lancashire Fusiliers and Aden House where the 23rd Manchesters had been decimated and pushed back to their start lines.[22] The 23rd Manchesters were just fifty other ranks strong. Later that afternoon some ground gained by the 35th Division was lost to a series of German counter attacks. To the rear the blockhouses and pillboxes, which seemed like a natural point to which casualties should be taken, were soon overcrowded and full. As the numbers of stretcher cases built up outside each concrete island many of these positions were shelled, the carnage and torture proving quite beyond the capabilities of any stretcher bearers to relieve. Dozens of men simply sank or were obliterated by the shells which searched around each pillbox. That night the remnants of the 23rd Manchesters were relieved, by the 4th Salford Pals, and were reformed about the area of Egypt House.

The Manchesters serving in the 7th Division would never return to Ypres. Following the collapse of Italian resistance at Caporetto the British Army dispatched

*On the right is Corporal Tom Andrews, 6946, an original Pal from the 1st City Battalion and brother of Albert, who served in the 4th City Battalion. After recovering from wounds received on the Somme, Tom had been transferred to the 2/5th Lancashire Fusiliers. He was killed in action at Epehy on 20 November, 1917. On the left of the photograph is Private Albert Andrews who survived the war and who would be invalided out of the Army in February 1918, suffering from the nervous debilitation of neurasthenia or shell shock. The two brothers had enlisted into the Manchester Pals on the same day, 7 September, 1914.* Capper

*Private James Redikin, 22016, 23rd Manchesters. Before the war James Redikin had been a spindle maker, for the many cotton spinning mills which dominated the area, living in a catholic family in the Ancoats area of the city. Like all the original bantams Private Redikin was of short stature, just 5'2" tall. The contrast with his seven brothers, photographed outside their home at No 5 Day Street, shows up clearly. For the Manchester bantams Houthulst Forest would be their last severe action as an original unit. The 23rd Battalion was destined to be disbanded in February 1918. Private Redikin was transferred to the 2nd Manchesters, Wilfred Owen's battalion, who had been brigaded with the 1st and 2nd Salford Pals, as part of the 96th Brigade in the 32nd Division. In the final year of the war his service culminated in his being awarded the D.C.M. The citation reads, 'For devotion to duty at all times, often under the most intense fire, particularly in the attack leading up to and the crossing of the Oise-Sambre Canal in early November, 1918.'* Murphy

two divisions immediately to help restore the position. Initially the 23rd and 41st Divisions were sent, quickly followed by the 7th and 48th Divisions, who began their move on 14 November. They were later followed by the 5th Division. These five divisions were a loss which the British Army could ill afford.

During the coming three months decisions were reached which were radically to alter the shape of divisional and brigade organizations. The most notable of these was the decision to reduce the number of battalions in each brigade from four to three. For the Manchesters still serving within the 30th and 35th Divisions this meant the end of the line for a number of battalions. On 11 February 1918 the 17th Manchesters were transferred to 21 Brigade of the 30th Division. The 18th Manchesters were effectively disbanded, as were the 19th Manchesters and the 23rd Manchesters. In many cases the men serving within the disbanded units were sent as drafts to the surviving Manchester battalions. In the case of the 19th's men, half went to the 16th and half to the 17th Battalion. 90 Brigade now consisted of the 2nd Bedfordshires, 2nd Royal Scots Fusiliers and 16th Manchesters. Of the 18th Battalion's men a number were taken on the strength of the 17th Entrenching Battalion with whom they were amalgamated on 19 February at Haut Allaines. The Manchester battalions which had travelled to Italy were unaffected by these changes.

## Notes

1 From the diary written by Private Bill Mathers, 47972, 21st Manchesters.

2 The centre of the 21st Manchester's attack running through the shallow valley under the railway embankment at T.24.d.7.3. and on to the Croisilles – Bullecourt road. See sheet 51B. SW4. Corrected to 2 February 1917.

3 One of the most highly decorated of Manchester's original Pals. Joseph Lucy, 19443, was awarded the Military Medal gazetted on 17 June 1919, the Miltary Cross with Bar gazetted on 26 November 1917 and 6 April 1918, and the Distinguished Conduct Medal gazetted in March 1917. Before the outbreak of war he had completed his service with one the Regiment's two regular battalions. Joseph Lucy continued to serve within the Manchesters after the war.

4 30th Operation Report. P.R.O. ref: WO95/2311.

5 16th Manchesters War Diary. P.R.O. ref: W095/2339.

6 P.R.O. ref: WO95/2311.

7 The 17th Manchester's Battalion War Diary for this specific day identifies the casualties as: 2 Officers KiA, 11

officers wounded in action, 10 OR KiA, 105 OR wounded in action and 168 missing.

8 P.R.O. ref: W095/2329.

9 Although all were accorded a burial along with many other men from the Manchesters, the identifications of three of the company commanders' graves were later lost. Captains Megson, Wilson and 2nd Lieutenant Ingram are therefore commemorated in Bay 7 of the Arras Memorial. Captain Hook's grave is in Wancourt Cemetery, Plot 5, Row E, Grave 9. Nearby are the graves of a number of men killed in the same action including Harry Ogden of whom Elstob speaks in his letter to Hubert Worthington. Wancourt Cemetery was created by the concentration of many small battlefield burials after the end of the war. Today it holds the graves of nearly 1500 soldiers.

10

| | Killed | | Wounded | | Missing | | Total | |
|---|---|---|---|---|---|---|---|---|
| | Officers | Other Ranks | Officers | Other Ranks | Officers | Other Ranks | Officers | Other Ranks |
| 16th Bn. | 4 | 23 | 8 | 81 | - | 62 | 12 | 166 |
| 17th Bn. | 2 | 11 | 11 | 112 | - | 184 | 13 | 307 |
| 18th Bn. | - | 18 | 6 | 189 | 9 | 132 | 15 | 339 |
| 19th Bn. | 3 | 11 | 3 | 58 | - | 22 | 6 | 91 |
| Total | | | | | | | 46 | 903 |

Source: P.R.O. ref: Appendix IV. 30th Division's narrative. The figures compiled by 30th Division's HQ for the ten day period up to 29 April are notably innacurate in that they do not detail, for example, the officers from the 18th Manchesters who were later known to have been killed in their Battalion's attack on 23 April. In fact all the nine identified as missing were killed: 2nd Lieutenants S D Adshead, N B Gill, F A Emington, B A Westphal, S J L Wyatt, H Duncan, J E M Taylor, G H Doughty and S M Shirley. All of the battalion figures for men killed during these actions are an underestimate, caused by the fact that the withdrawal left very men dead, wounded and unnacounted for in No Mans Land when roll call was held later.

11 During the course of these events the command of the 21st Manchesters passed to Major Charles Matthew Kemp on 11 May, during the period of Lieutenant Colonel Norman's promotion, temporarilly, to the command of 91 Brigade. On Brigadier-General Norman's formal farewell to the battalion, on his leaving to take command of the 89 Brigade, on 15 June 1917, it was discovered that there were still 81 members of the original 6th City Pals serving with the battalion. He was succeeded as C.O. of the 21st Manchesters by Lieutenant Colonel Lomax.

12 During these operations the Messines-Wytschaete Ridge, south of Ypres, had witnessed the unprecedented use of vast quantities of explosives which, when detonated from nineteen mines, had terrified the German defences and opened the way for a substantial advance and improvement in the British position. During these actions the Manchesters within the 30th Division had been held in reserve to Plumer's Second Army. It was, in the depressing context of 1917, an extraordinary and brilliantly planned success.

13 The map references relating to the 30th Division's attack on 31 July 1917 refer to Sheet 28NW4 and parts of NE3.

14 As men belonging to 53 and 54 Brigades of the 18th Division were sent up in the vain hope of continuing the attack. The 18th Division's attack was designed to be made after leapfrogging through the positions taken by the 16th Manchesters and then on towards objectives in Polygon Wood. Because of communication difficulties a number of these battalions, in the 53rd Brigade, later continued to press the advance, even though the protective barrage had long since dissappeared over the Gheluvelt plateau. Very little knowledge of these events and the failure to reach beyond the first objectives seems to have been known at either battalion or brigade level. The Brigade Major of 90 Brigade, Captain C W M Norrie, undertook an extraordinary personal reconnaissance which took him through the centre of all the battalions actions this morning, but his reports sent by pigeons commandeered from a F.O.O. in the 18th Division never reached his Brigadier, J H Lloyd. See W095/2337.

15 See Military Operations. France and Belgium. 1917 Vol 11. pp 178.

16 The British Official History, Military Operations. France and Belgium. 1917. Volume II, records the total casualties between 31 July and 12 November as 244, 897. The text concludes by saying that, during the same period, 'There seems every probability that the Germans lost about 400,000.'

17 The 19th Reserve, the area's original garrison, had been reinforced by units of the 45th Reserve and 4th Guards for the purpose of their intended attack.

18 The 21st Manchesters then held from J.6.c.1.2. to J.12.a.1.9. with the 22nd Manchesters to their right up to J.12.a.2.6. and thence along a defensive flank to J.12.a.0.5., facing Judge Copse.

19 PRO ref: WO95/1668.

20 During the October of 1917 the 21st Manchester's casualties amounted to 28 officers and 494 men.

21 His account later appeared in print under the title, Agony's Anguish. (Pub: Alf Eva, Manchester, 1931.)

22 See pp 150-153 of the Salford Pals for a full description of the part played by Captain Swarbrick's men in this, and subsequent actions, at Houthulst Forest. These attacks on 22 October left 173 men of the 23rd Manchesters 'missing'.

## Chapter Eight

# 1918, The Last Year of War

*'I have a rendezvous with Death*
*On some scarred slope of battered hill*
*When Spring comes round again this year*
*And the first meadow flowers appear.'*[1]

The Manchester battalions still remaining in France faced an unattractive prospect in the spring of 1918. For the small band of original Pals this year marked their fourth successive one in military service, far beyond these men's initial expectations. The collapse of Russia, following the Bolshevik Revolution, meant that Germany's armed forces on the Western Front were being steadily reinforced by divisions no longer needed in the east.[2] Pressure from France would soon result in the British lines being extended further south along the Western Front towards St. Quentin and beyond. The necessarily defensive posture of the British Army, therefore, meant that these areas could only be defended using a zonal system, in which the forward positions would be formed by a collection of defended, but lightly held, localities incorporating more heavily defended and manned redoubts. This forward zone was, therefore, itself sub divided into a line of observation, which consisted of widely separated observation posts; the line of resistance which was protected by a single but continuous belt of wire roughly ten yards

*The town of St Quentin in 1917. The cathedral dominated the area, which by 1918, had been reduced to a roofless and silent shadow of its former splendour.* Taylor

deep, and finally a line of redoubts. The gaps between each redoubt were covered by protective artillery fire. Troops holding this forward zone were expected to fight it out at all costs. The purpose of the lines of resistance and the redoubts was to break up and disorganize any major attack before it could reach the Battle Zone positions which were located a mile or more back. The Battle Zone positions were a series of interlocking and strongly defended localities, behind which counter attack troops were available to reinforce positions where any breakthrough, following a major attack, seemed imminent. Some miles to the rear of the Battle Zone it had been intended to create a rear zone or reserve position. This, however, had proved impossible to construct in the time available.

In March 1918 the area opposite the German salient at St. Quentin would be manned by XVIII Corps, under the command of Lieutenant General Sir Ivor Maxse. The 30th

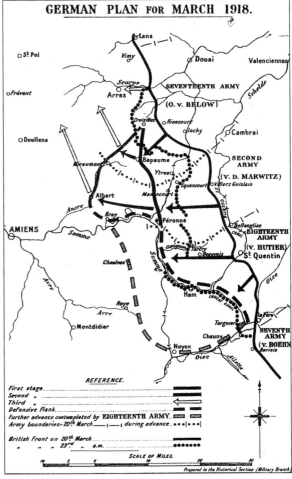

Division arrived here to take over its sector on 23 February. Within 30th Division's area, the 16th Manchesters would establish themselves at an important redoubt known as Manchester Hill.[3] During the coming weeks all of these men had the advantage of digging the trenches which they knew they would have to fight in, as well as constantly rehearsing the attack, defence and counter attack of each position. They each knew their locations and roles intimately. They knew that their post was one of a series of well-sited intermediate position redoubts which ran from the banks of the Somme canal, a mile and a half west of St. Quentin, in a northerly direction.[4] The redoubt on Manchester Hill commanded a magnificent field of fire and overlooked the town of St. Quentin, whose cathedral and roofless suburbs were clearly visible to the east. It was an imposing defensive position, well served by deep dugouts and protected by thick belts of barbed wire. A long spell of dry weather during the first three weeks of March meant that movement was easy.

> *This enabled the Field Artillery to act as mobile guns: horses were kept close up and one section per battery moved about the gun area and came into action daily from different positions.[5]*

A special S.O.S. 'Red Smoke' was kept in Manchester Hill redoubt. Arrangements had been made that, in the event of this particular S.O.S. being sent up, a barrage of all guns, both field and heavy, should search and sweep the area between each redoubt and its lines of resistance before forming a protective box around the redoubt itself. Inside the command dugouts on Manchester Hill a number of notices had been posted,

> *This S.O.S. is not to be used unless the safety of this Redoubt is endangered — misuse of this Signal will be a Court Martial Offence.*

Cables had been buried to a depth of eight feet, from the redoubt to Brigade HQ in the rear, making communication from Wilfrith Elstob and other battalion commanders reasonably secure. Only the thickest of fogs and failure of visibility would make the defence of these positions problematic.

The German plan of action was to employ their numerical strength in a surprise attack which would sweep into the area north of the River Oise towards Amiens. This was their great gamble, a last desperate throw of the dice before the arrival of ever increasing numbers of American soldiers loaded the odds insurmountably against the Germans. The decisions to press this attack were taken before the early spring of 1918 and the arrangements put together with impressive speed. By March the German forces arrayed against the southern end of the British positions consisted of the Seventeenth, Second and Eighteenth Armies. Outside St. Quentin IX Corps would be responsible for attacking towards Beauvois past Manchester Hill. Opposing the British 30th Division were the German 50th and 187th Divisions, whose start lines lay north of the St. Quentin canal. The task of the storm troops who led the assault was to press forward quickly, ignoring what was happening to the right or left and allowing the following battle groups to engage and overcome pockets of resistance. Air power was to be employed in low flying ground attack groups, whose purpose was to attack columns of men, artillery and transport. There was to be no prolonged large scale preliminary bombardment. Instead, in front of St. Quentin, the bombardment would last just five hours the first two of which would be devoted to the systematic gassing of the British artillery batteries. Thereafter, the remaining three hours were devoted to a comprehensive shelling of all the positions in the forward, main battle and counter attack positions. At 9.40 am the infantry attack would commence with a powerful creeping barrage, behind which the storm troops would be expected to be well up,

> *...regardless of shell splinters. A single enemy machine gun which survives the bombardment does more harm than any number of our own shell splinters.*[6]

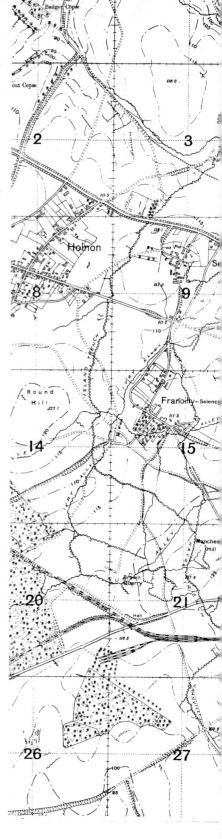

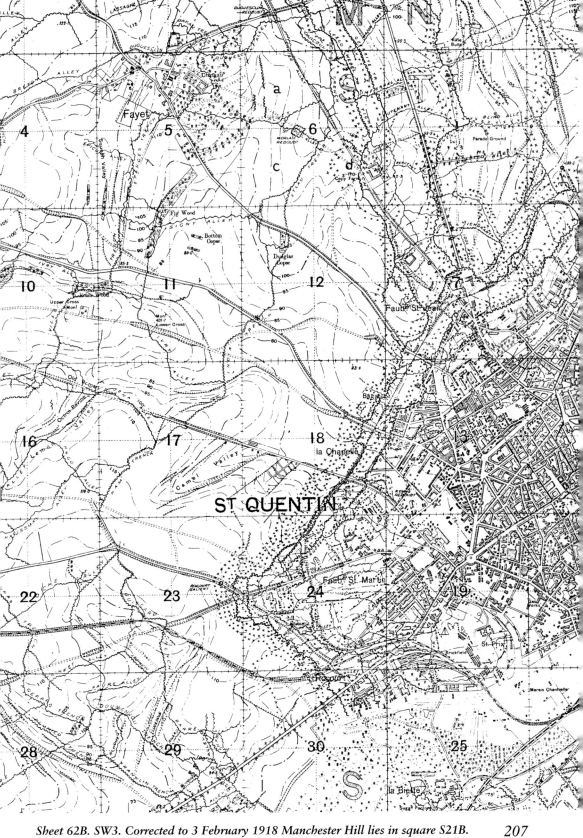

*Sheet 62B. SW3. Corrected to 3 February 1918 Manchester Hill lies in square S21B.*     207

On 18 March the 16th Manchesters relieved the 17th Manchesters in the redoubt and front line positions. Private Charlie Heaton had just returned from leave in England. It had been a lousy leave as he told his companions in the medic's dugout.

> *There's no beer, there's no cigarettes and the bloody women are top price, although I couldn't afford one meself!* Private Charlie Heaton. 16th Manchesters.

The area to be defended was substantial, a width of front line trenches almost 2,000 yards in extent and a depth, back to the rear counter attack platoons, covering almost as great a distance. Before leaving Savy dug outs, Wilfrith Elstob had explained his expectations to the men in great detail. The men were confident, and few were aware that he felt very few of them would survive the inevitable German attack. During their march up from Savy to take position in the redoubt the 16th's platoons were reviewed by the Divisional Commander, Major General W. de L Williams, to whom Elstob remarked that the band would be 'the only fellows that would come out alive.' A Company moved into the right front positions under command of Captain Edward Ashe with B Company on their left under the command of Captain John Guest. The very front line observation trenches on the 16th Manchester's exceptionally broad front consisted of a line from India Trench at S.11.d, past Ham Trench to Guiscard Trench, where it cut the St. Quentin Savy road at S.23.c. The bulk of the strength of A and B Companies were located further back in the line of resistance, running from Upper Cross, at S.10.d.5.7, to Gerard Trench, at S.22.c.9.0. C Company were split into platoons, providing tactical support to the front line companies in their role as counter attack troops. Two platoons of C Company were, therefore, located just south of the redoubt on the other side of the Savy road, whilst two other platoons were located in Francilly-Selency. D Company occupied the redoubt's main defences under the direct command of Lieutenant-Colonel Elstob. Battalion HQ was located in the bunkers within the quarry, although they were expected to move forward to the redoubt itself in the event of an attack. The battalion's strength was 23 officers and 717 men. Four machine guns of 90 Brigade's Machine Gun Company were located at the redoubt commanding the lower valleys either side. To the rear of the redoubt were two 6″ Newton Trench Mortars, in emplacements on the lip of the quarry. Linked by telephone from the Observation Post were two 18 pounder batteries, the 148th and 149th R.F.A positioned in the eastern fringe of Holnon Wood and around Savy, whose guns were to support the infantry manning Manchester Hill.[7] The whole location seemed impressive, although the very large frontage made it a daunting prospect to hold in the face of a determined attack. The surrounding countryside made a pleasant change to eyes tired of the devastation of the Somme, Arras and Ypres. In early spring the grass was already greening and was relatively unmarked by the scars of shellfire.

Nevertheless, concern about the imminence of the German attack led to a Divisional conference at 9.30 pm on the 19th to discuss plans for meeting the expected attack. That night, at 10.00 pm, a great volume of gas was discharged from the division's gas projectors onto St. Quentin in the hope of forestalling any concentration of German troops there. The following day was again quiet. On Manchester Hill the time was passed in closing any gaps in the wire around the redoubt and distributing vast quantities of ammunition. However, in the late afternoon of 20 March artillery observers in Holnon Wood and in the observation post on Manchester Hill began to be hampered by the development of a ground mist. Initially it lay in the hollows around the St. Quentin canal but it gradually rose until the bulk of the area occupied by the British Fifth and Third Armies was under its cover. As the evening progressed the mist thickened, until by 9.00 pm it was a dense fog, blanketing everything in a silence and making any visual observation impossible. The patrol which left the

Manchester's lines of observation just north of the St. Quentin Savy road found no enemy presence. However, a number of other British raids that night had captured prisoners who proved very anxious to be sent to the rear, suggesting that an attack was imminent. At 2.30 am the British artillery behind 90 Brigade began a bombardment of known German positions, shooting by map co-ordinates. An hour later a number of the British battalions in the rear of the line of redoubts set about the process of manning their battle positions, even though the formal order to do so had not been issued. One of the units behind the 16th Manchesters was the 17th Manchester Battalion, whose battle zone positions lay in the area between Savy and Roupy, approximately two miles to the rear.[8] In their intermediate position on Manchester Hill Wilfrith Elstob's men knew that they were expected to defend the locality without chance of early

*Overwhelming concentrations of German troops were assembled in St. Quentin prior to their attack on the morning of 21 March 1918. On that morning the superiority of the German artillery and the fortuitous intervention of a dense spring mist meant that their advance was relatively unhindered by the British defence whose plans were thrown into disarray.*

reinforcement. The system of defence demanded that,

*It must be impressed upon all troops actually allotted to the defence of any position, whether in the outpost system or the main battle position, that so far as they are concerned there is only one degree of resistance, and that is to the last round and to the last man.*

Wilfrith Elstob's instructions were clear. Everyone knew that his rallying point was to be the Battalion's battle headquarters.[9] He had described it with devastating simplicity. 'Here we fight and here we die.'

At 4.40 am the German artillery opened its massive and immensely well co-ordinated bombardment. His target selection was uncannily accurate and many of the telephone junctions behind the British redoubts were hit immediately. The artillery positions were swamped with lachrymatory gas. However, the telephone line from Manchester Hill to 90 Brigade HQ remained open. Out in No Man's Land the platoon patrol of the 16th Manchesters found itself cut off by the enormity of the German barrage. At 4.48 am the order to man the battle stations was issued to the men of 2nd Bedfordshires immediately behind Manchester Hill redoubt. Five minutes later the 30th Division's artillery, firing blindly, put a barrage down on No Man's Land in front of the 16th Manchester's front line observation positions. A further three minutes later, according to plan, the barrage was brought back to a position just in front of the lines of resistance. At 5.38 am German gas shells began to fall on Manchester Hill redoubt and the men were now forced to undertake all their duties within the suffocating constriction of their respirators. As dawn broke it became clear to these men in the redoubt that their position was going to be very desperate. Visibility in pockets of clear air was at best fifty yards, often much less, and nothing could be seen of their front companies through the murky greyness in the east. The valleys, which should have been death traps covered by the machine guns on Manchester Hill, now provided cover and invisibility to the German troops moving in hushed columns out from St.Quentin. By 7.00 am the platoon patrol which had been trapped in No Man's Land had still seen no signs of the masses of German troops, and began to work its way westwards across the empty line of observation posts towards the lines of resistance. However, the patrol was unable to get in because of the barrage in front of those lines by the British artillery. The gas shelling of the redoubt continued past 7.00 am. Nevertheless, half an hour later both A and B Companies reported that everything was still quiet in front of their positions. The men on the right front positions were visited by Elstob; his adjutant, Captain Sharples, visiting B Company on the left. Soon afterwards telephone communication with the posts in the lines of resistance was severed as the intensity of the German high explosive barrage on these positions increased. At this time Elstob moved his HQ forward to the battle position. The redoubt was now manned by the battalion administrative staff, cooks, military police and signals section men together with men of D Company.

By 8.50 am the gas was quickly dispersing from around the top of Manchester Hill and the shells were now mostly 5.9″ high explosives (falling along a line S.21.b.7.0 to S.15.d.4.0. and on northwards towards Francilly). Manchester Hill seems to have been one of the places where the German infantry assault was undertaken in advance of the main assault due at 9.40 am. The reason was simple and effective. It would have been foolhardy not to take advantage of the excellent cover provided by the dense fog, worsened by the smoke of shellfire. As the Brigade diary so concisely reported,

> All our careful preparations and organisation to meet the attack appear to have been nullified by the fog, which permitted the enemy to approach in overwhelming strength unseen.[10]

The German 50th Division's orders showed their line of attack to correspond almost exactly with the forward positions held by the 16th Manchesters and the Battle Zone positions held by the 17th Manchesters. The 50th Division would attack with two Regiments in the first line and one in close support; each of these Regiments in their turn attacking with two battalions in line and one in close support. The 16th Manchesters were therefore going to be confronted by nine battalions of infantry. Meanwhile, as the time of the infantry assault approached, the 30th Division's artillery were ordered to carry out a second counter preparation barrage at 9.30 am. It was, understandably, not long before news came by runner to the 16th Manchester's HQ that the line of resistance positions were already being overwhelmed. In some cases men in these positions were killed at their posts. A significantly greater number were taken prisoner. A few managed to fight their way back towards the central redoubt or were pressed further back towards Savy and Etreillers. By 9.40 am the left and right positions of the redoubt itself were being engaged by German troops using rifle grenades and machine guns. After 10.00 am only the most determined local counter attacks by the men within the redoubt were able to keep their positions secure. During these tense hours virtually nothing could be seen, but at 11.00 am patches of the mist began to lift and streaks of sunlight revealed the first Germans, who were seen advancing in strength from beyond the Old Roman Road towards Francilly-Selency, which lay approximately 1,000 yards to the north of Manchester Hill redoubt, behind B Company's positions. At the same time men in field grey were also seen in strength on the Savy road, just a few yards south of the redoubt. As a fighting unit A Company had been virtually wiped out. The artillery bombardment which was being fired by the Germans onto the redoubt and by the 30th Division's artillery in front of the lines of resistance now began to change. At 11.00 am the British artillery began to shorten its range and at 11.20 am placed the 'Red Smoke' barrage around the 16th Manchesters in the redoubt, unfortunately catching some pockets of men belonging to A and B Companies who were still holding out in isolated places in the lines of resistance trenches. The barrage had been fired on receipt of the telephone call from Elstob to 90 Brigade's battle HQ in Vaux[II] saying that it was now possible to see Germans streaming past both sides of the redoubt in the direction of the Battle Zone. Shortly afterwards Captain Guest and his men in B Company were attacked from the rear, many of this group also being taken prisoner of war during the afternoon as they were forced back to their Company HQ. There was now little doubt that the 16th Manchesters from D Company and the HQ details were utterly surrounded, although the final assault would, according to the German principles of infiltration, not be undertaken until later that day.

*They used to fire at the horses legs as the transport and light guns came up. I don't know whether it was Colonel Elstob that said, 'better to fire at the horses legs than the men, they can get plenty of men to take their place but they can't get a horse'. So, as they came up, we fired at the horses and the horses with broken legs screamed and everything went down. The Germans on top, if they weren't hit, were off with their mess tin and cuttin' slices off the flanks of these horses that wasn't dead, they were that 'ungry for meat, and they little knew that twenty yards away there was our battalion's daily grub, not touched and never will be.* Private Charlie Heaton. 16th Manchesters.

One of the first penetrations into the central redoubt came along Havre Trench. Here Elstob built a block between the attackers and his HQ dug out which he defended tenaciously with both his revolver and grenades. His opponents were Westphalians, men of the 2nd Battalion of the 158th Regiment. When these Germans abandoned the Havre Trench route and organized attacks over the top from near to No. 2 Post, Elstob again led his men by example in organizing the defence by rifle fire. Elstob now received his first wound, a grenade splinter, after some Germans had reached Havre Trench. However, after receiving treatment from the Medical Officer, Captain Walker, Elstob was soon back and organizing the defenders. Incredibly, when ammunition ran low, Elstob could be seen running across the quarry with boxes of grenades and small arms ammunition, his great physical strength serving him well. During the hours between 11.00 am and 2.00 pm Elstob was wounded twice more, yet still continued to exhort and encourage his men. By early afternoon the action had almost run its full course. The artillery, whose protection was so vital, was about to pull out from Holnon Wood, fearing that its position was soon to be overwhelmed by infantry attack. By 12.45 the advanced guns of the 148th R.F.A, south of Holnon and north of Round Hill, had already been passed by advancing German storm-troopers. The former Prime Minister's son was one of the subalterns with the unit.

*In the early afternoon our battery was ordered to retire into the Battle Zone, and one section remained behind with its teams and limbers hidden in the trees in order to cover the retirement. When we had fired off all the ammunition that was left, this section was also limbered up and went back to the battle position near Etreillers.*[12]

The patrol of the 16ths who had originally been trapped in No Mans Land had, by 2.00 pm, fought their way back to Francilly-Selency. They later reported that two machine guns to the west of that village had killed many German troops and that Manchester Hill was still fighting a heavy engagement. By this time very few of the 16th's men were still un-wounded and Elstob's telephone conversations with Brigade HQ confirmed that hand to hand fighting inside the redoubt had left the men exhausted. Sergeant Archer Hoye, 6630, the Lewis Gun section sergeant and an original Pal who had served with Elstob throughout was killed at his post on the western edge of the quarry. He had fired continuously until the Germans overran his position. Hoye was shot dead whilst changing the drum on his Lewis Gun. With the redoubt now open to attack from the rear across the quarry, there could be only minutes left

*Lieutenant Colonel Wilfrith Elstob.*

for Elstob's rapidly dwindling band of cooks, transport men, signallers and riflemen. On the bank which formed the eastern lip to the quarry, RQMS Jenkins and two young recruits were manning a Lewis Gun post only fifty yards behind his battalion's battle headquarters. In the middle of the afternoon the last few minutes of the action were being fought out.

*The Germans advanced down the [Havre] trench, in spite of our rifle fire as the bullets only bounced off their helmets. Fortunately for us a shell plunged in the ground between them and us, filling the trench and causing the Germans to retire. No Germans came over the top. We concentrated on cover for HQ and [on] the snipers in a ruined building.* RQMS P.E. Jenkins. Originally of the 21st but serving in 16th Manchesters by March 1918.

In the dugout in the quarry the medical officer, his staff and many wounded men were about to be taken prisoner.

*I think we'd moved about twenty seven wounded from the trenches into the dugout that we'd taken over from Colonel Elstob. It was getting about 3 o'clock, and we were still going round doing odd jobs and carrying a few bombs for them so as not to be seen. Then a hand grenade came down, it was only a jam stick. It came down the steps and fell on the floor. Well, we had a little wire-haired fox terrier, little "Whizz Bang", in the doctor's quarters and we'd feed it and it happened to be down in this dugout and it ran to the grenade thinking it was a bone. Anyway, it wouldn't run after another one. The dugout was now black 'cause the bomb had blown all the candles out. So we heard a voice on top then shouting to us to come out. There was a young Lieutenant there, I don't know who he was but I think he was a bit windy, so I said that I would go out. We reassured the lads who had been dressed saying that we'll get someone here to see to you.* Private Charlie Heaton. 16th Manchesters.

In front of the quarry a number of field guns had been dragged into positions just sixty yards from the final rallying point in the redoubt. His last conversation with Brigade was at 3.22 pm, when Wilfrith Elstob confirmed that the end was in sight. His last message was, 'Goodbye'. Shortly afterwards he was called upon to surrender.[13]

Wilfrith Elstob's reply was as expected of such a man.

*I saw Colonel Elstob rise to lob a grenade at the snipers but they shot him. Captain Sharples then tried to pull the Colonel's body into the trench and he too was killed. Later on our ammunition gave out, a shell plunged in the ground in front of us covering us with earth, so we scrambled on our bellies under the barbed wire to the quarry. As we reached the quarry a German officer in field cap covered us with a pistol. I levelled my empty rifle at him when someone shouted, 'Don't shoot, you'll have us all killed'. At that time there was about a dozen prisoners in the quarry but afterwards there was quite a procession brought of the line. In the hot afternoon we were marched to St. Quentin carrying the wounded slung in blankets.* RQMS Jenkins.

Wilfrith Elstob had been an extraordinarily brave, cheerful and resourceful man who had wanted to serve and if necessary die with his battalion. One of his last letters, written from

Ypres to the man who had been his first company commander and boyhood friend, Hubert Worthington, had recommended the poetry of a young American, Alan Seeger. In Seeger's writing Wilfrith Elstob found a special power. One particular poem he had written out, drawing attention to his pleasure in its stark message.

*I have a rendezvous with Death*
*On some scarred slope of battered hill,*
*When Spring comes round again this year*
*And the first meadow flowers appear.*

*God knows 'twere better to be deep*
*Pillowed in silk and scented down,*
*Where Love throbs out in blissful sleep,*
*Pulse nigh to pulse and breath to breath,*
*Where hushed awakenings are dear*
*But I've a rendezvous with Death*
*At midnight in some flaming town,*
*When spring trips north again this year*
*And I to my pledged word am true,*
*I shall not fail that rendezvous.*

Among his command of more than 700 men, 74 other ranks and four officers had been killed this day. However, very significantly more men had been taken prisoner, more than five hundred were certainly in the bag'[14]. As he moved forward with a signaller to get clearer observation on Round Hill, to the north of Manchester Hill, the former Premier's son saw clearly that the end had come.

*In front of Holnon Wood the ground slopes gradually upward to the Round Hill, then there is a slight dip in the land, and beyond it are the lower slopes of Manchester Hill. On my way up the Round Hill, I found that the mist was dissolving, especially on the higher ground, and here we were no longer troubled by gas. A dead corporal lay on the slope, and half way up the hill a platoon of our infantry were returning in open order towards the battle zone. When I reached the crest, I saw that our outpost redoubt at the Brown Quarry, that held out so gallantly against the full tide of the attack, was now cut off on the north and west by the German infantry: a large number of grey misty figures, easily recognised as Germans by the shape of their helmets, stood halted on the skyline of Manchester Hill. Asquith.*

### The retreat from Manchester Hill

Of Wilfrith Elstob's compatriots within the redoubt just two offcers and fifteen other ranks had survived unscathed. Of B and C Companies rather more men were still effective, although the bulk of those who had escaped death or being taken prisoner of war had been forced to make their way back towards the Battle Zone, through the Bois de Savy and along Victor Hugo Alley communication trench into Etreillers. Twelve of the Battalion's officers were taken prisoner. The defence of Manchester Hill had most certainly delayed and disorganized the German advance towards Savy and Ham and as such was all that had been expected and hoped of the men. Now many small parties were moving eastwards. One group of men from the quarry were trudging through the sunken lane, dropping down to the Rocourt Salient on the outskirts of St. Quentin.

*Fourteen of us were going down this sunken road when we 'eard a voice a few yards off the road. 'Englander, come here.' He was a Colonel in charge of the guns. And there*

*British casualties and prisoners of war being dealt with by German troops during their advance.*

was another young tall officer, he could speak English as well as you or I, and he was second-in-command. He said, 'This way boys, the colonel just wants to 'ave a word with you. He wants to know on this chart where you've been holding out.' And like a lot of bloody fools we told 'im. Well, 'e went up in the air about his horses. He was cursin' away. So this other officer, a decent sort of fellow, lower in rank than this other fat old begger, he said that, 'He's sent for a machine gun and you've got to line up here and he's going to have you shot.' Well, it so happened, with it being so late in the afternoon, quarter past three, all their machine guns had gone forward, they'd be mile and a half in front goin' towards Ham. So this officer said to me, 'I'm going to have a word with this colonel and while I'm talking to him his back will be turned to you, break off quietly, don't let him hear you and you walk quietly away He doesn't look like gettin' a machine gun.' And I don't suppose any individual would have shot fourteen fellows. So of course we did and before we got to St. Quentin we saw a couple of men in white coats, German doctors, who told us to get hold of this man and that man, their wounded. They put us in a large building with a naval gun at the side of it, being fired about every quarter of an hour. It so shook the place we thought it would come

*Captain and Quartermaster J.T. Ball, MC, who was badly wounded in the area of Etreillers on the morning of 21st March. Etreillers, at the centre of the battle zone, was subject to a powerful German box barrage through which Ball was attempting to get the 16th's battalion stores to safety. The wounding of Captain Ball then left one remaining original officer with the 16th Battalion, Lieutenant R.K. Knowles who, later promoted to the command of B Company, established a record in having served with the battalion continuously from its inception in September 1914 to the very end of its involvement in the war.* MRA

*down. The next day we started marching towards Belgium. Nothing to eat, nothing to drink. When we came to a village the inhabitants would put a bucket of water out for us but Gerry saw to it that we didn't get any water. The officers on horseback backed their horses into the buckets to knock them over. We came to one spot where there was a tap. There was about 4,000 fellows on the march. Nobody had had any water. Instead of saying, 'Form up and have a drink each', they were all round the tap and nobody could get a drink.* Private Charlie Heaton. 16th Manchesters.

Meanwhile, even before the redoubt on Manchester Hill had fallen, the fighting in the Battle Zone to the rear had become more intense. Now that the fog no longer concealed troop movements above ground the communication trenches running back towards Savy and Etreillers were the most obvious ways forward for the German Storm Troops. However, although Savy village was occupied by German troops after 1.00 pm, this proved to be the furthest advance made by the German Army behind Manchester Hill on 21 March. Later that afternoon stragglers from the 16th Manchesters were collected by 2nd Lieutenant F.J. Smith north of Etreillers, more than two miles behind Manchester Hill. At 8.00 pm they reported to Brigade HQ in Steen Wood at Vaux and then proceeded to Villers St. Christophe.

The 21 March also saw the 17th Manchesters brought into the thick of the action, in the defence of the line between Roupy and Savy. This area of the Battle Zone was defended by the 21st Brigade, of whom the 17th Manchesters were now a part. Before the German attack the 17th Battalion had been in Savy dug outs and at Vaux. Since early morning, when they had received the order to man battle stations at 4.50 am, and throughout the afternoon, the 17th Manchesters held Roupy Trench, 1,200 yards east of Pommery Chateau. On their left were the 2nd Bedfordshires of 90 Brigade, and on their right the 2nd Yorkshires. Following the German occupation of Savy, soon after 1.00 pm, the quarry just south west of the village, at F.4.b.5.8, was lost at 3.00 pm. The counter attack company of the 17th Manchesters, B Company, were ordered to retake the quarry, which was proving a fatal attraction for many desperate German soldiers. At one point in the late afternoon there were over 1,000 men

*A column of British troops marching eastwards. The interminable length of the column and the obvious relief on many of the men's faces now that they are Prisoners of War gives a clear idea of the initial success of the German assault. The photograph was probably taken in St. Quentin on the afternoon of 21 March, 1918.* Middlebrook/Bavarian State Archives

*During their March offensive the German Army's advance took them westwards towards Noyon, Ham, Albert and regained all of the ground lost during the British Somme offensive of 1916.*

sheltering there when machine guns from the 17th Manchester's front ripped into them, causing horrific and heavy casualties. The first counter attack was held up by machine gun fire, after which a heavy trench mortar was turned onto the quarry. At 5.45 pm the 17th Manchesters attacked again and re-took the quarry, thirty one prisoners being captured and twelve British soldiers who had been held there being liberated. During the afternoon many further waves of advancing Germans were seen moving forwards from the Bois de Savy astride the St. Quentin-Savy road. However it proved possible to hold these attacks by the use of well directed artillery and lewis gun fire. By nightfall the 17th Manchesters were still in possession of Roupy Trench.

The following morning, 22 March, again dawned shrouded in mist. South of Roupy part of the 36th Division's front had been pulled back to conform with III Corps' withdrawal towards the Crozat canal. At 8.00 am the Germans were again seen massing for an attack. At 9.00 am a heavy bombardment was launched all along the front between Savy and Roupy but by noon, following the fog's gradual clearing mid-way through the morning, the infantry attack was broken up by the concentrated machine gun fire brought to bear on the waves of German soldiers. Throughout the afternoon further German attacks in strength continued to

*British prisoners of war idle the time of day in a collecting 'cage'. For the first few days of their captivity, before their arrival in organized and hutted prisoner of war camps in Germany, the men were often kept out in the open during a time when the weather was still distinctly cold at night. Since the majority of these men had been captured without their full kit, the experience was harsh and depressing.* Middlebrook/Bavarian State Archives

*Major R.E. Roberts. Rupert Edward Roberts was an original officer of the 16th Battalion. In the spring of 1918 he had been attached to 90 Brigade's instructional school of which he was commandant. During the retreat he had valiantly led small detachments of stragglers from the 16th Manchesters and other units in the defence of positions along the Nesle-Noyen canal, between Buverchy and Ramecourt. He was severely wounded on the morning of 26th March and died of his wounds later that day.* MRA

be pressed against the 17th Manchester's positions, which still held firm. However, at 4.00 pm the Germans again attacked the front companies, and this time broke through towards Goodman Redoubt. B, D and C Companies were overrun and surrounded, and many of the surviving men taken prisoner. In the early evening, at about 6.20 pm, with many dead and all ammunition expended after close fighting within their trenches, A Company and some members of the HQ staff were pulled out from Goodman Redoubt. In fact a general retirement had already begun along the whole 30th Divisional front at 5.45 pm. Those few of the 17th Battalion who managed to escape collected at Bunny Wood, at F.7.c, and then withdrew towards Muille Villette.[15] All the Battle Zone positions on the 30th Division's front were being overrun, and the 36th Division on their right were retiring. By 2.30 pm 90 Brigade's men had already been ordered to retire towards Ham through the 20th Division, who were now holding the rear areas of the Battle Zone. Soon after midnight, in the early hours of 23 March, the tattered remnants of the 16th Manchesters arrived at Verlaines near Ham, where they held positions at Buverchy and Ramecourt on the Canal du Nord, under orders to hold the position to the last. On 24 March these men, collected together by Major Roberts, were still on the western bank watching the last of the British rearguard troops over the two bridges at Ramecourt, just east of Moyencourt, when groups of German troops outflanking their positions were seen. These seventy or eighty men of the 16th Manchesters held on for a further twenty four hours before the collapse of their flanks compelled them to fall back towards Cressy. During the next three days the rapidly dwindling groups of men of the two senior Manchester City Battalions were pushed further back in a series of enforced withdrawals, as small scale actions by exhausted, isolated and outflanked ad hoc units tried desperately to hold up the German advance. In the late afternoon of the 26 March the 16th's men were evacuated from Roye, marching along the Amiens road to Bouchoir. On 27 March they were shelled out of Bouchoir. By this stage every man was dazed and weakened. Officers at Brigade were aware that it had become impossible to keep the men in position under shellfire, battalion staffs had simply ceased to exist. Although there was no sign of panic, and attempts to withdraw were quite orderly, the surviving men 'appeared to have lost the sense of reasoning and it was difficult to make them understand.'[16] The men were literally asleep on their feet. The following morning the words all ranks had longed to hear were delivered to 90 Brigade's HQ.

G.O.C., 90 Brigede. Je suis satisfait que les elements de la 30' Division dans le secteur FOLIES-BEAUFORT peuvent sortir sans deranger les arrangements. Veuillez retirer vos troupes aussitot que possible. [I am satisfied that the elements of the 30th Division in the FOLIES-BEAUFORT sector can leave without upsetting the arrangements. Please retire your troops as soon as possible.] 28 Marz 1918. 11h.50. Le colonel Hoff Cdt.le D13. P.O.L'Officier d'Etat-Major.

At 2.00 pm that afternoon the exhausted men moved back, through French troops, past

Mezieres and Moreuil to Rouvrel. In both the 16th and 17th Battalions' cases these actions during the last ten days of March 1918 saw the virtual extinction of both battalions. In the case of the 16th Battalion their battle casualties during the period 21-30 March had reduced their ration strength from twenty three officers and 717 men to one officer and 116 men. In excess of 700 men from the two battalions had been taken as prisoners of war, at a time when the impact of the allied naval blockade and severe privation meant that their circumstances within these camps would be exceedingly harsh and spartan. In many cases those who had been wounded had to make do with little or no medication. Many of these men would unfortunately die as prisoners, without seeing their families again.

*Corporal Ernest Stockton, 26809, 17th Manchesters, seated left front row. Like many others within the Pals battalions, Ernest Stockton had passed through the Training Reserve Battalions before being sent out to France. Corporal Stockton was taken prisoner near Savy soon after the actions here on 22nd March. Ernest's left wrist was shattered by shrapnel and he was, for many weeks, in danger of having to lose the arm.* Stockton

Three days later XVIII Corps' very highly respected commander, Lieutenant General Sir Ivor Maxse, wrote to each of the 30th Division's units which had been under his command throughout the fighting during late March. In that letter, dated 3 April, he spoke of his admiration for the soldiers qualities and sacrifice, although making it clear that, in view of the territorial losses which had been incurred, the war had still to be won.

> *Orders have been received for the move of the 30th Division from the XVIII Corps to another area, I wish to place on record my appreciation of the services rendered by the Division during the arduous operations and strenuous fighting in which it was engaged from 21-29 March, 1918... During these operations the 30th Division has gained a reputation for hard fighting and I wish to thank all ranks for their gallant spirit, and would wish to remind them that still greater efforts will be required of them during the coming months. May good fortune attend the Division in the future.*

At a more personal level, amongst the men and officers who had survived, attention was now focussed on what had happened to the men who had been left behind. Were they wounded, dead, what had happened to the men posted as missing? One letter from an officer to Hubert Worthington summed up these feelings.

> *...I quite agree with your ideas about Ben [Wilfreth Elstob]. I do not believe he is killed, I think wounded and a prisoner and I am hoping for the best, for I too think the world of him, and I do not think there is a braver man in the British Army and I am also very proud of him and also very proud of the 16th for they fought like heroes. Yes, Roberts was hit in the stomach, died of wounds and I believe was buried at Rouen. I was hit by a piece of shell in the left elbow and left thigh, but I am doing very nicely and walking about the ward. I was hit on 21st, so I have been in hospital nearly a month and am absolutely fed up with it.* Captain and Quartermaster J T Ball in a letter dated 19 April 1918

## Prisoners of War

For the prisoners of war the shipping blockade on Germany meant unremitting hardship and a lack of medical care. Those who did receive food parcels on a regular basis were indeed fortunate, but the incidence of disease and infection amongst the men was high. The numbers of prisoners in the camps had been swollen dramatically as result of the German spring offensive, and the procedures for feeding and housing captured soldiers were stretched to their limits. Nevertheless, a close relationship built up between the Manchesters and their prison guards. In some cases the obvious privation and hardship which the guards themselves were suffering meant that a few blocks of chocolate or biscuits would cement a friendship which lasted many years.[17]

In Manchester the response of the City Council was one of shock and horror. A certain casualness had seeped into people's belief that the war, now the USA was 'in', would soon be over. The 16th Battalion had been especially close to the heart of the city. A memorial service, to be held in the Cathedral, was arranged for the afternoon of 15 April. Its purpose was to record the passing of the city's premier Pals battalion, believed to have been almost totally wiped out. The address would be given by Bishop Welldon, never one to stint in the almost vitriolic hatred which he reserved for the German 'nation' in his harangues from the pulpit. Contrasting what he referred to as the 'sublime characteristics' of the ordinary men who had fought under such overwhelming odds and with no little heroism at Manchester Hill, Bishop Welldon denigrated their opponents in the savage manner which he had allowed, all too sadly, in his sermons to characterize the response of the church in Manchester.

> *They were just ordinary men—men in the street they were sometimes called, but it is the heroism of the ordinary man which is supreme. Human history presents no parallel to the German character today, in its strength, its education, its organisation, its selfishness, its unscrupulousness, its inhumanity, its discipline, its fortitude, its patriotic duty and in some strange sense its religion. Our gallant boys at the front have saved us and are saving us. The enemy, if it could, would destroy Great Britain and the British Empire, and would strike at the heart of humanity.* Bishop Welldon as reported in the *Manchester Evening News*, 15 April, 1918.

It was, strangely, still the same rather bombastic rhetoric as that spoken four years earlier from many pulpits in the Salford and Manchester areas. The actions at Manchester Hill were

**This postcard sent to his younger brother by Captain Guest from his officer prisoner of war camp at Karlsruhe, Baden. The message on the reverse asked, 'How's cricket going down?'** M Guest

*The PoW camps were harsh and spartan. The impact of the Allied blockade meant that food was scarce and of poor quality. Many Manchester men were destined to die as Prisoners of War.*

*The arrival and distribution of food parcels in one of the Munster PoW camps. This photograph is one of a series depicting camp scenes, sent to his family in Chorlton-on-Medlock, by Corporal Albert Willmot, 47284 17th Manchesters.* MRA

*Right: Corporal Ernest Stockton amongst his friends in the camp at Saarbrucken.* Stockton

*Art class. Summer 1918 in the Munster POW camps.* MRA

already being portrayed by the City as a glorious last stand to the last cartridge or death. The reality had been rather different, although no less meritorious. There was, in Bishop Welldon's address, no reference to the 17th Battalion whose engagement at Savy and Roupy behind Manchester Hill had been almost as severe a trial.

In Germany itself some of the wounded and weaker prisoners of war died during the summer and autumn of 1918, influenza and secondary pneumonia being rife. The other men were occupied in the manufacture of boots and repair of clothing, writing letters and waiting, interminable waiting. Lieutenant John Clarke of the 16th Manchesters, who had been D Company commander at Manchester Hill, died in Cologne on 24 October, just two weeks before the end of the war. A number of men were repatriated on an exchange basis, usually because of persistent medical conditions and severe shell shock. Amongst the exchanged was Sergeant Major George Evans of the 18th Manchester Battalion. For those unwounded who were well enough to cope, some opportunities to trade for food arose. Charlie Heaton, as a non smoker, arranged a steady supply of potatoes in return for the cigarettes which one young boy regularly brought to the camp. One day, however, the weakness of Germany's military position was revealed when the young man spoke across the wire:

> *'I'm being called up.' he said. 'I want to be a prisoner like you.' I said, 'It all depends who you get in front. If you get in front of the English you've no need to be afraid. Just go over and say, "German prisoners calling!"'* Private Charlie Heaton.

### The Spoil Bank

Early in April the 16th's handful of men had marched into Kempton Park camp near Ypres and been designated as the Brigade Reserve, under the command of Major W H Colley of the Yorkshire Regiment. On 19 April the men of the 16th and 17th Manchesters were formed into a composite battalion, and then manned the front lines at Spoil Bank, at I.33. central, on the south side of the Ypres-Comines canal, 1,500 yards south east of Bedford House. On 24 April this composite battalion was relieved and moved back into the close support positions around the Spoil Bank and Lock 8. The following morning, 25 April, an attack by the Germans south of the canal at 10.00 am led to severe fighting in which the German line was pushed forward to a line running from The Bluff, through Oosthoek Farm and past Shelley Farm. D Company of the composites (made up from C and D Companies of the 17th Battalion) counter attacked at Oosthoek Farm to restore the situation, whilst C Company formed the defensive flank with its left on the St. Eloi to Trois Rois road with B Company with its right on this road and its left at Shelley Farm. These positions were isolated and utterly without any wire protection to the front of the men. On 26 April, in a thick mist at 9.30 am the forward posts, to whom the Manchesters were in reserve, were overwhelmed. C and D Companies of the composite battalion (all of whom were the old 17th Battalion's men) were surrounded and either killed or taken prisoner. A Company found themselves trapped within the Spoil Bank tunnel as large numbers of German troops attacked from the direction of Norfolk Lodge and Oosthoek. Only two platoons of A Company managed to get out on the south side of the Spoil Bank. Almost all of these men exiting on the south side of the tunnel were either killed or wounded by the artillery barrage and machine gun fire which was being directed on the tunnel exits as they tried to assemble to make their counter attack. The remainder withdrew across to the north of the canal, suffering heavy casualties in a further barrage, eventually arriving at Lock 8 where the line was held on the north bank of the canal. The following day, the 27 April, was quiet, apart from two heavy barrages which the remnants had to endure. On the 28 April at 7.00 pm, after a day in which the few remaining

*The Band of the 16th Manchesters photographed in early June 1918, before the Battalion's return to England, its amalgamation with the 29th Battalion of the Manchester Regiment and incorporation into the 14th Division.* MRA

*The Spoil Bank area, SW of Zillebeke, where the remnants of the 16th and 17th Manchesters were reduced to a strength of less than 20 men during the fighting between 25-28 April 1918.*

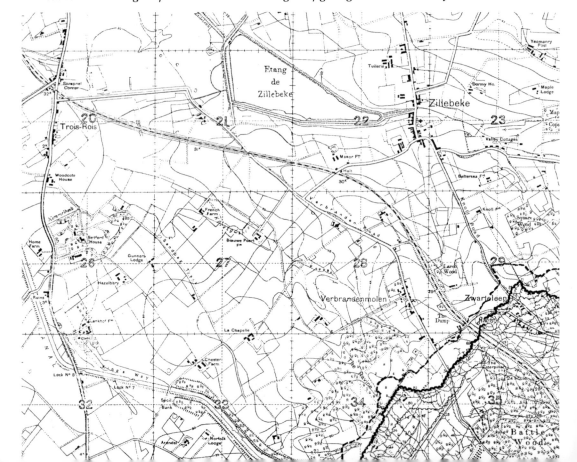

men had engaged lines of German troops advancing in files towards the canal, the Manchesters composite Battalion withdrew from the area of Lock 8 towards trenches occupied by the Leicesters. They were three officers and twelve men strong! As a fighting force the battalion had simply ceased to exist, and these men of the composite battalion were temporarily absorbed into No. 4 Battalion of the 39th Composite Brigade. During the following two days a few dozen more men, who had become separated, straggled in to rejoin their unit. It was clear that the battalion's willpower and morale were at an all time low. Losses and battle weariness had jaded every man's powers. At least nine of the composite battalion's officers were taken as prisoner of war[18] as had been hundreds of men. Four days later the composite battalion was formed into a composite company, which manned the trenches at Ouderdom. During the three day's battle prior to 28 April the 17th Battalion's men were reduced by 212 casualties and the 16th Battalion's men by 236.

But in Cologne, Berlin and Hamburg German civilian resolve was starting to crumble. Of that weakness the British prisoners of war knew only too well. The sparcity of food and clothing revealed all too clearly the effectiveness of the Allied naval blockade. The German hopes which had been put so extravagantly into the single basket of their spring offensive had now cracked and soured as the advance failed to crush the combined British and French will to resist. The 'Black Day' of 8 August's battle outside Amiens revealed that Germany's war effort was in desperate trouble and in danger of giving way. The fighting however was not yet done with, and the numbers of casualties incurred during the desperate fighting of late summer and autumn of 1918 were enormously heavy. In the meantime, however, during the period after the actions in front of Savy in March and at the Spoil Bank in April, the 16th Battalion was reduced to a skeleton training cadre on 13 May, followed two days later by the 17th Battalion, each unit lending their experience to the training of newly arrived American troops. For the 17th Battalion this was effectively the end of their service as a recognized separate unit of infantry. On 19th June the few men within this cadre were transferred to the 66th Division, and later absorbed into the 13th Battalion of the Manchester Regiment. For the 16th Battalion however, their reduction to a training cadre was not to be the end of their service. On 18 June the Cadre was placed with 42 Brigade and crossed the Channel to Dover, from whence they moved to Aldershot. At Aldershot these few dozen men of the 16th Battalion were amalgamated with the soldiers of the newly raised 29th Battalion of the Manchester Regiment. On 4 July 1918, as part of the 42nd Brigade of the 14th Division, the newly reformed 16th Manchesters arrived back in Boulogne, where they had first arrived as the 1st City Battalion nearly three years earlier. Fortunately, as the year of 1918 unfolded into high summer, the position of the German Army itself began to weaken and the 16th Battalion's casualties were relatively light, with deaths from influenza and other infections far exceeding the numbers of men who were killed in action.[19]

## Italy

Germany's closest aid in the war had always been the Austro-Hungarian Empire, against whose troops the British 7th Division had been engaged since their arrival in northern Italy six months earlier. Of the three Manchester battalions who went to Italy with the 7th Division, in November 1917, only the 22nd Battalion remained in Italy throughout the remainder of the war. The 20th and 21st Battalions left the 7th Division, on 13 September, to join the 25th Division in France. The campaign in Italy was never marked by the same ferocity for which the Western Front had become infamous. Austria-Hungary, as the junior partner in her alliance with Germany, was rather reluctant to pursue the war with all of her available resources. The casualties suffered by the Manchesters in Italy were therefore light, and even those raids undertaken by the 22nd Battalion, to make identifications, would give rise to numerous prisoners easily taken from the ranks of the Austrian troops opposite, who by late 1918 were demonstrably becoming less committed after the Battle of Asiago in mid June.[20]

One unique and dramatic raid was organized on the village of Canove di Sotto as part of a series undertaken along the whole of the 7th and 48th Divisions' fronts across the River Ghelpac, towards Canove and Asiago. At this point there was a considerable distance between the two front lines, and the Manchesters were able to move freely at night in No Man's Land to rehearse their dispositions and moves prior to

*Two winners of the Military Medal celebrate their awards in Italy. The man on the right is Lance Corporal Crawley, 20th Manchesters.* Pawson

the raid. In reality these events were almost a full scale battle, involving more than 4,000 British troops, whose purpose was to provoke an Austrian withdrawal towards Gallio, Mount Catz and Mount Rasta north east of Canove. These raids were due to take place on the night of 8/9 August. Alongside the 20th Manchester's men would be the 2nd Borders on their left and the 1st South Staffordshires on their right. The arrangements were quite radically different from those predictable events which featured so unremittingly on the battlefields of France and Flanders. An entire week was devoted to rehearsal of the plan. Artillery preparation would be brief but devastating, less than a minute on the front lines but then lifting to form a protective box around the occupied trenches. The raiding parties would occupy those Austrian trenches for at least two hours. Counter battery fire would continue for three hours after zero. Indirect machine gun fire would continue on important strong points around Mount Ambrosini beyond the left flank of the Manchester's raid as well as positions on either immediate flank of the trenches being raided, for two and a half hours after zero. Illumination to aid the raiders would be provided by huge searchlights whose beams would be reflected off the cloud cover. The signal to withdraw would be the lighting of a massive fire on Mount Lemerle, two miles south of the points being raided. The blaze would also show the troops their route back. Special parties were detailed to search the enemy's dead and to bring back documents, papers and identifications from dugouts.

The two Companies due to undertake the attack left Carriola Camp at 6.00 pm, marching to their appointed positions. The night was dark and moonless. At ten minutes before midnight both A and C Companies were already assembled, utterly silently, within fifty yards of the Austrian wire. Chewing gum had been issued to help keep the men's throats clear and prevent the sounds of coughing. As soon as the artillery opened fire the men moved forwards, and quickly overran Gordon and Gwent Trenches. Fifty one prisoners, including two officers, and three machine guns were taken, many enemy killed and numerous dugouts destroyed. Trench mortars were systematically destroyed along with their teams. After about ninety five minutes two rather half hearted counter attacks developed which were easily beaten off with rifle fire. About twenty minutes later, exactly two hours after the raid had begun, the fire was seen burning fiercely on Mount Lemerle and the raiders withdrew. Just three men had been

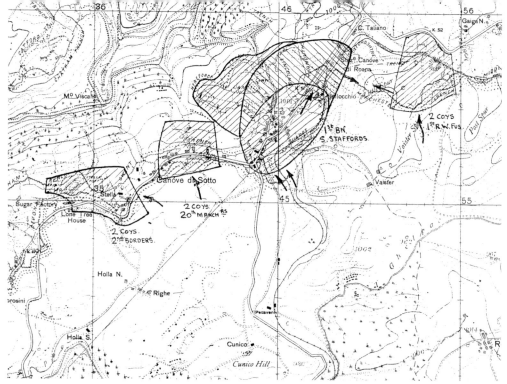

*Detail of the Canove area trenches showing disposition of the Borders, 20th Manchesters and South Staffordshires during the raid on the night of 8/9 August 1918.*

killed and a further two were missing. One officer and eleven men were lightly wounded. All along the front the story was the same, great success for the raiders and light casualties. That night the men were addressed by the Divisional Commander and, as the War Diary records, 'Major HRH the Prince of Wales called on the CO to congratulate him on the success of the Raid.' In all eight battalions along the British front made raids on this night. Eight Austrian officers and 304 other ranks were taken prisoner. One week later the Austrians withdrew to a prepared position north of Asiago known as the 'Winterstellung'.

## The crossing of the Piave

As war on the Western Front ground towards the defeat of Germany, Austria's reluctance turned to abject

*An artillery officer directing the fire of his battery according to his forward observation officers's direction. This photograph was taken somewhere on the Austro-Italian Frontier'.* Taylor

*Men of the 2nd Gordon Highlanders guard Austrian troops who had been taken prisoner during the 7th Division's crossing of the River Piave in late October 1918.* Taylor

*Troops in the trenches in Northern Italy. This period contrasted starkly with the harshness and grim circumstances of the Western Front.* Taylor

despair, collapse and defeatism. On 23 October the British 7th and 23rd Divisions were already fixing plans for the crossing of the River Piave across the Grave di Papadopoli, the north western part of which was already in British hands. The following morning, 24 October, the remainder of the island was reported captured, at 4.50 am, by men of 22 Brigade. Unfortunately it proved impossible to capture the far bank, as heavy rain caused the river to swell making further progress impossible. Throughout the 25 and 26 October, the few Austrians holding out on the island were mopped up, and the construction of the pontoon bridge from Salettuol to the west bank of the Grave di Papadopoli continued under a welcome blanket of fog and rain.

From the east bank of the Grave to the left bank of the River Piave were about 200 yards of gravel banks and shoals of rapid water between three and four feet deep at the centre of each channel. Beyond this was a further 150 yards of scrubland, laced with barbed wire and deep trenches before an embankment known as the Bund which hid the main Austrian position. Emplacements on top of the embankment gave machine gunners and riflemen an impressive field of unrestricted fire. Dug into the rear of the Bund were many shell-proof dugouts. It was a formidable defensive position.

On the 26 October the 22nd Manchesters, who were to be the assault troops, left their assembly positions at Maserada and crossed onto the Grave at 7.00 pm. Half an hour before midnight the British bombardment of the embankment began. In the darkness rain began to fall heavily, and was still falling when the men moved forward at 6.25 am. The air was bitterly cold. The attack on the Austrian positions above the east bank began at 6.45 am on the 27 October, the 22nd Manchesters being the front line unit of 91 Brigade's attack. On the right were the 2nd Gordon Highlanders as the assault unit of 20 Brigade, and on the left were the 8th Yorkshires. The undergrowth on the island and the far banks was so dense that only the smoke shells fired as part of the barrage made it possible to keep direction. Once the men emerged from the undergrowth and moved across the shingle they were exposed to intense machine gun fire from the Bund, roughly three hundred yards away. From right to left the formation was A, B and D Companies with C in close support. As the men splashed into the

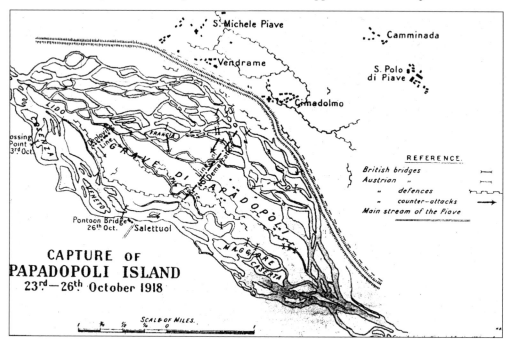

water many were swept off their feet and washed away whilst attempting to wade across. Many of the men were forced to take cover under the shelter of the far banks. A few of the most resolute pushed on, within the cover of the deep undergrowth, as trench mortar shells began crashing amongst them. There was continuous rifle and machine gun fire to hamper their attempts to cut through the wire in front of the Bund. The 22nd Manchester's commanding officer, Lieutenant Colonel Ramsbotham, knew his troops were in trouble and requested support. As the 1st South Staffordshires came up the breach of the wire cut by the 22nd's men enabled the troops of both battalions to stream through and clamber up the face of the Bund. Hundreds of Austrians were seen running away through the vines to the east. The few that remained surrendered or were killed. On the Manchester's left a number of machine gun posts in three houses in the area of St. Michelle Piave were routed by determined attacks under the cover of Lewis Guns. One hundred and sixty prisoners were taken by the 22nd's men. Numerous machine guns and trench mortars, together with their complete teams were captured as well as nine artillery pieces. By midday, the advance of the 7th Division had secured a solid bridgehead and the 22nd Manchesters had advanced to the road running between Tezze and Rai just north of Borgo Zanetta. Here the Manchesters had captured five more guns.

The following morning, the 28 October, an Austrian counter attack on the 22nd Manchesters was broken by rifle and Lewis Gun fire before the Battalion again moved forward across the River Piavesela towards Vazzola, coming across almost no organized opposition. In the coming days, as the men pushed on in the direction of Sacile, the rout of Austrian resistance was complete. On the 29 October the Battalion Commander's narrative describes how Austrians would wade across rivers towards the Manchesters in their enthusiasm to surrender before any fire at all had been directed at them. Nevertheless, during the period 26-29 October the Battalion's casualty returns record five officer casualties, two of whom were killed, sixteen men having been killed, 115 as wounded and twelve missing. During three days the men had fought and marched almost continuously, with little rest and almost no substantial rations other than the eggs and vegetables which were gratefully offered by the liberated villagers. However, by comparison with many events which the battalion had been engaged in during their stay in France and Flanders, these casualties seemed almost superficial. This, however, was not the last time that any of the battalions raised in 1914 as the Manchester Pals saw action in the Great War.

### The Last Days

The very last actions undertaken by any of the Pals' units during the war were those made by the 20th and 21st Battalions during their service with 7 Brigade of the 25th Division. By the end of September, having been transferred from their service with the 7th Division in Italy, the men were marching through Millencourt and Henencourt west of Albert. On 1st October the men passed through Guillemont, though very few members of the two battalions recognized it as their old stamping ground of 1916, en route for Beaurevoir and Pouchaux. Here they attacked on the 4 October and subsequently on each of the four successive days. During this period of German retreat the casualties suffered by these two battalions, throughout the period of October and November, were substantial and included more than two hundred fatalities as well as over six hundred other casualties. The 20th Battalion alone lost eighty one killed in action, together with twenty seven missing and 223 wounded in October. Twenty two of these wounded would die later from their wounds. It was a time of mobile and intense fighting, and the contrast with the relatively static and peaceful sojourn experienced during their stay in Italy could not have been more marked.[21] As the winter weather worsened so did the awful conditions under which these men were ordered to fight. The roads were desperately muddy, and rations were only provided on an intermittent basis as supply lines became over extended during the advance. German machine gunners still exacted their toll before any progress could be made, and the move forward was by no means an easy one. In November the battalions passed through Happegarbes and Landrecies at the Sambre-Oise canal on their way towards Dompierre, which was reached on 6 November. The casualties suffered on this day, as the village was cleared, included four men who were killed, the last men to die in action whilst serving with the Manchester Pals. Although three of these men had been transferred into the 20th Battalion from other units as drafts, one man was an original Manchester Pal. He was Lance Sergeant John Edwin Crompton, 20552, D.C.M. Just five days later the armistice, forced on the German Army by the collapse of its ability to resist and the end of support for the war at home in Germany, brought a halt to the fighting.

## Notes:

1 Copied from a poem written by Alan Seeger.

2 Thirty-three extra divisions at the start of the year and rising each week.

3 See sheet 62B.SW3. Corrected to 3 February 1918. Manchester Hill was located within square S21, 1000 yards east of Savy Wood. XVIII Corps covered a frontage running from Gricourt in the north to Itancourt, south east of St. Quentin.

4 On the morning of the German assault here the redoubts were held by the 2nd Wiltshires at l'Epine de Dallon, the 16th Manchesters at Manchester Hill which lay one mile north of l'Epine de Dallon and the 2/8th Worcesters who held the next redoubt north, located one mile east of Holnon. The name 'Manchester Hill' does not stem from the action involving the 16th Battalion here in March 1918 but rather from actions which had been undertaken here by the 2nd Manchesters during 1917.

5 See 30th Division's narrative in PRO ref W095/2313.

6 See *Military Operations France and Belgium 1918 Vol I* pp 159/160 for details of Lieutenant Colonel Bruchmuller's detailed artillery plan.

7 30th Division's Battle Zone was covered by the Fourteenth Army Brigade artillery. Also available were anti-tank guns, 8 x 9.2″ howitzers, 4 x 8″ howitzers, 16 x 6″ howitzers and 6 x 60-pounders.

8 The 17th Manchester's positions in D South Sector, south east of Etreillers, lay behind l'Epine de Dallon which was the 21st Brigade's intermediate position redoubt. The 90th Brigade's battle positions were in Savy village and westwards to Etreillers.

9 Elstob's battle HQ was located at S.21.b.2.2. at the junction of Havre Trench and the right hand communication trench running out of Brown Quarry. For a full description of the instructions given to military units by GHQ and Fifth Army before 21 March, see Appendices to *Military Operations in France and Belgium, 1918, Vol 1*.

10 90th Brigade War Diary. PRO ref: W095/2338.

11 A hamlet just behind Savy, not to be confused with the Vaux on the Somme marshlands where the 3rd City Battalion had held the front soon after their arrival in late 1915.

12 Asquith. H, *Moments of Memory*. Hutchinson. London. 1937. pp 320.

13 The course of events along the whole of XVIII Corps' front was similar. The three divisions of XVIII Corps were opposed by 14 German Divisions. In the 30th and 61st Divisions opposite St. Quentin almost all the forward defences were overwhelmed after a short but desperate engagement. Further back the line of redoubts made a more lengthy resistance. The redoubt south of Manchester Hill, l'Epine de Dallon garrisoned by 2nd Wiltshires, held out until 2.30 pm. To the north the redoubt situated a mile east of Holnon, garrisoned by 2/8th Worcestershires, held out until 5.15 pm.

14 The officers taken prisoner were Major R N R Gibbon, Captain J Guest, Captain O T Prichard, Captain P H Heywood, Lieutenant E T Hollins, Lieutenant J Clarke, 2/Lt F Hayes, 2/Lt J A Birchenough, 2/Lt W Dean, 2/Lt J A Bentley and 2/Lt W Quinn. Although a very considerable proportion of the battalion had been taken prisoner of war, there were a number of gallantry awards made to the men and officers of the battalion. Apart from the award to Wilfreth Elstob these awards included 3 DCMs, 12 Military Medals and 3 Military Crosses.

15 The officers of the 17th Manchesters taken prisoner this day included Captain W G Woodward, Captain J L Clayton, Lieutenant G Dunscombe, 2/Lt F V Harrison, 2/Lt C S Miles, 2/Lt T Longworth and 2/Lt S A Jackson. Over 300 other ranks were described as 'wounded and missing' or 'missing'. The 17th Battalion's casualties for the period 21 March to the end of the month amounted to 471, including seventeen officers.

16 See 90th Brigade Operation Reports. PRO ref: W095/2338.

17 These friendships even endured past the Second World War. In 1949 Private Herbert Thomas, 32669, who had

served in the 21st Manchesters and been captured at Bullecourt received this letter from one of his guards. 'After a long time I look at the photos I got from my dear English prisoners at Gettorf and Birkenmoor in the year 1918, and I ask me if you perhaps remember your old guard Hoffmann, who never has forgotten you. You were younger than I, and I hope you are still alive and well. I am now seventy-three years old, and my force is disappearing; but I am always enjoying to work little things in my electrical profession. My dear wife died in January 1940, and now I am alone with my younger sister, who is also a widow since the first war, without children. It would be a great joy for me to hear from you.' [Lamb]

18 2/Lt A Woodacre, 2/Lt H T Ringham, 2/Lt E Jones, 2/Lt E Bradwell, 2/Lt W H Smith, 2/Lt L Rathbone, 2/Lt S W Cannon, 2/Lt J Hillian and 2/Lt C T M Marshall were all taken prisoner. However, a number of men and officers did receive gallantry awards as a consequence of the very brave parts they played at Spoil Bank. One award of the DCM was made to Sergeant W Brookes, 11760, originally of the 19th Manchesters. The trench map references relating to the Spoil Bank actions are taken from Zillebeke, 28 NW4 and NE3 parts of.

19 The battalion was actually disbanded during June 1919 at Herseaux where, at this stage in the battalion's story, the Nominal Roll showed that, there were just three original members of the 1st City Pals still serving. They were 6694 C.Q.M.S. A J Tyldesley, who had originally enlisted into VIII platoon of B Company as a L/Cpl, 7269 A/Cpl J Jones, originally of XIII platoon of D Company and 7258 Pte H Shannon, originally with XV platoon in D Company.

20 During the year 1918 there were less than forty fatal casualties within the ranks of the 22nd Battalion, whilst it was serving in Italy, most of those incurred at the crossing of the River Piave in late Octoher.

21 These events almost certainly mark the last occasions on which original members of the Manchester Pals received awards for valour undertaken whilst serving with a Manchester Pals unit on the Western Front. eg; 17459, C.S.M. H Perry, DCM. 19110, Sgt. F Evans, MM. 17842, C.Q.M.S. H Cadman, MM. 17195, C.Q.M.S. A Phippen, .MM 14783, Pte S Taylor, MM. 14065, Pte W Summerscales, MM. 7688, Pte C Johnson, MM.

## Chapter Nine

# A rather rusty old tin box...

### 'Things have altered while you have been in the Army'

The men who had served within the Pals battalions established a bond of comradeship which would stretch across many decades. The cost to the city of Manchester had been enormous. In human terms the loss of so many people of such distinctive character and quality proved irreplaceable throughout the depressed years of the late 1920s and the '30s. In the autumn of 1914 almost 10,000 of Manchester's best had enlisted into the Pals. As the conflict progressed and casualties mounted the recruitment net had been widened to include men from every walk of life in the city and its surrounding areas. Four thousand seven hundred and seventy six men had died whilst serving with Manchester's Pals battalions.[1] The inclusion of their officers takes the total to 5,000. Many thousands more were physically maimed and mentally blighted for life. The death toll among the Manchester Regiment as a whole was 13,000 men. The Lancashire Fusiliers, recruiting in the industrial areas north of Manchester and in Salford, lost over 13,600

Lance Corporal Wilfred Chadwick, 43844 16th Manchesters (seated), together with his brother Alexander of the 5th Battalion. Also shown is the scroll, issued by the Borough of Leigh, to those men who had served within the armed forces together with the certificate of 'Disembodiment' on Demobilization which marked the end of every man's service within the Manchester Pals battalions.

Chadwick

*Emily and James Hayes, proud parents of three brothers. Seated centre is James Hayes, carefully hiding the loss of his fingers on his left hand. His two brothers Fred, of the Royal Engineers, and James, wearing the RFC insignia, survived the war without wounds. James Hayes had enlisted, on the 2 September 1914, into A Company of the 2nd City Battalion.* Hayes

dead. Many other regiments as well as artillery, naval and airforce units drew heavily on Manchester's willingness to involve itself totally in the war effort. Any estimate, even the most conservative, would say that the Manchester and Salford area paid for the Great War with the lives of more than 22,000 young men killed and more than 55,000 further casualties. Every family was touched in some way by the consequences of war. Some men, with skills and sound body, were able to prosper.

A few commercial companies knew more than a little about how to take advantage of the sympathy felt towards the men who had served. Taylor Chapman returned to work as a commercial traveller for Hodder & Stoughton, seeking trade behind the carefully worded introductory card with which his employers equipped him, stating that 'Our Mr Chapman, after four years in the services, has now returned to us, and will be calling upon you for your requirements. We hope you will receive him well.' Within weeks of demobilization he was on the road seeking subscriptions for a new John Buchan novel. Before the war he had seen a steady stream of orders invoiced as thirteen for the price of twelve which he and his office colleagues regarded as a sound order. Now things were changing.

*I remember going into a book-shop called Allens in Newcastle. I was rather green and didn't know much about what was happening. The manager's method was that he used to see the traveller in the morning and write the order out to be picked up about a quarter to four in the afternoon. On this occasion when I picked the order up ready to send into the firm at night I hadn't the courage to do so because he'd ordered two hundred and fifty copies. I thought he'd made a mistake and that it was twenty five! I went back the next morning and pointed this out to him. 'Oh it's all night young feller' he said, 'Things have altered while you've been in the Army.'* Taylor Chapman

*Opposite: 1. Miss Annie Smith with her intended husband Private John Alfred Burns.*
*2. John Alfred Burns of the 1st City Battalion and another soldier.*
*3. Jim Dale, probably serving with one of the reserve battalions, the 25th, 26th or 27th Manchesters.*
*4. Private John Burns' platoon at Heaton Park, late autumn 1914.*
*5. A section of men, outside their billets in Morecambe, in the spring of 1915. Jim Dale is seated next to the Corporal on the front row.* Walker

**3**

**1**

**2**

**5**

*13*

**WILL.**

In the event of my Death
I give the whole of my property
and effects to any inting
wife Mrs Annie Smith
98 South St
Openshaw
Manchester
July 27 19?
Signature John Burns
Rank and Regiment Pte Manch Regt
Date July 27 1917

Proficiency Pay

Service Pay ...    ...

Corps Pay or Engineer Pay ...

Total ...

*Deduct* Allotment or Compulsory
Stoppage

† NET DAILY RATE FOR ISSUE—

(words)

Date and Station

† Subject to amendments (if any) on page

Corps 16th H.L.I. Bn Manchester

Battery or Company "C"

Rank Private

full Burns Jno alfred

Attestation 11-1-15. and

on Enlistment 21/3/20. 5 mths

appointed to a unit formed on Mobilization,
designation of such unit should be clearly stated

NOTE.—The account of the soldier while on
active service will be kept in the Office of the
Paymaster paying the Base Depôt of his Unit,
or by the Paymaster at the Record Office Station of
his Unit, and all communications relating to his
accounts should be addressed accordingly.

*The Paybook and will of Private John Alfred*
*Burns.* Walker

233

The human aftermath included a social revolution in which many of the surviving men took advantage of their relative scarcity to make marriages above their economic and social status, a situation which would have proved impossible before the war years. Even seventy-five years on the consequences were, sometimes, clearly and painfully visible. In September of 1993 I was contacted by a lady who had lived in Openshaw, just east of Manchester's city centre, for all her life. Although soon to turn seventy years old she found time to write, saying that after the recent death of her husband she was having a clear out. Would I like to look at the contents of 'a rather rusty' tin box which she wondered might be of interest. For me the contents of that box came to epitomize the very sadness of the Great War's ultimately human cost, and our frail hold on the personal and family links which bind us to the story. At first the cracked and faded photographs revealed little, the soldier's shoulder titles were indistinct and their names simply abbreviated into familiar short forms, Jim and John and others. A torn paybook, for use on active service provided the first clue. 'John Alfred Burns, CofE, 16th S.Bn.Manchesters. C Company. 7346. Private.' In the back, on page 13, was his will dated 20 March 1917, and a second will dated 27 July 1917, both made in favour of Miss Annie Smith of 98 South Street, Openshaw, Manchester. Amongst a collection of distinctive birthday greetings were cards from Jim to Sarah, together with a photograph of a soldier in uniform, signed on the reverse 'from Jim to John'. And there, on a group photograph taken outside a billet in Morecambe, was Jim again, smiling out from a group of men wearing the distinctive Pals' shoulder titles, probably belonging to a reserve company of one of the second Brigade's battalions left at Morecambe. So Jim, who was in the City Pals, knew John who was definitely an original member of the 1st City Pals. Soon another of Tuson's ubiquitous Heaton Park group-shots, No 597, emerged from the rusty box. There, sure enough, was John, next to the end of the back row, looking immaculate.

But there was, clearly, another close friend or relative whose confident and clean features looked out of the portrait alongside John. The lady, within whose box the photograph was found, thought it was probably John Burns' brother. Perhaps it is too late now to know for certain who this man was. We do, however, know that Private John Alfred Burns had been wounded, at least twice, and on each occasion returned to his unit. We do know that he was taken prisoner during the actions at Manchester Hill in March of 1918. And we did now know for certain what were the circumstances in which Lance Corporal John Alfred Burns had died. A letter sent, five months after the war's end, on 9 April 1919, to Annie Smith confirmed all her worst fears. The grim news was recorded by a fellow soldier who had been an inmate with John Burns at Weidenau Prisoner of War Camp. Lance Corporal Burns' last few days were revealed in all their loneliness.

> The two pay books and photos are all that L/Cpl Burns had, as he, in common with most of us, lost everything when he was captured. It was a very long time before we started receiving our parcels and he seemed to lose heart as time went on. Then he caught the influenza or Spanish grip as we called it, and that seemed the last straw. He refused all food, and appeared unable to eat anything. We did everything we could for him, you may depend, but he appeared to have given up all hope. The Germans had no medicines to give him and even when they took him to hospital he was not much better off and only lived thirty six hours after his removal there. Letter from Vincent A Watson to Miss Annie Smith, dated 9 April 1919

The photograph of John and his 'intend wife', as his will so aptly described Annie, was all that she would have to treasure. Four years later, in July 1923, Lance Corporal Burns' next of kin received a letter from the Imperial War Graves Commission to inform them of an important decision relating to the graves of British soldiers who were buried in the military cemetery at Weidenau.

*I am now directed to inform you that in accordance with this decision the bodies of the British soldiers buried in Weidenau Cemetery on the Haardterberg, have been exhumed and re-buried in the South Cemetery, Cologne, Rhine Province... I can assure you that the re-burial has been carefully and reverently carried out.*

John's body is in Plot 14, Row D, grave number 26. Like so many women of her generation Miss Annie Smith never married, living with her sister who was mother to Ida, until her death in the 1950s. One of Annie Smith's sisters, Sarah, who had been the recipient of the metal birthday cards from Jim, also had cause to be terribly sorrowed by the impact of war. Her husband was Jim Dale. Soldiers Died in the Great War records a Private James Dale, born in Manchester, enlisted in Manchester and who died of wounds at home on 22 July 1916. Had Jim and John survived the war they would have been brothers-in-law. However, all that was now left of the story was the box. Yet, with its sepia photographs cracked and partly eaten by years of age, the rusty box was in reality a treasure trove of family history, but one whose documentation was incomplete.

Such boxes and forgotten papers are still, undoubtedly, duplicated in many thousands of lofts, cellars and box rooms around Manchester, just waiting to be rediscovered and researched. Because many thousands of people like Annie Smith bore their grief silently and with fortitude, and then preserved their memories of the Great War in some small package of photographs, I do sincerely hope that people who come later, in the history of Manchester, will resolve to continue and expand the preservation of this unique and telling social heritage.

For the remainder of the 16th Manchesters who had served alongside John Burns at Manchester Hill during March 1918 very few of those who had been killed were ever recorded as having a known grave. Wilfrith Elstob's body was almost certainly stripped of his regimental insignia, badges of rank and wallet in the search for information and souvenirs which was routinely conducted by soldiers of all sides to the conflict. Just four of the men killed at Manchester Hill have a known grave, all being buried at Chapelle British Military Cemetery in Holnon. After the war, Elstob's friend Hubert Worthington searched the area of Manchester Hill repeatedly, digging within the confines of the redoubt and its immediate surroundings. All his efforts were, however, to no avail and it is therefore quite possible that the 16th Battalion's commanding officer is buried under a simple headstone bearing the words 'A Soldier of the Great War, Known unto God'.

In great part the award of the Victoria Cross to Elstob was due to Worthington's unflagging efforts to bring the selfless bravery which had been shown on Manchester Hill to the attention of the War Office.[2] The unfortunate side effect was to propagate a somewhat unreal and rather false history of the actions in front of St. Quentin, which has lingered for far too long in Manchester mythology.

As with every unit whose history was forged in the heat and desperation of the Great War, the Manchester Pals would continue to meet and support each other through their annual reunions and the less formal gatherings which constituted the various Pals' Associations. The public display of the battalion's colours was an essential symbol to the men of their real comradeship. Amidst great ceremony the colours of the Pals Battalions were enshrined in the Cathedral in 1920, a perpetual reminder of the sacrifice that had been given.[3] More informally, one group which flourished for a while, whilst youth lasted, was the City Comrades football club which fielded teams in a number of local Manchester leagues during the early 1920's. Later in the 1920's there were a number of tenth anniversary reunions, including one at Heaton Park to mark the anniversary of the Battle of the Somme, which drew widely amongst the men who had served within the Pals battalions, together with their wives and children. Sometimes smaller groups would arrange further irregular meetings, the signals sections, the bombers, the machine gun companies and others in progressively dwindling numbers as the impact of the war's privations, habitual smoking and the after effects of wounds ensured a relatively shorter lifespan for many of the men who enlisted with such enthusiasm in 1914. The late 1920s and the 1930s became a period of industrial recession in Manchester, caused by the worldwide collapse of demand for her products and the consequent erosion of the city's massive manufacturing base. Coal, cotton textiles and engineering were all under challenge from either new products or new industrial areas whose costs were more competitive. The great ship canal, previously the main artery of the city's prosperity, began to founder as other ports and means of transport took away the reason for her existence. The city of Manchester's response was slow and ponderous. There was a lack of flair and imagination. A very considerable part of a generation was missing and the Pals had been the best part of that generation. The city's loss of so many skilled men, managers and entrepreneurs during the war years meant that Manchester found adjustment to the new world order a hard task. What the missing Pals' contribution could have been would never be known.

Nevertheless, reunion dinners continued for fifty years, many an old Pal arriving home without his scarf, gloves and brolly for obvious reasons! Fifty years on from the opening of the Battles of the Somme a final organized pilgrimage was made by these surviving but ageing citizen soldiers. Their visits must indeed have provided many poignant and moving moments for each and every one of the men who travelled.

Since 1919 there have of course been many hundreds of thousands of other informal visits and pilgrimages to the area, often simply known as The Somme, where the original Manchester Pals arrived in late 1915. It is quite impossible to spend a quiet moment here without thinking about what awfulness and heroism has been seen within the later history of these places. From almost any vantage point today the beautifully maintained white cemeteries often draw the eye's attention, the register revealing a little about what each location saw and suffered in the years 1916 and 1918. One Manchester name whose intimate

*City Comrades A.F.C. 1919-20. On the back row, wearing the striped shirt, is William Albert Willmot, ex 2nd City Battalion and prisoner of war until his repatriation earlier in 1919.* Willmot/MRA

Ben Leech serving in 1915 with the 25th (Reserve) Battalion. Also shown is a card recording his work for the Resistance (1940-1944). Leech

Taylor Chapman, together with his wife and daughter, photographed in the year of the 10th anniversary of the Battle of the Somme. Chapman

link with the battlefields of France has remained virtually unbroken since the Great War is that of the Leech family. In November of 1914 Benjamin Leech, 27354 enlisted into the 25th Reserve Battalion of the Manchester Regiment, then feeding drafts and replacements into the Manchester Pals, with whom he later served. After the war was over Ben Leech returned to the area of Miraumont and Serre where he settled to his job with the Imperial War Graves Commission, working on the establishment, building and maintenance of the numerous cemeteries in the Serre, Thiepval and Beaumont Hamel areas. During the Second World War Ben Leech was an active member of those groups engaged in the secret and dangerous work of smuggling out and repatriating Allied airmen who had been shot down over northern Europe, many of his charges taking refuge in the gardener's huts and buildings located at the rear of the magnificent Serre Road Number 2 cemetery. Since that era many other men of this family have also served with the Commonwealth War Graves Commission, continuing the links between Manchester and the perpetual memory of the cemeteries. It has been, quite clearly, a labour of love.

The debate about the leadership which had been exercised over the men who served within the British and Empire Armies was inevitably and deeply felt in many northern towns and cities. Manchester was, of course, no exception. The *Manchester Guardian's* literary coverage of the post war era was edited by C E Montague, author of *Disenchantment* and a man not disposed to speak lightly of the inadequacies of Britain's military leadership and of the futility

*One of the 4th City Battalion's reunion dinners, held during the 1930's in Manchester.* Capper

of war. In the *Manchester Guardian* Montague responded to the publication of G A B Dewar's book which dealt with 'Sir Douglas Haig's Command'.[4] Dewar's words had been written as an essentially supportive and approving text, describing the patience and sincerity of Haig's attempts to manage what he saw as an impossible situation. On 29 November, 1922, the book received a reasoned and balanced criticism in the *Manchester Guardian*. Haig, the review concluded, was unlikely to be placed,

> *...among the greatest of Generals. But he showed himself a man of great qualities, and he came through a most extraordinary test of self will and self control without ever losing balance or treating anyone unworthily. He was at any rate able to stand among some of the greatest events of history and never look dwarfish or grotesque in that tremendous company... We incline to think that intellectually he was only a good*

*Fifty years on, the Manchester Pals leave for the Somme outside the city's Town Hall.* MRA

It was one of the those extraordinary moments. The years had taken their constant toll and now in 1993 it was time to unveil a permanent memorial at the site of Heaton Park. Tuesday, 7 September. The wording reads, 'The 16th, 17th, 18th and 19th PALS BATTALIONS of the Manchester Regiment trained at Heaton Park between September 1914 and April 1915.' Present to witness the event were a number of stalwart men, Sergeant Joe Fitzpatrick of the 2/6th Manchesters, Private Albert Birtwistle of the 1/5th East Lancs and the last surviving original Manchester Pal, Albert Hurst, who enlisted into and served with the 2nd City Battalion, the 17th Manchesters. Seventy-nine years had elapsed since his enlistment. Author

The Great War was also the start of an extraordinary interest in and trade of artifacts. Some are mundane. Some are priceless and unique. Amongst the latter is this watch – solid gold – a gift to Private J Redikin, originally of the 23rd Manchesters, from his workmates at F A Fitton & Sons. It records his service and the award of a D.C.M. It is still, of course, a much treasured possession of his daughter and family.

specimen of a certain type, the standardized product of the pre-war educational and social ideals of England, with its sobriety and stability, and also with its limited power of grasping new facts and devising or accepting new expedients to meet them, and its rather hampered and chilled imagination. Mr Dewar hates the word, but war is a science, and the scientific imagination, which is quite a distinct thing, is a necessary condition of the first eminence in it. But morally we should incline to rank him much higher, as an individual of uncommon strength and loftiness of character... *Manchester Guardian*. 29 November 1922

From a newspaper whose community had suffered intensely as a consequence of its commitment to, and support for, the war effort these words were indeed fair. Such a statement does balanced justice to Haig's determination and limitations, and to that of the pre-war middle class Edwardian society which gave rise to the original Pals in Manchester. However a judgement of this nature would be inappropriate were it applied to the selfless sacrifice to which all the men and families associated with the city's battalions are bound in history. Each man was, of course, 'only a good specimen of a certain type, the standardised product of the pre-war educational and social ideals of England, with its sobriety and stability...' That, however, was what made the Pals and it was that shared outlook and intense comradeship which held them together through all the terror, desolation and tragedy of the Great War.

### Notes

1 As a rule of thumb most of the battalions seem to have been employed on average during five periods of severe action resulting in significant casualties in excess of that perhaps expected during the normal course of attrition.

2 The Victoria Cross, Distinguished Conduct Medal and Military Cross awarded to Manchester's most decorated soldier of the Great War are now kept for posterity at the Museum of the Manchesters, located in the Town Hall at Ashton-under-Lyne. Like many of the men who were killed during the fighting in 1918, and whose bodies were never recovered, Wilfreth Elstob is commemorated on the Pozieres memorial on the Albert to Bapaume road. Another magnificent memorial to the memory of the men who served within the Manchesters during the Great War exists inside the Chapel of the Manchester Regiment and the King's Regiment at Manchester Cathedral. This chapel was built in 1513 and later dedicated to the memory of the Manchesters in 1936. The chapel was however devastated by the explosion of bombs, during an air raid, on the 23 December 1940. In the ensuing years the chapel was restored and given greater character by the work of Sir Hubert Worthington and a team of master craftsmen whose efforts are well worth a long journey to visit, contemplate and rest awhile within.

3 A tablet within the Chapel records the destruction of 13 colours in 1971. These colours had been damaged by the prevailing acidity of Manchester's atmosphere and were destroyed when it was discovered that they were beyond repair. The colours of the Salford Pals are located in Trinity Church on Chapel Street in Salford, less than a quarter of a mile from Manchester Cathedral.

4 Sir Douglas Haig's Command. George A B Dewar assisted by Lt. Col. J H Borraston. Constable. London. 1922.